The Memory of Love

The Memory of Love

Sūrdās Sings to Krishna

Translated with
an Introduction and Notes by
John Stratton Hawley

OXFORD
UNIVERSITY PRESS
2009

OXFORD
UNIVERSITY PRESS

Oxford University Press, Inc., publishes works that further
Oxford University's objective of excellence
in research, scholarship, and education.

Oxford New York
Auckland Cape Town Dar es Salaam Hong Kong Karachi
Kuala Lumpur Madrid Melbourne Mexico City Nairobi
New Delhi Shanghai Taipei Toronto

With offices in
Argentina Austria Brazil Chile Czech Republic France Greece
Guatemala Hungary Italy Japan Poland Portugal Singapore
South Korea Switzerland Thailand Turkey Ukraine Vietnam

Published by Oxford University Press, Inc.
198 Madison Avenue, New York, New York 10016

www.oup.com

Library of Congress Cataloging-in-Publication Data
Suradasa, 1483?–1563?
[Surasagara. English. Selections]
The memory of love : Surdas sings to Krishna / translated with an
introduction and notes by John Stratton Hawley.
p. cm.
Includes bibliographical references and index.
ISBN 978-0-19-537398-1; 978-0-19-537399-8 (pbk.)
1. Krishna (Hindu deity)—Poetry. I. Hawley, John Stratton, 1941– II. Title.
PK1967.9.S9S8213 2009
891.4'3—dc22 2008031794

9 8 7 6 5 4 3 2 1
Printed in the United States of America
on acid-free paper

For Laura
In love and memory

Acknowledgments

This book has a parent—in fact, two parents. One is a translation and poem-by-poem analysis of compositions in the *Sūrsāgar* that can be said with reasonable or, in some cases, complete certainty to have been known in the century when the poet to whom they are attributed, Sūrdās, actually lived. A second parent accompanies the first, namely, a critical edition of those same sixteenth-century poems that has been produced by Kenneth E. Bryant and his associates. These two parent works are to be published by Oxford University Press, New York, under the common title *Sūr's Ocean*. My efforts appear as volume 1; Bryant's, as volume 2. But these are only the end-products of a long and complex endeavor in which many other people have also played important roles. I could never have produced the book that follows without the deep involvement of a host of colleagues and friends over a period of time that now stretches to a quarter of a century.

The first and in many ways the most crucial person to mention is Kenneth E. Bryant, with whom I shared the task of locating and photographing the manuscripts that became the basis of our common work. Early on, we divided the labor that lay before us. Ken took on the vast challenges provided by the edition itself, while I directed myself to its translation, annotation, and literary analysis.

The formidable job of accurately transcribing the earliest dated (or datable) manuscripts containing poems attributed to Sūrdās fell principally to Thomas Ridgeway of the University of Washington. Tom's knowledge of orthographic styles and conventions, his ability to make sometimes difficult judgments about the proper boundaries between words, and his savvy assessments of the design of individual manuscripts were foundational to the project. He was ably assisted by Mandakranta Bose of the University of British Columbia, who went on to help Ken Bryant in the early stages of preparing the edition itself. She was soon joined by Vidyut Aklujkar, also of UBC, who became Ken's close editorial collaborator. In that role Vidyut brought to bear her remarkable command of Sanskrit, Hindi, and Marathi, and her deep interest in the literature of bhakti. She used that same wealth of knowledge to provide a detailed review of my draft translations and notes, urging precision, suggesting alternative interpretations, and correcting errors both major and minor on virtually every page. As she and Ken discussed the text and meaning of each poem, I also benefited from analyses and corrections put forward by Ken.

Teachers, colleagues, and friends in India often provided a very different set of perspectives, mixing scholarly rigor with intense personal commitment. Krishna Chaitanya Bhatt drew on his unparalleled knowledge of the religious culture of the Braj area as he read and discussed many of these poems with me. Braj Vallabh Mishra provided a helpful second review. The third reader was my friend and mentor Shrivatsa Goswami, whose quiet but piercing insights shed new light on poem after poem. Often Shrivatsa would start with a question or observation about a single word or verse, as if to test the water, and by the time we were done, both of us often felt that we had bathed in the entire poem. It was my special pleasure to pass on Ken Bryant's edition to Shrivatsa, who began to use it as his criterion when he integrated Sūrdās into his increasingly frequent and influential week-long expositions of the *Bhāgavata Purāṇa*.

I presented my first verse translations from the *Sūrsāgar* to my examining committee as I submitted my Ph.D. dissertation on "The Butter Thief" to Harvard faculty in 1977. I will never forget the book Daniel H. H. Ingalls had tucked under his arm as he walked into the exam—a volume of Matthew Arnold's poetry—or the effect of hearing him read aloud from it as a way of giving me some sense of how my own verse sounded. Clearly there was serious work to be done, and Mark Juergensmeyer was the person who did the most to help me crawl out of the nineteenth century and into the twentieth, even the twenty-first. Ultimately Mark reviewed every poem that appears in this book. Numerous choices of word and rhythm were originally his. Linda Hess also blessed the manuscript with occasional strokes from her expert editorial pen.

My students through the years have often had fine insights to share about individual poems, including especially Paul Arney, Amy Bard, Nadine Berardi, Elaine Fisher, Joel Lee, James Lochtefeld, Till Luge, Gurinder Singh Mann, Travis Smith, and Hamsa Stainton. Two other students, Anne Murphy and

Rupa Viswanath, gave close readings of the Introduction, making thoughtful suggestions about how it might be extended and improved. Christian Novetzke had particularly good proposals for further reading on my part. In all these interactions it was often hard to tell who better deserved to be called the student—they or I?

I was fortunate in being able to direct questions about individual poems to experts such as Purushottam Goswami (§433), Gurinder Singh Mann (§419), Philip Lutgendorf (§433), Suresh Pandey (§373), and Rupert Snell (§§19, 337–341), and I benefitted from their answers each time. Winand Callewaert and Michael Shapiro offered suggestions about a range of matters, and steady encouragement along the way. Discussions about the *Sūrsāgar* at a number of institutions have buoyed me up through the years—at the Conference on Religion in South India, the University of Chicago, Rice University, the University of Texas, and the University of Washington. For sustained collegial give-and-take here at home, I am especially indebted to Allison Busch, Vidya Dehejia, David Lelyveld, Gurinder Singh Mann, Rachel McDermott, Mary McGee, Philip Oldenburg, Sheldon Pollock, Fran Pritchett, Gary Tubb, and in memory, Barbara Miller.

At a crucial moment late in the game, Aditya Behl and I read each other's book manuscripts. His detailed comments on my Introduction opened a whole new set of questions about the larger cultural context in which Sūrdās poems might have been performed in the sixteenth century. Allison Busch has played a similar role, expanding my horizons still further and making numerous helpful suggestions about the book. Other colleagues and friends shared their expertise about questions of performance and historical musicology. Vidur Malik performed a set of poems in the *dhrupad* tradition and offered a running commentary. Shubha Mudgal took the time to compose memorable renditions of certain poems and performed them in an intimate, happy atmosphere provided by Veena Modi. Peter Manuel commented knowledgably on a draft of the musicological section of the Introduction, and it was my great privilege to speak with Prem Lata Sharma about matters of performance and interpretation in what turned out to be the last months of her long and productive life.

I am indebted to those who have helped me with clerical and technical aspects of the project: Paul Arney, Greg Hansbury, Kristie Contardi, Maureen Dillon, Akinyi Okoth, Tynisha Rue, Mary Ellen Tucker, and Karin Zitzewitz. Generous grants from the National Endowment for the Humanities were critical for launching the project in the first place, and supplemental awards from the American Institute of Indian Studies, the John Simon Guggenheim Foundation, the University of Washington, Barnard College, and the Leonard Hastings Schoff Fund of the University Seminars at Columbia University have sustained its progress over a very long haul. In recent years I have benefited from the advice and encouragement offered by Patrick Olivelle as editor of the series in which *Sūr's Ocean* is published, and from Sean Pue's brilliant work in converting that manuscript to camera-ready copy. Cynthia Read at Oxford University Press, New York, has over the years set a standard of competence and loyal friendship that is hard to match; I am grateful to her junior colleagues as well. And it has been my great good fortune that Margaret Case, formerly my editor at Princeton University Press and long an advocate of the *Sūrsāgar* project, was willing to be enlisted as copy editor when this volume finally came to fruition.

Finally there's my family. I wish to thank my daughter Nell for fending off the shadow of the *Sūrsāgar* with more than a little humor as she flourished so determinedly in the first twenty years of her life. To my wife Laura Shapiro I am indebted for an exquisite quality of patient impatience as she lived with Sūrdās year after year, and once again for the deft and timely editing of my prose. But that is only the beginning. Only the beginning.

Contents

Transliteration, xiii
Abbreviations, xvii
Manuscripts Consulted, xix
Introduction, 3

Poems from *Sūr's Ocean*

1. Krishna Growing Up, 47
2. The Pangs and Politics of Love, 79
3. Krishna Departs for Mathura, Never to Return, 107
4. The Bee-messenger, 127
5. Lordly Encounters—and Others, 147
6. Rāmāyaṇa, 167
7. The Poet's Petition and Praise, 175
8. To the Holy Rivers, 195

Notes, 199
Bibliography of Works Cited, 285
List of Poems by English Title, 291
List of Poems by Brajbhāṣā Title, 297
Index, 303

Transliteration

No simple set of conventions provides definitive guidance about how the sixteenth-century *Sūrsāgar* should be presented to readers of English living five centuries later. The *Sūrsāgar* is not really a text but a collection of texts—manuscript versions of poems that would most likely have been performed independently of one another—and these in turn record (and doubtless reshape) a band of utterance that was primarily oral, not written. How best to represent such a matrix in transliteration?

First of all, the standard system for transliterating the *devanāgarī* syllabary into the Roman alphabet has to be modified so that it can represent Brajbhāṣā rather than Sanskrit. Only in instances where Sanskrit is being quoted or the context of discussion clearly concerns works composed in Sanskrit (such as the *Bhāgavata Purāṇa*) will the standard system be adopted in its fullness. Otherwise, I have two complementary aims. The first is to allow readers to reconstruct the exact text of the Bryant critical edition when we refer to it in our discussion of individual poems. The second is to "tune" that discussion in such a way that it does not sound strange to speakers of Modern Standard Hindi. This requires a set of compromises.

In notes on the first poem, for example, I retain the neutral *a* at the end of *dīnadayāla* and *dāsa* because I am quoting from the edition itself: the vowel would be pronounced in singing or reciting the poem, and is necessary for its metrical structure. Yet when I depart from direct quotation, I hope to move to a level of discussion that would seem natural to speakers of Modern Standard Hindi, where the final vowel is unpronounced except after consonant clusters that demand it. Thus I present the name of Mathura's usurper king as Kaṃs, not Kaṃsa. Often this shift from direct quotation to general reference will appear on the page as a shift from words that are contained between parentheses and words that take their place in the diction of the commentary itself. Finally, at a third level, I present the name of Kaṃs's slayer as Krishna (not Kṛṣṇa or Kṛṣṇ) both because that form has become so familiar in English as to be standard and because when the cluster *ṣṇ* is pronounced in Hindi or Brajbhāṣā, it takes a subsequent *a* to render it audible. The same is often true when the retroflex *ṇ* appears by itself in the final position; hence I allow *nirguṇa*, for example, to alternate with *nirguṇ*.

Nasalization is normally indicated in *Sūrsāgar* manuscripts by the simple practice of positioning of a dot above the vowel in question. In transliteration this is notoriously hard to reproduce. I have settled for the standard Sanskritized possibilities (*ṃ, m, ṅ, ñ, ṇ, n*) when the nasalized vowel precedes an interior consonant, and give *ṅ* uniformly when nasalization occurs at the end of a word.

I hope readers will quickly become accustomed to this layered system of transliteration, and will not regard it as offputting because it fails to adopt an invariant policy throughout. Yet one detail does merit advance warning, especially to speakers of Modern Standard Hindi. Our manuscripts almost always represent the gutteral aspirant *kh* as *ṣ*, which in other contexts can represent the lingual sibilant, as in Modern Standard Hindi. When quoting from the *Sūrsāgar*, I have followed this system so as to allow readers to reconstruct exactly the critical edition or one of the manuscripts upon which it is based (for example, *muṣa*, meaning "face" or "mouth"). If, however, I use this word while commenting on a poem, I will revert to the more familiar Hindi form *mukh*.

I have also tried to follow this layered approach to transliteration in rendering words that are not necessarily drawn from the *Sūrsāgar* itself. With place names that have come into common usage, I accept the English spellings that are usually assigned: e.g., Lanka, Agra, Mathura, Dvaraka, Varanasi. If such names are sufficiently unfamiliar that readers may not know the correct pronunciation, however, I do supply diacritics: Kānthā, Cātsu, Ghanorā, and so on. In giving references, I spell the place of publication in a fashion that was familiar at the time the work was published (for example, Banaras during British rule; Varanasi thereafter). I confess that I find the official spelling of the place hallowed by Krishna's youth (Vrindaban) to be sufficiently far from its usual spoken sound (Brindāvan) that I have preferred an anglicized rendering which has largely gone out of fashion—Brindavan—except when repeating others' usage.

Similar patterns appear in other realms—for example, the naming of languages. If a language or dialect has achieved a standard English form, I leave aside diacritics (Hindi, Avadhi); otherwise I retain them (Hindavī, Brajbhāṣā). With persons, the scale moves from more or less standard English usages (Krishna, Shiva, Vishnu, Ganges) toward a realm that represents normal Hindi speech (Jarāsandh, Kālīdās, Rūp Gosvāmī, Bhaum), even if the name in question occurs in a context that suggests Sanskrit conventions would also be appropriate (Jarāsaṃdha, Kālīdāsa, etc.). If the name is a title of a work written in Sanskrit, however, Sanskrit conventions apply (*Bhāgavata Purāṇa*, *Rāmāyaṇa*). Writers of Hindi or Brajbhāṣā are represented with diacritics (Parameśvarī Lāl Gupta) unless they also write frequently in English and have established conventional spellings for their names in that milieu (Prem Lata Sharma). English words adopted into Indic titles are spelled in the English way (Saṅgīt Nāṭak Academy). The neutral vowel is dropped in compounds where it is generally inaudible in normal speech (Braj+bhāṣā>Brajbhāṣā), unless that omission might lead to a confused reconstruction of the Hindi original (Pāras+nāth>Pārasanāth).

Punjabi spellings are chosen in preference to Hindi ones where the context suggests it. When discussing the epic figure Arjuna as he appears in the *Sūrsāgar*, I call him Arjun, but the name of the fifth Sikh guru is spelled Arjan.

Abbreviations

§	Designates a poem (*pad*) as numbered in the Bryant edition of the *Sūrsāgar.*
App.	Appendix 1 in the Nāgarīpracāriṇī Sabhā edition of the *Sūrsāgar*
BhP	*Bhāgavata Purāṇa*
Brj.	Brajbhāṣā
C.E.	Common Era (equivalent to A.D.)
HV	*Harivaṃśa*
Mbh	*Mahābhārata*
MSH	Modern Standard Hindi
NPS	Nāgarīpracāriṇī Sabhā (i.e., Kāśī Nāgarīpracāriṇī Sabhā). May designate the NPS version of a poem that also appears in the Bryant edition or, more commonly, a poem that is absent in the Bryant edition.
RCM	*Rāmcaritmānas* of Tulsīdās
Skt.	Sanskrit
V.S.	*Vikram Saṃvat,* a lunar calendrical system that provides a date usually corresponding to C.E.+57
VP	*Viṣṇu Purāṇa*

Manuscripts Consulted

Basic information about the manuscripts referred to in this book is presented in the list that follows. It includes a brief description of each manuscript, together with the abbreviation by means of which it is designated, both here and in the full critical edition to follow. Where possible, the abbreviation assigned to a manuscript in the edition of Mātāprasād Gupta (*Sūrsāgar*, Agra: Agra University, 1979) is also given.

(1) J1. MS no. 49 in the Hindi collection of the Maharaja of Jaipur. v.s. 1639 (1582 c.e.); written at Fatehpur; 163 folios and 411 *pads*, of which, once 23 repetitions are subtracted, 239 belong to Sūr; untitled. This manuscript has been published in a facsimile edition edited by Gopal Narayan Bahura and Kenneth E. Bryant: *Pad Sūrdās kā/The Padas of Sūrdās* (Jaipur: Maharaja Sawai Singh II Museum, 1984).

(2) B1. Hindi MS no. 156, Anup Sanskrit Library, Bikaner. No date (ca. v.s. 1655–1685) or other colophon information. 150 folios, 423 *pads*, untitled. Resembles Mātāprasād Gupta's "Bi. 4."

(3) B2. Hindi MS no. 157, Anup Sanskrit Library, Bikaner. v.s. 1681, copied at Burhanpur, in the Deccan, probably by a scribe in the entourage of Maharaja Surya Singh of Bikaner, 161 folios pertaining to Sūr, 492 *pads*, untitled. Gupta's "Bi. 1."

(4) B3. Hindi MS no. 149, Anup Sanskrit Library, Bikaner. v.s. 1695, no place given, 132 folios, 480 *pads* of Sūr, untitled.

(5) U1. Hindi MS no. 575/2396, Rajastan Oriental Research Institute, Udaipur. v.s. 1697, at Ghānorā (near Banswara?), 202 folios, 812 *pads* of Sūr, entitled *Sūrsāgar*.

(6) B4. Hindi MS no. 158, Anup Sanskrit Library, Bikaner. v.s. 1698, Mathura, 109 folios, 615 *pads* of Sūr, untitled but with divisional headings. Gupta's "Bi. 3."

(7) J2. Hindi MS no. 6732(2), "Khās Mohar" collection, Maharaja of Jaipur. Before v.s. 1718 (the date of its acquisition by the House of Jaipur), 150 folios, 503 *pads* of Sūr, untitled and without divisional headings.

(8) J3. Hindi MS no. 3538, "Khās Mohar" collection, Maharaja of Jaipur. Before A.H. 1059, the date of the first seal it bears (i.e., v.s. 1706), acquired by the House of Jaipur A.H. 1075 (v.s. 1722), 188 folios, 681 *pads* of Sūr, untitled but with divisional headings.

(9) G1. Hindi MS. no. 1057, K. M. Hindi Institute, Agra University. The manuscript is composite and the Sūrdās section bears no date, but the section that follows immediately afterward, containing the *Rāsapañcādhāyī* of Nandadās, continues the Sūrdās pagination apparently in the same hand and is dated v.s. 1713, at Meḍtā. In the Sūrdās section are 98 folios, 533 *pads*, and the notation that the scribe wrote in Gokul.

(10) J4. Hindi MS no. 1979, "Khās Mohar" collection, Maharaja of Jaipur. v.s. 1733, at Cātsu (near Jaipur), by a scribe of Gokul, 305 folios, 1400 *pads* of Sūr, entitled *Sūrsāgar*, divisional headings.

(11) J5. Hindi MS no. 3387 (1), "Khās Mohar" collection, Maharaja of Jaipur. v.s. 1734 (?) at Ajavgaḍh (Alwar District): 34 folios contain 100 *pads* of Sūr under the general title *śrī sūrdās jī kā pad.*

(12) A1. MS no. 76/220, Allahabad Municipal Museum. v.s. 1743, no place given, 213 folios, 690 *pads* of Sūr, entitled *Sūrsāgar*, sporadic divisional headings.

(13) K1. Hindi MS no. 3335, Rajasthan Oriental Research Institute, Kota. v.s. 1758, at Pachor, originally 64 folios, 209 *pads* of Sūr, entitled *Sūrsāgar*, divisional headings. Gupta's "Pa."

(14) U2. Hindi MS no. 133/1954, Rajasthan Oriental Research Institute, Jaipur. v.s. 1763, at Udaipur, 30 folios, 170 *pads* of Sūr, entitled *Sūrsāgar*, divisional headings. Gupta's "Śrī."

When manuscript readings are cited in the pages that follow, reference is made to the abbreviations listed above. If no manuscript is mentioned, the citation is to the critical edition prepared by Bryant, et al. Only on very rare occasions is reference made to a critical reading that differs from the Bryant edition.

The Memory of Love

Introduction

Ask someone who lives in the West to name an Indian classic, and the answer is almost foreordained: the *Bhagavad Gītā*. This poetic work, depicting a didactic encounter between an exemplary human being and the god Krishna, has been translated into European languages hundreds of times. Yet surprisingly few inhabitants of the populous states of north India can recite more than a phrase or two of the Sanskrit original. The Krishna they know as the subject of classic poetry is apt to come from quite another source: Hindi poet-singers of the early modern period, and the greatest of these is Sūrdās. Like Homer, he is remembered as having been blind. Like Shakespeare, he has infused a tradition of living performance. And the Krishna to whom he sings is largely the god of love rather than the key to life's other battles, as in the *Gītā*. Why then is Sūrdās still so little known outside his homeland? It has to do with the definition of a classic.

When European scholars and colonial administrators tried to make cultural sense of India in the late-eighteenth and nineteenth centuries, they typically started their quest by studying Sanskrit. Latin and Greek were what made for a serious education in Europe, so as it became clear that these two had a sister language in Sanskrit—"more perfect than the Greek, more copious than the Latin, and more exquisitely refined than either," as Sir William Jones famously proclaimed in 1786—it was natural that this ancient tongue should be accorded a parallel place of honor.[1] Persian entered the picture, too. After all, it had been at the core of the Mughal administrative culture that the British were eager to supplant. But nothing rivaled Sanskrit. As a Western canon of Indian literature began to emerge, works like Kālīdāsa's *Śākuntala*, the *Bhagavad Gītā*, the *Bhāgavata Purāṇa* (in an abridged version), and the Upanishads led the way.

These were classics, no doubt, and Sanskrit was certainly a learned language, but for many centuries it had ceased to be anyone's mother's tongue—if ever it was. Sanskrit means "refined," and a significant part of its vocation had always been to ride above the unruly rhythms of ordinary, local speech. So if you were a Britisher living in north India, you would have to turn to some other medium if you actually wanted to communicate with the people who surrounded you. Some version of Hindi would be your best bet, and indeed Hindi is customarily reckoned as the fifth most widely spoken language in the world today. Yet it took European scholars a while to appreciate the fact that Hindi too had its classics. These long-cherished works speak to the people of north India—then and now—as Shakespeare speaks to the British or Molière to the French.

Modern Standard Hindi, the national language that is taught as a compulsory subject in schools across India, has existed as such for only about a hundred years. Its grammars, dictionaries, and textbooks draw on a register of common speech called *khaḍī bolī*, which has come to have a literary aspect, but only since the early years of the twentieth century. Hindi's more venerable classics tend instead to be drawn from two linguistic streams that have flowed strong and hard for half a millennium, reaching back to the days when the Mughal Empire brought much of India under a common rule, and even before. These two streams are conventionally called Avadhī and Brajbhāṣā. Their labels associate them with particular geographical regions, though as literary idioms they could be adopted by writers and performers living far away from these regional centers.[2]

1 Jones, "Third Anniversary Discourse Delivered to the Royal Asiatic Society of Bengal," as recorded in *The Works of Sir William Jones*, ed. A. M. J. [Anna Maria Jones], vol. 1, p. 26. More was involved in the comparison of these classical languages than the mere matter of common philological origins, exciting as that was—from the sixteenth century onward—to establish. For Jones and others, as Arthur Dudney has emphasized, the classics were perceived as affording access to a field of analysis that made it possible to locate Indian and European culture within a single frame, a common cosmopolitan culture whose glory had been tarnished with the passing of time. See Dudney, "Colonial Knowledge and the Greco-Roman Classics," especially pp. 25–53; on the distinction between this point of view and that of Raymond Schwab, whose masterwork *The Oriental Renaissance* (French original 1950, English translation 1984) first surveyed the field, see Dudney, pp. 32–33. In Schwab, see especially pp. 4–20, 51–80.

2 A general and very helpful review of the subject is presented by (Ronald) Stuart McGregor in "The Progress of Hindi, Part I: The Development of a Transregional Idiom," in Pollock. ed., *Literary Cultures in History: Reconstructions from South Asia*, pp. 912–957. Also worthy of note is Rupert Snell's *The Hindi Classical Tradition: A Braj Bhāṣā Reader*, especially pp. 29–36.

Avadh or Oudh is the Gangetic region southeast of Delhi. Its cultural capitals included Jaunpur, Banaras, and Lucknow, but Sufi centers such as Jais and Kalpi also figured in the mix. Hindus, though, often conceive the capital of Avadh to be Ayodhya (you can hear the resemblance), since Ayodhya is regarded as the city where the god Rām held sway. It was the Hindu poet Tulsīdās who, writing toward the end of the sixteenth century, crystallized the epic of Rām—the *Rāmāyaṇa*—in a vernacular form that many people consider to be Avadhī's greatest classic. Yet in doing so, Tulsīdās made use of epic and poetic conventions that had been established by Avadhī writers whose subjects were less Hindu than Sufi.[3] Examples are Maulānā Dāūd's *Candāyan* and Mañjhan's *Madhumālatī,* written in 1379 and 1545. Interestingly, these two authors called the language in which they composed Hindukī or Hindavī, that is, Hindi or simply "Indian." The more restrictive label Avadhī was applied only considerably later.

The other major stream that contributes to the literary and linguistic confluence we recognize today as Hindi is Brajbhāṣā. It rose somewhat farther west and, like its eastern cousin, was designated only generically in its earliest phrases—as *bhāṣā,* "what is spoken," by contrast to the more self-consciously literary idioms of Sanskrit and Persian. Brajbhāṣā is "the speech of Braj," and Braj is the region south of Delhi where the river Jamunā flows. Its ancient cultural capital is Mathura, birthplace of Krishna. Mathura sits directly between Delhi and Agra, two of the three cities (with Lahore, farther north and west) that became principal axes for the Mughal Empire. As the Mughals established their hegemony across north India in the sixteenth century, they worked closely with several Rajput kings, including especially the Kachvāhā rulers of Amber (later Jaipur), in modern-day Rajasthan. Mānsingh Kachvāhā served as a general for the great Mughal emperor Akbar (r. 1556–1605) in his Gujarat campaigns of 1572 and 1576, and he and his father were later dispatched by Akbar to govern Kabul, Lahore, and Bihar and Bengal; they also helped bring a number of other Rajput rulers within the Mughal orbit. The culture of Braj was a major beneficiary of this system of alliances, since from the sixteenth century onward the rajas of Amber were staunch—though not exclusive—devotees of the god Krishna. They regarded themselves as Krishna's servants and protectors, and they played a major role in constructing in Braj some of the most impressive temples where Krishna could be worshiped in image form. Through a series of land grants and administrative

3 Aditya Behl has stressed this point in "Presence and Absence in *Bhakti:* An Afterword." Further on the *premākhyān* genre and its intertextual relations, see Behl, "The Magic Doe: Desire and Narrative in a Hindavi Sufi Romance, circa 1503."

protocols, in fact, and acting together with his Kachvāhā courtier-colleagues, the emperor Akbar came to be reckoned as a temple patron himself.[4]

The legendry of Krishna locates him firmly in Braj. As the story goes, he was born several thousand years ago into the royal family of Mathura, just before the disintegration of the world age that preceded our present era. Because of a cruel, usurping uncle—a Herod if ever there was one—Krishna had to flee the city on the night of his birth. He was ferried across the Jamunā and raised as a cowherd in the surrounding Braj countryside. Almost by definition he must have spoken Brajbhāṣā in one of its earlier forms. When Krishna reached adolescence, he set out to liberate his natal city, returning the rightful monarch to the throne, and from there went off to assume a throne of his own at Dvaraka on the shores of the Arabian Sea. With that as a base, he brokered the cataclysmic conflict reported in the epic *Mahābhārata,* a battle fought just northwest of Delhi.

Krishna was to Brajbhāṣā what Rām was to Avadhī—in fact, even more so. His charmed life, clever exploits, and expertise in the arts of love and war made him a principal focus of cultured speech, song, and art throughout India in the first millennium C.E., and the Braj region always asserted a special claim on his personality. Hence it is no surprise that when Brajbhāṣā rose to literary prominence in the fifteenth and sixteenth centuries, the poetry of Krishna was very much to the fore. It was not, however, alone. From early on, Brajbhāṣā also supported a broader tradition of courtly aesthetics.[5] Similarly, although it offered itself as an intrinsically appropriate vehicle for expressions of devotion to Krishna, Brajbhāṣā exercised no monopoly in that sphere. The Sufi poet Malik Muhammad Jāyasī felt quite at home composing his version of Krishna's life, the *Kanhāvat,* in Avadhī. Finally, in the same spirit, it cannot be said that the Braj region was solely responsible for the ascent of the language that would in time be named after it; Gwalior, farther south, also played

4 The several aspects of this process can vividly be seen in Case, ed., *Govindadeva: A Dialogue in Stone.* Particular attention might be drawn to the inscription dated 1590 found on the temple of Vṛndādevī, immediately to the north of the great temple of Govindadev and completed in the same year. It recognizes Akbar as the "maker" of the latter temple and gives the names of several of the officials in charge of the building project. This and other relevant inscriptions are reproduced and translated by Gopal Narayan Bahura, "Śrī Govinda Gāthā," in Case, ed., *Govindadeva,* pp. 200–202. Also of note is the imperial decree (*farmān*) of 1565 documenting direct imperial support for the temple in an earlier period. See Mukherjee and Habib, "Akbar and the Temples of Mathura and Its Environs," p. 235. A retrospective *farmān* issued in 1598 describes what Mukherjee and Habib call "the entire scheme of grants" that had by then emerged from the throne in support of major religious institutions in Braj, with Brindavan the major focus (ibid., articles 4.6–4.8, pp. 240–241).

5 Allison Busch has eloquently made this point in a series of works: "Questioning the Tropes about '*Bhakti*' and '*Riti*' in Hindi Literary Historiography," "The Anxiety of Innovation: The Practice of Literary Science in the Hindi/*Riti* Tradition," and "Hindi Literary Beginnings."

a major role. Yet it is striking that Brajbhāṣā attained its particular place of privilege among the vernaculars of north India in a context that had a true geographical bias in favor of Braj. The ascent of Brajbhāṣā as a widely shared literary medium occurred only once it became part of the cultured diction of the Mughal court—and the Mughals ruled, essentially, from Braj.[6] Given the Kachvāhās' special religious interest in the region, it is perhaps no wonder that the poetry of Krishna emerged as central to the enterprise, even through the Mughal emperors, to whom the Kachvāhās gave daughters in marriage, remained Muslim.

In cooperation with the rajas of Amber, the Mughal rulers doled out extensive grants in the Braj heartland, helping to create a dense temple culture that became home to a new wave of Krishna worship. Anchored in these temples and mapped by a series of devotional demographers who typically traveled great distances to do so, Braj quickly became a much more important focus for pilgrimage than it had been in preceding centuries. The Mughal roads, well kept and well defended, helped make it so; and the most important artery of all passed directly through the Braj country. It connected the imperial establishments at Agra and Delhi before proceeding farther north to Lahore and Kabul. Hence we have what many would regard as a great irony. It was a polity developed by Muslim rulers that largely made it possible for the language and worship of Krishna to flourish as never before.[7]

Some historians have characterized this transformation as a renaissance of Braj culture, and to be sure, the arts of Mathura and its environs have ancient roots that were waiting for such a restoration. Yet in a more meaningful way, this sixteenth-century transformation actually created Braj as we know it today. It was then that the region and the language associated with it attained the cultural, linguistic, and religious paramountcy they were to enjoy for centuries thereafter. It was then that Brajbhāṣā became a "classic" literary culture—one of the two, with Avadhī, that speakers of Hindi would come to think of as their linguistic birthright.[8]

6 See Busch, "Hidden in Plain View: Brajbhasha Poets at the Mughal Court."

7 If one regards Hindi as a language that is in some special way Hindu, then one finds a parallel irony in regard to Avadhī and Hindi generally, as Aditya Behl and Allison Busch have both remarked. Busch puts it starkly, referring to Maulānā Dāūd's *Candāyan*: "yes, the first major Hindi text (what an embarrassing thing for Hindi-wallahs) is by a Muslim!" (Busch, "Hindi Literary Beginnings," p. 6 [in draft]). Behl casts this issue in a somewhat broader frame in "How Newness Enters the World: Inaugurating a Genre," pp. 5–7.

8 The work offering the best overview of these developments in Braj is Alan W. Entwistle's *Braj, Centre of Krishna Pilgrimage*. In Hindi one has the landmark trilogy by Prabhudayāl Mītal: *Braj kā Sāṃskṛtik Itihās, Braj ke Dharma-Saṃpradāyoṅ kā Itihās*, and *Braj kī Kalāoṅ kā Itihās*.

The "Sun" of Brajbhāṣā Poets

By common consent, the poet regarded as the epitome of literary artistry in Brajbhāṣā is Sūrdās. His name means literally "servant [*dās*] of the sun [*sūr*]," but in Braj he is seen as the sun itself. Indeed, his name is often shortened to Sūr. Sūrdās, whose exact sixteenth-century dates cannot be determined, was confirmed in this position of eminence in the 1920s and 1930s, when an influential group of scholars associated with the Nāgarīpracāriṇī Sabhā (Society for the Propagation of [Languages Written in] the Nāgarī Script) worked in Banaras to define a literary canon that would support Hindi's claims to literary worth—as against English and Urdu, which represented competitors and oppressors in different ways. No voice was more important in this struggle than that of Rāmcandra Śukla, whose *History of Hindi Literature*, first issued in 1929, still serves as the backbone of Hindi curricula throughout the country. Śukla regarded Sūr as second only to Tulsīdās in the firmament of writers he saw as constituting Hindi's literary past, and some of Śukla's peers were bold enough to reverse the order: "Sūr is the sun; Tulsī, the moon," as a familiar Brajbhāṣā verse had it.[9] Compared to Sūr and Tulsī, the verse continues, only one other poet even deserved mention—Keśavdas, who qualified as "the stars." The rest merely "flickered around like fireflies."

Rāmcandra Śukla and his cohort were hardly the first to see Sūrdās as the dominant literary figure of Brajbhāṣā. One can trace that estimation right back to the close of the sixteenth century itself, which must have been Sūr's own. At that point an author named Nābhādās endeavored to create a different sort of canon from the kind Śukla had in mind—more religious than literary, but a canon nonetheless. As Nābhādās assembled his influential *Bhaktamāl* (Garland of Lovers of God), he singled out Sūrdās for a special sort of praise. Other poet-saints might be lauded for their personal fearlessness (such as Mīrābāī) or for their defiance of the rules of caste and class (such as Kabīr), but when the subject was poetry itself, Sūrdās had no peer:

> What poet, hearing the poems Sūr has made,
>   will not nod his head in pleasure?
> Turns of phrase, epigrams, assonance, description—

9 Śukla worked out the comparison between Sūrdās and Tulsīdās at many points in his oeuvre, e.g., *Sūrdās*, pp. 118, 154–157, 186–193. An interesting digest of quotations culled from Śukla's extensive writings in which he compared the two poets is to be found in Kumār, ed., *Ācārya Śukla Vicār Koś*, pp. 232–234. A recent treatment of the subject in English is provided by Milind Wakankar in "The Moment of Criticism in Indian Nationalist Thought," and in "The Prehistory of the Popular: Caste and Canonicity in Indian Modernity," pp. 153–167.

in each regard his standing is immense:
Speech and loving sentiment he sustains,
conveying their meaning in wondrous rhyme.
In words he expresses Hari's playful acts,
which are mirrored in his heart by divine vision:
Birth, deeds, virtues, and beautiful form—
all are brought to light by his tongue.
Others cleanse their virtues and powers of insight
by tuning their ears to his fame.
What poet, hearing the poems Sūr has made,
will not nod his head in pleasure?[10]

Nābhādās tells us that Sūr was able, in words, to "express Hari's playful acts" *(hari līlā bhāsī)*. The name Hari can designate any of the aspects of divinity that we associate with the god Vishnu, whether or not we think of these as being formally Vishnu's avatars. In the sixteenth century, the term Hari was also frequently used as a designation for God in an even more general sense—the sort of God who loved to help those who loved him, and had designed the world as a theater in which that sort of action could be performed. So Hari can mean many things, but when Nābhādās speaks of Hari in connection with Sūrdās, he is clearly thinking of Krishna, the deity whose trademark is his "playful acts," his *līlās*. For Nābhādās, as for Rāmcandra Śukla and countless others, Sūrdās is first and foremost a poet of Krishna. To be sure, Sūr addressed a series of lovely compositions to Rām and his consort Sītā, and he loved to evoke other aspects of the *Rāmāyaṇa* as well, but his primary narrative métier was the world of Krishna.

A widely distributed twentieth-century poster illustration captures this nicely. Published by S. S. Brajbasi & Sons, Bombay, it shows the poet sitting somewhere in Braj, singing to Krishna (Figure 1). And who should be listening? Krishna himself. Sūrdās has his clacker-cymbals in one hand and his one-stringed *ektār* in the other, and the infant deity, mesmerized, puts aside his own instrument, the flute, to hear the poet sing. A temple in the background provides a nice connection between the two figures: there, presumably, Krishna is worshiped in image form and the poems of Sūrdās are sung. But in the foreground we see that the poet and his god inhabit their storied world not by virtue of the ritual patterns made possible by organized religion, but in an absolutely immediate way. This absence of obstacle is made possible, ironically, because

10 Jhā, *Bhaktamāl: Pāṭhānuśīlan evam Vivecan*, part 2, p. 27 [§72]; cf. Nābhādās, *Śrī Nābhādās kṛt Śrī Bhaktamāl*, edited by Sītārāmśaraṇ Bhagavānprasād "Rūpkalā," p. 557.

FIGURE 1. Sūrdās sings for Krishna. Poster illustration printed by S. S. Brajbasi & Sons, Bombay.

Sūrdās struggles against a handicap. He is blind. He can "see" Krishna in his songs and not be distracted by the fact that Krishna sees him at the same time.

This is not merely a modern conceit. Already in the opening decades of the eighteenth century artists were portraying Sūrdās, unlike other poets, as a direct participant in Krishna's world. Somewhat earlier, in the mid-seventeenth century, collections of poetry attributed to Sūrdās had come to be called *Sūr's Ocean*—*Sūrsāgar*—and by the eighteenth century we begin to see miniature paintings that were originally attached to manuscripts of the *Sūrsāgar*. In Figure 2 we have a page that has survived from a *Sūrsāgar* apparently painted in the Mewar region of western Rajasthan. Here Sūrdās watches as Krishna and his beloved Rādhā cross-dress and exchange the gendered roles they traditionally play in the game of love; the cross-dressing too is a longstanding aesthetic conceit. In a way that is sometimes approximate, sometimes exact, the two lovers act out the sentiments expressed in a poem on this subject that is attributed to Sūrdās. The painter apportions a bower to each scene, beginning with the one in which Rādhā asks to play Krishna's flute Muralī, and he ends with a bower devoted to Sūr himself. Just as the poet typically announces his own name—his "seal" *(chāp)*, it is called—in the

FIGURE 2. Sūrdās observing—from the lower right-hand corner—a series of scenes in which Rādhā and Krishna exchange garments and roles. Illustration for the poem *lāla tumārī muralī naiṅka vajāuṅ* ("Dear, let me play your Muralī for a moment"), which bears the signature of Sūrdās but is absent from the Nāgarīpracāriṇī Sabhā edition of the *Sūrsāgar*. Mewar, ca. 1720 C.E. Courtesy of the Los Angeles County Museum of Art: M.71.1.11; formerly belonging to the Nasli and Alice Heeramanick Collection.

last verse of the poem, so the artist reveals the identity of the poetic observer in the lower right-hand corner. That final bower seems to ensure that no mortal might intrude upon the intimacy of the divine couple, but evidently the poet's blindness also removes that danger. The physical constriction symbolizes spiritual freedom of motion.

We do not know exactly when it became popular to think of Sūrdās as being blind, but we know that the story of his blindness was told in a number of forms. In one version Sūr is granted a vision of Krishna and then requests the deity to remove his faculty of sight so that nothing he might see subsequently could dilute the splendor of what he had witnessed.[11] In another version of the tale, Sūr's blindness is with him from birth. This is the form the story takes when told by the religious community that has positioned itself since at least the mid-seventeenth century as Sūr's most influential interpreter: the Vallabh Sampradāy or Puṣṭimārg (Path of Fulfillment), a group whose worship is focused entirely on Krishna and whose members revere the theologian Vallabh (or more formally, Vallabhācārya—Master Vallabh) as their founder. One of Vallabh's grandsons, a man named Gokulnāth, is traditionally believed to have been the author of an interconnected series of religious biographies called *Caurāsī Vaiṣṇavan kī Vārtā*–"Accounts of Eighty-four Vaishnavas," including Sūrdās. This is the Sūrdās biography everyone knows, and the singing of Sūr's poetry—along with that of other poets regarded as constituting the "eight seals" (*aṣṭachāp*) initiated by Vallabh into the sectarian fold—is one of the central acts of Vallabhite worship.[12]

In his late-seventeenth-century commentary on the "Accounts of Eighty-four Vaishnavas" Harirāy, the nephew of Gokulnāth, makes it clear that Sūr was blind from birth, but a series of internal considerations argues against our regarding this deeply theological text as a simple report of historical fact. Not surprisingly, then, if we look at the corpus of poetry that had come to be attributed to Sūrdās in the sixteenth century, we discover that only a few compositions allude to the poet's blindness, and among these even fewer suggest he was blind from birth. The following poem (§399) is perhaps the most prominent example. In it, Sūrdās addresses the Deity as Rām, using the term in roughly the same broad sense we have seen for Hari. He joins his own name to a list

11 This occurs in Miyāṅsiṃh's *Bhaktavinod* (in Hindi), which in turn serves as background for the Marathi *Bhaktavijaya* of Mahīpati. See Abbott and Godbole, trans., *Stories of Indian Saints*, vol. 2, 33:37–39, p. 18.

12 I give an English précis of the *sūrdās kī vārtā* attributed to Gokulnāth in my *Sūr Dās*, pp. 3–14. In regard to questions about the status of the text from which it is drawn (Parīkh, ed., *Caurāsī Vaiṣṇavan kī Vārtā*), see Hawley, *Sūr Dās*, p. 7, and *Sūr's Ocean*, vol. 1, p. 7, note 14.

of persons who have received divine mercy. But this is his list. He asks what's wrong with him—or God—that he hasn't been included on God's list, as well:

They say you're so giving, so self-denying, Rām,
That you offered Sudāmā the four fruits of life
  and to your guru you granted a son.
Vibhīṣan: you gave him the land of Lanka
  to honor his early devotion to you.
Rāvaṇ: his were the ten heads you severed
  simply by reaching for your bow.
Prahlād: you justified the claim he made.
  Indra, leader of the gods, you made a sage.
Sūrdās: how could you be so harsh with him—
  leaving him without his very eyes?

This poem is attested in the oldest manuscript where poems attributed to Sūr are collected (J1, dating to 1582 C.E.), but it is not too clear just what sort of blindness is meant—blind from birth or only later? Blind in a physical sense or something more spiritual?[13] Other poems are more explicit. In one of the most graphic, which appears in a manuscript dating to 1736 C.E., it seems plain that the poet's blindness comes upon him not at birth but as one of the curses of old age:

Now I am blind; I have shunned Hari's name.
My hair has turned white with illusions and delusions
  that have wrung me through till nothing makes sense.
Skin shriveled, posture bent, teeth gone;
  my eyes emit a stream of tears;
    my friends, a stream of blame.
Those eyes once ranged as free as a cat's,
  but failed to measure the play of Time
Like a false-eyed scarecrow failing to scatter
  the deer from the field of the mind.
Sūrdās says, to live without a song for the Lord
  is courting death; his sledge stands poised
    above your waiting head.[14]

13 A full discussion of this issue appears in Hawley, *Sūr's Ocean*, vol. 1, Introduction, chapter 1, "Sur's Blindness."

14 Relevant notes, together with a transliterated version of the original text, are given in Hawley, *Sūr Dās*, pp. 180–181. The poem appears on folio 102a of a *Sarvāṅgī* (Complete Works [contained in the liturgical repertoire

Here, as in many similar compositions, it is hard to tell whether a spiritual affliction is intended or a spiritual one—or both. But it is obvious that by this point in time blindness was a motif firmly associated with Sūrdās. The interest came in hearing how the poet would comment upon the disease. In this instance even more than in the earlier example. Sūr's blindness becomes a sign of his distance from Krishna/Hari, not a sign of his mysterious proximity, as in the Vallabhite story and the paintings we have surveyed. An important aspect of the difference is that here we have the poet purportedly speaking about his own condition, rather than being appraised by someone else.

This disparity is at the heart of the most influential biographical tradition associated with Sūrdās, the one maintained in the Vallabh Sampradāy. Vallabhites were eager to cast as less than worthy the entire range of *Sūrsāgar* poems where the poet speaks in his own voice—poems of humility, protest, and praise that are voiced in the first person and conventionally called *vinaya* ("petitionary") poetry. Around the middle of the seventeenth century, Vallabhite biographers thought that *vinaya* compositions such as we have just heard were to be understood as poems Sūr had uttered early in life—before he met Vallabh and felt the influence of his teachings about Krishna, becoming his disciple. It was only after his initiation by the great master that Sūr was able to see Krishna as he really was. Then his blindness came to have the meaning it was intended to have all along; it came to represent his direct apprehension of Krishna's *līlās*. Yet in another sense, this was only possible because an element of indirectness has been inserted into the account: Vallabh had intervened to supply Sūr with his access to the truth.

In other writing I have explained in detail why I am convinced that this Vallabhite version of Sūrdās's life cannot be accepted as historical truth, despite its widespread acceptance as such in the present day.[15] Readers may have already thought it odd that according to the Vallabhite scheme an old-age poem such as "Now I am blind" would have to be classified has having been composed when the poet was still relatively young. But there is much more. For one thing, none of the Sūrdās poems that circulated in the sixteenth century (unlike several that were added to the *Sūrsāgar* later on) makes any reference to Vallabh. It takes a good bit of fancy footwork on the part of Vallabhite hagiographers to make the record look otherwise. Another important fact is that no early manuscript of the *Sūrsāgar* places the first-person poems at the beginning of the collection; several, in fact, do the reverse. Finally—and on this point we will presently have a good bit more to say—one must factor in the reality that the authorial identity

of the Dādūpanth]) accessioned to the Maharaja Man Singh Pustak Prakash Research Centre, Jodhpur, as Hindi manuscript no. 1359/14, *pad saṅgrah*.

15 Hawley, *Sūr Dās*, pp. 14–22; also *Three Bhakti Voices*, chapter 8, pp. 181–193.

called Sūrdās actually describes a literary tradition that was many decades, even centuries, in the making. Manuscripts in which poems attributed to Sūrdās were collected tended to expand over the years as ever more poems were added to the corpus. All these carry a single signature—or rather a small group of signatures designating a single well-known poet—but very probably they were composed by a great many poets. The story of Vallabh meeting Sūrdās radically foreshortens this textual reality in the course of giving it biographical form.

In the end there is perhaps only one feature of the story that rings genuinely true. The Vallabhite embrace of Sūr does accurately reflect the fact that both the original Sūrdās and the many "Sūrdāses" who later took his name were overwhelmingly poets of Krishna. That emerges plainly from almost every early collection of works attributed to Sūrdās, and it is also evident in the representative selection that appears in this volume.

Translator of the *Bhāgavata*?

What are these poems? If we follow the Vallabhite narrative, the great majority—the Krishna poems—are in a certain way translations. They are narrativizations of Vallabh's theological views about how the universe should rightly be regarded—as an expression of the reality of Krishna. More specifically, however, Sūr's poems are understood by Vallabhites to be translations of the scriptural text to which Vallabh was most deeply devoted: the *Bhāgavata Purāṇa*, written in Sanskrit. According to Vallabhite hagiography, when Vallabh vouchsafed his theological vision to Sūr in the act of adopting him as a disciple, he transmitted to him in a miraculous, instantly accessible form the entire content of his commentary on the *Bhāgavata Purāṇa*. Sūr was made able to sing of Krishna with such insight and clarity because he had special access to the sum and truth of the Sanskrit text, which Vallabh had revealed.[16]

This explanation of how the Krishnaite portions of the *Sūrsāgar* came into being is intended to be understood as a compliment. It links Sūr's poetry to a text of unparalleled authority, thereby baptizing Brajbhāṣā speech in the water of classical Sanskrit. Simultaneously it enables the presumed Sanskrit Urtext to bask in the light of its vernacular reflection. Yet in another way this understanding of the *Sūrsāgar* has a bitter aftertaste. It devalues the potentialities of vernacular speech by accounting for them in other terms than their own.

16 Parīkh, ed., *Caurāsī Vaiṣṇavan kī Vārtā*, pp. 405–406; cf. Hawley, *Sūr Dās*, pp. 38–39.

We must reject this view of the relationship between the *Sūrsāgar* and the *Bhāgavata Purāṇa:* the actuality is far more complicated and interesting. If one looks closely at a number of compositions that appear in early versions of the *Sūrsāgar*—§336 and §356–357 are translated here—one sees that the poet delighted in playing with his and his audience's knowledge of the *Bhāgavata*. He pokes and probes and inverts rather than simply hauling the *Bhāgavata*'s contents over the linguistic divide into Hindi.[17] Many who listened to Sūr's poems may not have been able to read the Sanskrit text, yet they may have had a fine sense of its contents: we have no way of knowing exactly who his audiences were. It is clear, however, that the poet planned for a situation in which those who did know the *Bhāgavata Purāṇa* thereby gained access to a deeper appreciation of the subtlety of his own compositions in Bhajbhāṣā.

This intertextual dexterity is an important aspect of the virtuosity we find in the *Sūrsāgar*—part of what makes it a classic in its own right. This status has nothing to do with its being a translation in any ordinary sense. Later versions of the *Sūrsāgar* were organized in such a manner that they reflected the twelve-book plan of the *Bhāgavata Purāṇa,* but there is no indication that the poet himself would have arranged them this way. Nor did the early scribes and editors: the idea is completely foreign to any sixteenth- or seventeenth-century collections of Sūr's poetry.[18] Moreover, early Sūrdās poems often elicited moods and suggested theological positions that were very different from what we find in the supposed "parent" text.

Take, for instance, the celebrated poems that appear in the so-called "bee-messenger" (*bhramargīt*) section of *Sūrsāgar.* Time and again they make it clear that in Sūrdās's view the cowherd women who surrounded Krishna—the *gopīs*—had no use for the spiritualist philosophizing of Ūdho, the messenger whom Krishna sent to assuage the pain the *gopīs* felt in the wake of his absence. The *Bhāgavata* is much more even-handed in reporting the exchange between these two, and is often eager to promote the sort of truth that Ūdho purveys. In the *Sūrsāgar,* by contrast, Ūdho is just a joke—until he is converted to the *gopīs'* view of the bodily devotion that actually counts with Krishna. The poet effectively uses the *gopīs'* intractability as a way of urging that vernacular speech

17 See Hawley, *Sūr's Ocean,* vol. 1, "Intertextual Lineage and the *Bhāgavata Purāṇa,*" pp. 18–27; also the explanatory notes on §336, 356–357 in this volume.

18 See Hawley, *Sūr Das,* pp. 44–52. This is by contrast, for example, to the Brajbhāṣā version of the tenth book of the *Bhāgavata Purāṇa* that was undertaken (but not completed) by Nandadās in the latter part of the sixteenth century, and Nandadās may indeed have had a direct association to the Vallabhite sect, though this cannot be asserted with absolute confidence. See McGregor, *Nanddas,* pp. 31–34; Nandadās, *Nandadās-Granthāvalī,* edited by Brajratnadās, pp. 51–52, 189–278.

and "vernacular" styles of behavior are far superior to the high-minded, tongue-twisting subtleties for which Sanskrit and its Brahmin promoters are so often praised. In this way, with the *gopīs* as his paradigm, Sūr conveys the message that true classics emerge in conversation with everyday speech, and that the body itself is their most basic underlying text.

In its earliest form, the *Sūrsāgar* was strictly in the nature of an anthology—or rather, anthologies, since the poems included in one collection typically differed in substantial ways from those that appeared in another, as did the order in which they were presented. Clearly these lyrics had initially been performed independently of one another. They piped into a vast reservoir of knowledge about Krishna, but they did so episodically, apparently in response to what seemed right for this performative occasion or that. Although they were sometimes organized by themes that suggested a loose narrative progression, it was apparently not until around the turn of the nineteenth century that anyone tried to organize them in such a way that they would look as if they constituted a vernacular rendition of the *Bhāgavata Purāṇa*—a single sequential text composed of lyrics that led logically from one to the next. Only then do the first manuscripts appear in which poems attributed to Sūr are sorted out according to the twelve books of the *Bhāgavata*.[19]

It is hard to conceive that the image of Sūrdās as a translator of the *Bhāgavata* could have emerged from the speech of the original poet whose compositions served as the nucleus around which the ever-expanding *Sūrsāgar* was built. But with sufficient time this did happen. In one poem that seems to have made its way into the *Sūrsāgar* in the eighteenth century or later—it is absent in earlier manuscripts—Sūr is conceived as the endpoint of a lineage that starts with the gods themselves (NPS 225):

> Vishnu, from his sacred mouth,
>   explained four *ślokas* to Brahmā;
> Brahmā told them to Nārad,
>   and Nārad to Vyās in turn;
> Vyās told them to Śukdev,
>   setting them out in twelve books,
> And these Sūrdās told as songs,
>   sung in the common tongue.

Here Sanskrit is the language of the gods, and the finest thing one can say about the language people actually speak is that it stands in a derivative relationship

19 Hawley, *Sūr Dās*, pp. 39–40.

to Sanskrit. Sūrdās makes this happen by connecting it to the divine tongue through the *Bhāgavata Purāṇa*. The sage Vyās is its attributed author; Śukdev is his spokesman within the text itself; and the musical sage Nārad, who is said to have revealed the Purāṇa to Vyās, heard it from his father, the creator god Brahmā, who in turn heard its kernel—four Sanskrit verses called *ślokas* in which the eternal Vishnu describes his own nature (BhP 2.9.32–35)—from that very deity.

Thus Sūrdās is made out to be the vernacular mouthpiece of the Sanskrit document that flowers from the self-revelatory seed of sempiternal truth itself—a high compliment. Yet the actual textual history of the *Sūrsāgar* delivers this compliment in quite a different way. Here there seems to have been no embarrassment about "the common tongue." Poems attributed to Sūrdās were avidly collected—and celebrated—in their own terms, as we shall explain below. A theorist of bhakti such as Nābhādās seems to reflect that fact, and he was not alone. Sometime toward the end of the sixteenth century—perhaps somewhat earlier—his rough contemporary, the Braj poet Harirāmvyās, could be heard to lament that the age of great bhakti poets such as Sūrdās seemed to have passed.[20] His was a golden moment largely defined by what was happening in the vernacular. The Sanskrit writers Rūp and Sanātan Gosvāmī also figure among the spiritual exemplars (*sādhuni*) of the age Harirāmvyās is depicting, but they are the exceptions that prove the vernacular rule. About the *Bhāgavata Purāṇa* all is silence. Instead Harirāmvyās proceeds by lineage groupings, sectarian or otherwise, devoting a couplet to each. He awards Sūr a dramatic position at the end of his list, just before commencing his final couplet with a summary that refers to "all the rest" (*aura sakala sādhuni*). There we learn that Sūrdās was the master of the short lyrical form called *pad*, about which we will soon have quite a bit to say. Harirāmvyās links Sūr to another poet of his generation, Paramānanddās, who was also an exponent of the genre:

> With Paramānanddās now gone, who will sing of Krishna's playful acts?
> With Sūrdās gone, who among poets will carry on composing *pads*?[21]

20 The *terminus ad quem* can be fixed as 1618 C.E., when a memorial to Harirāmvyās was erected in Brindavan by Vīrsingh, king of Orcha, but on several accounts Heidi Pauwels is inclined to date the poet's *floruit* considerably earlier—to the mid-sixteenth century (Pauwels, *Kṛṣṇa's Round Dance Reconsidered*, pp. 2–11). As Pauwels freely concedes, the principal texts guiding any effort to assess Harirāmvyās's chronology are undated, hence I will be conservative and speak of the compositions that concern us as emerging from the latter half of the sixteenth century.

21 I follow the critically edited text published by Heidi Pauwels in her book *In Praise of Holy Men*, *pad* 32, pp. 84–85. She provides a translation of the entire poem on pp. 85–86.

Courtly Frames for Sūrdās

So far we have surveyed ways of framing Sūrdās that locate him firmly within a bhakti milieu, whether or not the *Bhāgavata Purāṇa* was conceived as its criterion. Yet there is more to the story than that. By the first quarter of the seventeenth century, not long after Nābhādās and Harirāmvyās, Sūr had evidently become so famous that the mention of his name was an effective way to establish the sophistication of a court lineage that had vied with the Mughals for supremacy in northern India. Muhammad Kabīr, a person of Afghan lineage who wrote his *Afsānah-i-Shāhāṅ* (Tale of Kings) during the reign of the Mughal emperor Jahāngīr (1605–1627), lauded the darbar of Islām Shāh by saying that Sūrdās performed there. Islām Shāh was one of the Afghan rulers who displaced the Mughals for a brief time in the middle of the sixteenth century (r. 1545–1555), a fact that Muhammad Kabīr implicitly celebrates by recalling the cultural greatness of his fellow Afghan clansman:

> Wherever he [Islām Shāh] happened to be, he kept himself surrounded by accomplished scholars and poets. Kiosks [*khūshak*] were set up, scented with "*ghāliā*" [a compound of musk, ambergris, camphor, and oil of ben-nuts], and provided with betel leaves. Men like Mīr Sayyid Manjhan, the author of *Madhumālatī*, Shāh Muḥammad Farmūlī and his younger brother, Mūsan, Sūrdās and many other learned scholars and poets assembled there and poems in Arabic, Persian and Hindavī were recited.[22]

A passage like this suggests a completely different way of locating Sūr's authority. Here the Krishna poet shares the stage with a series of Sufi writers, and the stage on which he performs is provided not by a temple but by a court. Note that the languages cited in the last phrase seem to be conceived as emanating from an Islamic core rather than an Indic one—first Arabic, then Persian, finally Hindavī. Sūrdās evidently enjoyed a sufficiently stellar reputation

22 The translation is by Behl and Weightman, *Manjhan: Madhumālatī, An Indian Sufi Romance*, pp. xii–xiii, emended from an earlier translation by S. H. Askari, "Historical Value of Afsana Badshahan or Tarikh Afghani," p. 194. It renders folio 151a of the British Library *Afsānah-i-Shāhāṅ* (Persian manuscript add. 24409). I am extremely grateful to Aditya Behl for alerting me to the mention of Sūrdās in this passage, and to Shakeel Admad Khan of Aligarh Muslim University for help in determining its precise location. A printed version of the Persian text in Devanagari transliteration, based on the rotograph copy held by Aligarh Muslim University, may be found in Kutuban, *Kutuban kṛt Miragāvatī*, edited by Parameśvarī Lāl Gupta, p. 39. Transliterations offered in the Behl text refer to standard forms of Persian words that appear somewhat differently in the manuscript original: *khośak* for *khūśak*, and *gāliyā* for *ghāliā*.

that Muhammad Kabīr wished to include him as an embellishment to this royal scene, or perhaps he had heard the scene described by others.

Either way it is hard to accept the historicity of the account. The *Afsānah-i-Shāhāṅ* is filled with episodes that feature genii as main characters, depict fabulous night journeys between Istanbul and India, serve a clearly panegyric rather than documentary purpose, and generally conflict with information that appears in other records of the time.[23] If we take the skeptical view and conclude that Muhammad Kabīr's report was probably fictitious in its depiction of what was going on in the mid-sixteenth century, it nonetheless reveals something important about what had happened by the time we got to the early seventeenth, when he wrote it. By then, clearly, Sūrdās was famous enough that no explanation was required to propose him as a symbol of literary excellence. If by some chance there is a kernel of historical truth in what Muhammad Kabīr reports, that merely indicates that the process began in the lifetime of the poet himself.[24]

Nor did it end with Muhammad Kabīr. When we come to the mid-eighteenth century, in the *Kāvyanirṇaya* (Verdict on Literature) of 1746, we meet quite a different sort of literary retrospective. This one is framed by Bhikhārīdās, a poet in attendance on a ruler named Hindūpati Singh, at Pratapgarh:

(kavitt)
Sūr, Keśav, Maṇḍan, Bihārī, Kālīdās, Brahma,
 Cintāmaṇi, Matirām, and Bhūṣaṇ are reputed.
Līlādhar, Senāpati, Nipaṭ, Nivāz, Nidhi,
 Nīlakaṇṭh Miśra, Śukhdev, and Dev are respected
Ālam, Rahīm, Raskhān, Raslīn, and Mubārak—
 remembering them, how can one praise them enough?
Living in Braj doesn't measure the language of Braj;
 It's only known by the words of poets such as these.

(dohā)
Tulsī and Gang—these two are master poets:
 Their poetry spans languages of different sorts.[25]

23 Siddiqi, "Shaikh Muhammad Kabir," pp. 59–69; Askari, "Historical Value," pp. 184–188.

24 A more extended discussion of these issues appears in Hawley, *Sūr's Ocean*, vol. 1, "Authorship—The Poet and the Poetry," pp. 32–39.

25 Bhikhārīdās, *Kāvyanirṇaya*, chapter 1, in the Javāharlāl Caturvedī edition, pp. 7–11; in the Ved Prakāś edition, p. 56. By Kālīdās is meant not the Sanskrit poet but probably the Kālīdās to whom is attributed the anthology of Brajbhāṣā verse called *Hazārā (Hajārā)*. The name Brahma refers to Bīrbal, Akbar's courtier. Other poets in the list are sometimes given shorthand designations; an explanatory key is provided by Javāharlāl Caturvedī on pp. 9–10. The term translated as "poetry" in the final line is *kāvya*. I am indebted to Allison Busch for drawing this passage to my attention, and to her perceptive discussion of it in "Hindi Literary Beginnings."

Bhikhārīdās's purpose in offering this bouquet of names is to establish for Brajbhāṣā a poetic genealogy that would make it amenable to the aesthetic categories that had been developed to describe the virtues of elevated Sanskrit verse *(kāvya)*. Although Muslim names are not absent from the list, as Allison Busch notes, we hear nothing of Sufi poets such as Qutban and Jāyasī. Does Bhikhārīdās regard them as belonging to a different canon? Similarly there is silence about *sant* poets such as Dādū and Kabīr. As *kavitt* leads on to *dohā*, Bhikhārīdās implicitly contrasts his roster of Brajbhāṣā poets with Gang and Tulsīdās, sixteenth-century poets who displayed their virtuosity by composing in more than one linguistic vein. With Tulsīdās, he is doubtless thinking of the fact that while Tulsī chose Avadhī as the vehicle of his great vernacular *Rāmāyaṇa*, he was equally at home in Brajbhāṣā, as demonstrated by the fine lyrics collected in his *Kavitāvalī* (Poems) and *Vinayapatrikā* (Petitions). For our purposes, though, it is not so much the end of the roster that matters as its beginning. Bhikhārīdās sounds as if he is repeating common knowledge, treading common ground, when he commences his list of well-respected Brajbhāṣā poets with Sūrdās and Keśavdās. As Busch observes, it seems unlikely that Sūr's position at the head of the list is accidental. If he was understood as the *ādikavi* of the set—the originary poet—it was probably in not just a temporal sense but an exemplary one, as well.

The record that emerges from the beginning of the seventeenth century onward, then, seems unanimous about the literary esteem in which Sūrdās was held. That this esteem was expressed in such different contexts—by authors with such different purposes—only strengthens the impression. But there is one potentially discordant note that we have yet to consider, and it comes from a crucial source. Abū'l-Fazl 'Allāmī, Akbar's court chronicler (d. 1602), provides us a list of singers and instrumentalists in his *Ā'īn-i-Akbarī* (Institutes of Akbar) and there too the name of Sūrdās appears.[26] Sūrdās is the nineteenth of thirty-six musicians whom Abū'l-Fazl mentions; almost all of those listed above his rank were also singers. In assigning such a relatively low rank to Sūrdās, Abū'l-Fazl seems clearly to show that his estimation of the poet's greatness fails to align with what we have learned so far. By contrast, he places the eminent musician Tānsen of Gwalior, Akbar's favorite, at the head of the list. Next comes a certain Bābā Rāmdās, also a singer. This man is especially noteworthy for our purposes because when Sūrdās is named later on, he is said to be Rāmdās's son—evidently part of the same Gwalior coterie that

26 'Allāmī, *The Ā'īn-i-Akbarī*, translated by Blochmann and edited by Goomer, *ā'īn* 30.60, pp. 681–682.

included Tānsen, whose son Tāntarang Khān also earns a place above Sūrdās on the list.

Are Abū'l-Fazl's Sūrdās and "our" Sūrdās one and the same? This is the position that was taken by Śivsiṃh Seṅgar, who wrote his *Śivsiṃh Saroj* (Śivsiṃh's Lotus) in 1878, and more recent scholars have sometimes also suggested this might be so.[27] Yet caution is advised. We learn from the *Bhaktamāl* of Nābhādās, which cannot have been written much later than the *Ā'īn-i-Akbarī*, that the name Sūrdās may have been quite common toward the end of the sixteenth century; hence the existence of two distinct poets named Sūrdās would not be strange. Indeed Nābhādās gives us portraits of not one Sūrdās but two, distinguishing the second from the first by adding the name Madanmohan, which connects him with a particular temple in Brindavan.

There are other problems, as well. Take for example the role played by Bābā Rāmdās, who turns out to be a rather confusing figure. The other major Mughal chronicler, the well-placed but distinctly unofficial 'Abd al-Qādir al-Badā'ūnī, disagrees with Abū'l-Fazl in his understanding of Rāmdās. He traces Rāmdās's earlier career not to Gwalior but to Lucknow, associating him not with Tānsen and his ilk but instead with Akbar's regent Bairām Khān, who is said to have been Rāmdās's intimate and generous patron. Badā'ūnī also tells us that Rāmdās had earlier been associated with the Afghan ruler Islām Shāh, but he fails to say what happened to Rāmdās after Akbar secured Bairām Khān's resignation as chief minister in 1560 and Bairām was killed. There is nothing to suggest that the poet joined Akbar's entourage.[28] It is therefore hard to know what to make of Rāmdās (if indeed these Rāmdāses were a single person) except to surmise that he had a career elsewhere before being recruited to what we might broadly call the Mughal court—Akbar's in the one instance, Bairām Khān's in the other. And, of course, there is the plain fact that both chroniclers take a far greater interest in Rāmdās than in his son. Badā'ūnī, in fact, does not even mention him.

One could well imagine that the standards of evaluation brought to bear by these writers of courtly Persian may have been quite different from those that shot Sūrdās to the top of lists fashioned by Brajbhāṣā writers, and considering factors of seniority, Abū'l-Fazl's ranking of nineteenth may not have been so uncomplimentary after all. Yet it certainly contrasts with what we hear from Vaishnava authors, and the poets they associate with Sūr are altogether different from Abū'l-Fazl's royal crowd. Tulsīdās, Paramānanddās, Haridās, Nandadās, and others who are frequently mentioned in company with "our" Sūrdās are

27 Vaudeville, *Pastorales par Soûr-Dâs*, pp. 35–37; to the contrary, Gupta, *Sūr aur Sūr Navīn*.

28 al-Badā'ūnī [al-Badaoni], *Muntakhabu-t-tawārīkh*, vol. 2, translated by Lowe, p. 37 [orig., 2:42].

simply absent from the Mughal record, while Vaishnava hagiographers for their part are silent about Bābā Rāmdās. No poet called Rāmdās seems in any special way to surface either in their accounts or in the early anthologies of poetry where Sūrdās's name appears.[29] We do have the intriguing fact that Badā'ūnī makes a connection between Islām Shāh and Rāmdās, while Muhammad Kabīr goes on to do the same with Sūrdās, but this is a tangled and probably tangential web.

No doubt Akbar welcomed to his palaces in Agra and Fatehpur Sikri the musicians who had once gathered at the Tomar court of Gwalior, by the same stroke recruiting the musical talent that flourished at the Shattari Sufi hospice of Shaikh Muhammad Ghaus in that city. The Sheikh's eminence was also relevant to Muhammad Kabīr's ex post facto attempt to burnish the reputation of the rival court of Islām Shāh. He was the spiritual guide of Mañjhan, whom Muhammad Kabīr mentions in the passage where Sūrdās appears, and he would have been a primary reason that Islām Shāh sometimes traveled to Gwalior, as Muhammad Kabīr tells us he did. Yet although it is easy enough to understand why the author of the *Afsānah-i-Shāhāṅ* might have wanted to make Sūrdās an ornament of the court of Islām Shāh, it is hard to see what this or the Sufi connection might have to do with the Sūrdās whose poems were amassed in the Fatehpur anthology of 1582 (J1: see below) and who was praised about then or soon afterward by Harirāmvyās and Nābhādās. There is nothing in the manuscript heritage of poems attributed to Sūrdās that suggests we could connect him with any of the courts we have so far mentioned, any more than they suggest a sectarian connection to Vallabh or a special tie to the *Bhāgavata Purāṇa*.

All we know is this. Sūrdās was very likely a sixteenth-century poet. He was apparently renowned both in Braj, as indicated by the testimony of Harirāmvyās, and around Amber, as indicated by that of Nābhādās, who seems to have resided in the Rāmānandī ashram at nearby Galtā. He was deeply celebrated by at least one member of the Kachvāhā royal family, a *ṭhākur* named Naraharidās who belonged to the Fatehpur branch, in the year 1582.[30] Evidently he was also a well-known poet somewhat before that time, since the Fatehpur anthology builds on at least two earlier collections, perhaps three. Two of the three distinct collections that make up the Fatehpur manuscript are very

29. In J1, for instance, the name Rāmdās is given as the seal of only one poem (#50) in a total of 411. Many poets other than, of course, Sūrdās have considerably more.

30. Gopal Narayan Bahura traces out the implications of the information given in the colophon of J1 in his introduction to Sūrdās, *Pad Sūrdāsjī kā/The Padas of Sūrdās*, pp. iv–v. Please note that the Fatehpur in question is to be found in the present-day Sikar district of Rajasthan and is entirely separate from the capital Akbar built at Fatehpur Sikri, which lies almost due east of Jaipur near Agra. We refer to the Fatehpur manuscript as J1 because it now exists as part of the collection of the Kachvāhā kings of Jaipur (J), where it is the oldest *Sūrsāgar* manuscript (1).

largely devoted to Sūrdās, one exclusively so.[31] But beyond that—who Sūrdās was apart from the ever-widening corpus of poetry that claimed his name in dated manuscripts that survive from 1582 onward—we simply do not know. All we can say for sure is that by the end of the seventeenth century the ocean of poetry associated with his name bubbles up in manuscripts written in Mathura, all over Rajasthan (on one occasion, at least, by a scribe who hailed from Braj), and as far south as Burhanpur in the Deccan. This does not give us much in the way of biographical detail, but in another way—a literary way—it is no small thing to say.

Collective Authorship and the Expanding Sūrdās Legacy

So far, I have many times implied that *Sūr's Ocean* is no single, linear text—no continuous narrative. It is not a poor man's *Bhāgavata*. Instead, from the earliest moment to which we have access, it is a collection of individual lyrics generating their own distinctive sense of life. They do largely concern Krishna, but in the earliest manuscripts available to us, they are organized in a variety of ways—by raga, by word or theme, and only sometimes by the progression of Krishna's life-story. Listeners are not expected to have heard one poem in order to be able to grasp the force and meaning of the next. Rather, early manuscripts of the *Sūrsāgar* are in the nature of anthologies.

The earliest *Sūrsāgar* manuscripts to which we have access are small; the oldest contains 239 poems attributed to Sūr. Only later does the collection assume the oceanic dimensions its familiar title implies. Not surprisingly, that title came to be applied to the corpus only after it acquired a certain magnitude. We first meet the designation *Sūrsāgar* in a manuscript dated 1640, which contains 795 poems.[32] Once applied, the title evidently stuck. Later manuscripts almost always make use of it, and they tend to expand this ocean of poems farther and farther with the passing of succeeding years. By the nineteenth century, we meet a manuscript containing almost 10,000 poems.

Who then "composed" *Sūr's Ocean*? One can answer this question in one of three ways. The traditional method is to say that a single individual was responsible for generating the entire corpus: Sūrdās composed the *Sūrsāgar*. This position forces one to explain the varying sizes of different anthologies,

31 That is, if we follow the editor in considering the poetic signatures Śyāmghan, Sūrij, Sūrijdās, and Sūrśyām all to designate the same poet. See Sūrdās, *Pad Sūrdāsjī kā*, "List of Padas."

32 U1. On its structure, see Hawley, *Sūr Dās*, pp. 47–48.

especially the smallest among them, as the result of insufficient efforts at collecting the vast number of poems that were actually available. In the Vallabhite tradition, this number is pegged at 125,000, and the final 25,000 are held to have been composed by Krishna himself. This was necessary, the story goes, because Sūrdās found himself exhausted after 100,000 and appealed to Krishna for help.[33] The numbers involved give us some hint of the mythical quality of this claim, not just because they are so large (even the largest manuscript does not begin to approach such sums) but because these numbers have an obviously honorific intent. If something is so praiseworthy that it exceeds what normally counts for perfect, it can be referred to as possessing still another quarter of itself. When the Mughal emperor Aurangzeb wanted to praise the young Kachvāhā ruler Jai Singh II, for example, he called him 1¼ of himself: Savāī Jai Singh. In a similar way the story about the size of the *Sūrsāgar* shows how Krishna took Sūr's perfection over the top—to the 1¼ mark.

This view of the facts is still repeated by connoisseurs of poetry attributed to Sūrdās and can handily be invoked whenever a previously unknown poem comes to light—perhaps in a newly examined manuscript. But at a serious level, it obviously will not do. It may well be that each of the earliest manuscripts, written in different places and at different times, captured only a portion of the Sūrdās poetry circulating in the sixteenth and seventeenth centuries. But this model of a huge *Sūrsāgar* produced by the poet himself and ever in the process of being recovered makes little sense of the fact that anthologies of poetry attributed to Sūr increased in size at a more or less regular rate through the years. Was it harder to remember the poet's utterances early on, when they were fresh, than in later years? A far simpler explanation would be to hold that as the years passed and the reputation of *Sūr's Ocean* grew, later poets wishing to be heard or otherwise to contribute to the genre added new poems to the preexisting sea.

This incremental understanding of how the *Sūrsāgar* became an ocean is supported by several other considerations. First, we know that a number of compositions earlier attributed to other poets were attracted into the *Sūrsāgar* in the course of time. In one or another manuscript they might contain the name of Paramānanddās or Hit Harivaṃś, but later the signature would change and they would show up in the *Sūrsāgar*.[34] One can well imagine how this could happen. Performers working without scripts were doubtless uncertain at times about who was supposed to have composed a given poem. In such

33 Parīkh, ed., *Caurāsī Vaiṣṇavan kī Vārtā*, chapter 10, pp. 434–435.

34 See Hawley, *Three Bhakti Voices*, chapter 9, pp. 206–207, and in regard to my indebtedness to Rupert Snell on this point, p. 375, note 42.

circumstances the performer had a bit of leeway. All it took was the alteration of a few syllables in the final line, where the oral signature appeared, to accommodate one poet's name rather than that of another.

Another consideration is the nature of the signature itself. In some instances, at least, we know very clearly that it was intended more to attest to the authority of a given composition than to designate the biological person who first gave it shape.[35] We can see this very plainly in the development of the roughly contemporaneous corpus of poetry that became canonical for Sikhs. All the Sikh guru-poets who contributed to the *Gurū Granth* adopted the signature of Nānak, who was the first and most important among them. A similar thing must have happened with Sūr, for the *Sūrsāgar* has continued to grow at a steadily increasing pace, yet still to register the signature of only one poet. Poets aspiring to the particular sort of excellence that the name of Sūrdās represented might well be expected to have taken his name as they contributed poems of their own composition to the genre, the way that students of Western classical music sometimes sit down and compose a Bach partita or a Mozart sonata.[36] Finally there is the fact that because of Sūr's reputation as the finest blind poet of all time, many another blind singer would certainly have called himself Sūrdās. This happens still today.

Suppose we grant, then, that *Sūr's Ocean* is not a static thing produced by a single poet, but rather a "Sūr tradition," as Kenneth Bryant was the first to say.[37] What does this make us conclude about the nature of its authorship? One approach would be to abandon any sort of language that would imply the agency of a single, original Sūrdās—the sort of person Nābhādās had in mind. Instead, we would adhere strictly to the conditions of our knowledge, admitting that nothing like an autograph copy can exist in a body of poetry that was largely the precipitate of oral performance. Plainly a multiplicity of Sūrdāses must have been involved in generating this multi-particulate opus, so why not cut to the chase and be satisfied with the notion of collective authorship, as Vinay Dharwadker has recently done for Kabīr?[38] This would be the second answer to the question "Who composed *Sūr's Ocean?*"—exactly opposite to the first.

This solution to the authorship problem is attractive in purely formal terms, and it comes close to describing what must have been the case for the

35 See Hawley, *Three Bhakti Voices*, chapter 1, "Author and Authority," pp. 21–47.

36 I am grateful to my musical wife for this comparison.

37 Bryant, *Poems to the Child-God*, pp. ix–x.

38 Dharwadker, *Kabir: The Weaver's Songs*, p. 60: "a community of authors." On difficulties Dharwadker encounters in employing this notion with complete consistency, see Hawley, *Three Bhakti Voices*, pp. 337–338.

vast majority of poems that were contributed to the *Sūrsāgar* as it expanded from its relatively modest sixteenth-century size to the ocean it is today. But it is not, in the end, satisfactory.[39] It does not explain how the name Sūrdās came to be associated with a particular poetical style and expertise in the first place. Nor does it register the fact that on the whole, poems that appear only in later iterations of the *Sūrsāgar* are less intricate, less dramatic, less convincing artistically than those whose manuscript pedigrees are more venerable. For this reason I believe we must retain a sense of a single excellent poet standing at the headwaters of the Sūr tradition. Perhaps, in this sense, the *Sūrsāgar* might better be thought of as a river than as an ocean—gathering strength in the course of time, but gradually growing more sluggish and losing a good bit of the purity that could be tasted farther upstream.

This is the third and, I think, best solution to the authorship problem, even if it forces us to speak in approximations. True, we do not know anything biographically reliable about the "original" Sūrdās. Yet by speaking about him as if we did, we can affirm the tradition's own sense—from early on—that a poet of special merit first sang the Brajbhāṣā songs that bear the signature Sūrdās and its metrical alternatives: Sūr, Sūrij, and so forth. In the current volume, we can speak in this approximate way with a clearer conscience than we might if we were referring to a much larger and later body of poetry attributed to Sūr. For the poems we present, unlike those assembled in any prior edition, can be said either conclusively or with reasonable certainty to have been in circulation in the sixteenth century itself, when the original Sūrdās undoubtedly lived. In discussing them in my explanatory notes, I will often allow myself to speak as if they were the product of a single creative mind.

As I say, this is an act of approximation. The true reference of the terms Sūr and Sūrdās is to the special logic and poetic art that are displayed in poems early collected in Sūrdās's name. All we have is text—no person—and no single text at that, but a series of anthologies whose contents overlap in complex

39 A thoughtful recent attempt to deal with this set of issues as they impinge upon the formation of several classes of South Asian texts is that of Ronald Inden. Inden mobilizes from R. G. Collingwood the interconnected notions of "complex agency" and "scale of text," both of which have resonances to the *Sūrsāgar*. See Inden, Walters, and Ali, *Querying the Medieval*, pp. 11–12; cf. 48–51. Inden finds an almost perfect alignment between the genre called *purāṇa* and Roland Barthes' idea of a "text"—by contrast to a "work," the latter term signifying "the closed expression of a particular 'author'" (p. 96). The textual history of the *Sūrsāgar* makes it more interesting than a *purāṇa* in this regard. One could argue that it has only come to be conceived as a "work" in Barthes' sense in the course of the last century and a half, yet it is equally difficult to assimilate it to the "open, authorless" end of the work/text spectrum. There are two reasons for this. First and perhaps more important, there is the insistent presence of the poet's signature in each poem and the authority that attaches to it in the minds of those who listen. Second, historical proximity to an implied (sixteenth-century) poet plays a major role in determining the size, shape, and tone of the textual corpus.

ways. Still, as a group they seem to radiate a particular poetic personality: someone tirelessly imaginative, and yet so scrupulous that he avoided repeating any word in the course of a single composition unless he intended the emphasis or irony it would command. It is a pleasure to follow tradition and call this person or persona Sūrdās.

Listening to the *Pad*

We will be meeting a particular poetic personality in these pages, yet it is important to realize that his chosen poetic genre has a great deal to do with making him who he is. To understand why Sūr's poems are considered classics, we must understand the rules of the genre that was his favorite.

With a single exception (§418, "Sūr's twenty-five"), all the poems collected in this volume are designated in Brajbhāṣā by the term *pad,* meaning literally "foot" or "pace." *Pads* are lyrics meant to be sung. On rare occasions they may also be recited, and in the case of the *Sūrsāgar* this practice is justified by the definite structure a *pad* possesses independent of any musical rendering. Manuscripts of the *Sūrsāgar* often differ in the ragas (*rāg*) they assign to any given *pad,* but the *pad* itself remains an integral entity. Of course, something is lost when the musical element is missing—as if one were quoting out of context rather than offering the real thing—but the central life of the *pad* remains. The formal structure stays intact.

Much of that structure is dictated by the few, relatively simple rules governing every *pad.* These are implicit, not the product of any written prescription, and for that reason all the more important to understand as one approaches the genre. They are as follows:

(1) The *pad* is rhymed at the end of each of its lines or verses, most often with a single rhyme that persists throughout the composition, but not infrequently by couplet, and very occasionally in a hybrid of the two.[40] A given word can appear more than once in a rhyme scheme provided its

40 In speaking of Brajbhāṣā *pads,* I shall use the terms "line" and "verse" synonymously. The English translation will be formatted so as to correspond to the layout adopted in standard Brajbhāṣā editions, including that of the Nāgarīpracāraṇī Sabhā, and in the Bryant edition upon which we rely here. When a line of English translation is positioned flush left, this means that a new verse—ending in rhyme—has begun in Brajbhāṣā. (Manuscripts of the *Sūrsāgar* often adopt a different numbering system, counting by couplet.) In translation it is usual for a Brajbhāṣā verse/line to yield two lines of English print, with this latter line division corresponding to the caesura in the original. Occasionally a third or even fourth line is required to convey the meaning of a single verse. Yet however many lines figure in the translation, I will continue to calculate a verse or line as that which appears in the Brajbhāṣā original.

repetition introduces a separate meaning, but this option, called *yamak*, is rarely exercised in the early *Sūrsāgar*.

(2) In part because it can be structured by couplet, the *pad* contains an even number of verses, with only rare exceptions.

(3) The overall length of the composition is not defined. *Pads* of six or eight verses are most common, but *pads* in the *Sūrsāgar* can have as many as sixty lines or as few as four. Genre is often determinative in this respect: it is unusual for a "riddle" (*kūṭ*) poem to contain more than eight lines, but *pads* appropriate to the season surrounding the festival of Holī typically have at least a dozen.

(4) The verses in a *pad* are of equal length, except for the first verse, the *ṭek* ("prop," refrain), which may be shorter.

(5) The length of a verse is normally calculated by "instants" or morae (*mātrā*), which may be either long or short, the former being twice the length of the latter. In the most frequently used meter (*sār*), all verses but the *ṭek* contain twenty-eight *mātrās*, with a certain margin of deviation to be expected from manuscript to manuscript and sometimes from line to line. The exact sequence of *mātrās* is not governed by formal regulation. Instead this becomes a feature that distinguishes one meter from another, with particular attention being paid by taxonomists to the last four *mātrās* in a verse.[41]

(6) Each verse contains a caesura (*yati*), which falls either exactly halfway through the line or, more frequently, at a slightly later point. In the *sār* meter, for example, it divides the verse into sixteen and twelve instants. In that case, the *ṭek* is normally equivalent in length to the portion of a verse that precedes the caesura (in *sār*, sixteen instants).

(7) The poet's signature (*bhaṇitā*) or seal (*chāp*) appears in the poem itself, usually in the final verse but sometimes in the penultimate verse instead. Strictly speaking, no syntax is required to relate it to other words in the line in which it appears, but often it forms part of a genitive phrase or can be understood as carrying with it the verb "says," which is occasionally expressed outright.

(8) The *ṭek* functions not just as a title line but also as a refrain, and is repeated at least once in performance—after the entire poem has been sung. Usually it is repeated more frequently, either in whole or in part, and is often sung after every couplet or even after every verse.

To see how these conventions come together in practice, let us consider a single poem in detail. It serves as an appropriate introduction to the *pad* in that

41 For further information in English, see Bryant, *Poems to the Child-God*, pp. 125–128, and Snell, *The Hindi Classical Tradition*, pp. 24–26.

it is today among the most frequently performed compositions in the *Sūrsāgar*.[42] Moreover, its structure is so pellucidly clear that it lends itself to "textbook" use. This is so despite (and in some ways, because of) the fact that it does not possess one of the best pedigrees in the early *Sūrsāgar*. Like many poems represented in our edition, it appears in only some half-dozen manuscripts, and these do not include the one manuscript (J1) that clearly dates to the sixteenth century itself. The poem's oldest datable attestation is in manuscript B2 (1624 C.E.), but it figures in our collection because it appears not only there but in several other early manuscripts that lie some distance from B2 on what we can loosely call the manuscript "tree." As with a number of poems included in our collection, the relatively wide dispersion of this *pad* in the seventeenth century implies with fair certainty that it was already in circulation in the sixteenth.

The poem in question commences with the words "Prince of Braj, awake," but in giving it a title, I have dubbed it simply "Awake!" It figures as §19 in the critical edition created by Kenneth E. Bryant (*Sūr's Ocean*, vol. 2) and in my own larger treatment of the text (*Sūr's Ocean*, vol. 1). A closely corresponding version of the poem appears as number 820 in the *Sūrsāgar* first published in its complete form by the Nāgarīpracāriṇī Sabhā in 1948 and edited by Jagannāth Dās "Ratnākar," Nandadulāre Vajpeyī, et al. For more than half a century this has been the most frequently used version of the *Sūrsāgar*—the standard edition, you could say—and it plays an important role in the general process of Hindi canon formation to which I alluded at the beginning of this introduction.

Now to the poem itself. On hearing its first words, a knowing audience would naturally identify it as being addressed to the child Krishna by someone in the cowherders' village (Gokul) where he grew up. Probably they would think of the speaker as Yaśodā, Krishna's foster mother and the wife of the village headman Nanda, for in other poems and in the religious plays (*rās līlā*) so frequently performed in Braj, where Sūrdās *pads* are sung, Yaśodā is often lovingly depicted in just this act of trying to wake her child. In the setting of a temple or home altar, this poem would be sung before an image of the deity just after daybreak. According to the system that is standard in Braj and in the Braj-focused religious groups that span from Gujarat to Bengal and beyond, this is the moment called *śṛṅgār āratī* or *śṛṅgār bhog*, the time when Krishna is dressed (*śṛṅgār*) for the day ahead. In a home, the poem would be sung by selected members of the family; in some temples, such as those of the

42 For example, it is the first poem that Dharmanārāyaṇ Ojhā mentions as being frequently performed when the deity is awakened at the first *darśan* of the day (*maṅgal*) in a Vallabhite temple. See Ojhā, *Sūr-Sāhitya meṅ Puṣṭimārgīya Sevā Bhāvanā*, p. 378.

Vallabh Sampradāy, by one or two professional musicians; and in others, as in the Caitanya Sampradāy, by a larger, somewhat more informally constituted group of singers.

In what follows, I present the *pad* in three forms: in its critically edited version, given in transliteration and with the caesura marked by a slash; in a literal interlinear translation of the individual words involved; and in a full translation into English verse.

1	*jāgau*	*braja*	*rāja*	*kuṅvara*	/	*kaṅvala*	*kosa*	*phūle*
	awake	Braj	king	son		lotus (of day)	sheath	blossom
2	*kumudini*	*muṣa*	*sakuci*	*rahī*	/	*bhṛṅga*	*latā*	*jhūle*
	lotus(es) (of night)	face(s)	ashamed	remain		bee	vine	swing
3	*tamacura*	*ṣaga*	*rora*	*sunat*	/	*bolata*	*ban*	*rāī*
	rooster(s)	bird(s)	din	hearing		speak(s)	forest	line (or king)
4	*rambhati*	*vai*	*madhur*	*dhenu*	/	*bacharā*	*cita*	*dhāī*
	low(s)	that (or those)	sweet	cow(s)		calf(ves)	mind	run(s)
5	*bidhu*	*malīna*	*rabi*	*prakāsa*	/	*gāvata*	*braja*	*nārī*
	moon	dull	sun	brightness		sing(s)	Braj	women
6	*sūr*	*śrī*	*gupāl*	*uṭhe*	/	*ambuja*	*kara*	*dhārī*
	Sūr	blessed	Cowherd	arose		lotus	hand	bearing

1 "Prince of Braj, awake!
    The lotuses of day blossom from their sheaths
2 And the lotuses of night hide their faces.
    Vines swing, heavy with bees.
3 Roosters and birds make such a din
    that it seems the very forest is speaking.
4 Cows produce their sweet, lowing sound
    as they ruminate on their calves.
5 The moon is dimmed, the sun shines bright,
    and the women of Braj sing."
6 And then, says Sūr, the blessed Cowherd stirs—
    he who bears the lotus in his hand.

Let us begin by observing how this poem satisfies the requirements placed on any *pad*, as we have listed them above. It rhymes by couplet; it has six verses, about the number most frequently encountered; the verses are of equal length, although one must scan two syllables from the first line in the optional "short" form to achieve this exactly; the caesura divides each line into components of twelve and ten *mātrās*, respectively; and the poet's signature appears at just the point where one most frequently encounters it, at the beginning of the final line. The brevity of the meter is unusual, and this accords with another somewhat atypical feature of the poem, namely, that its first or "refrain" line is as long as any of the other verses. But aside from these features, everything in this *pad* is as standard as could be wished—except, perhaps, that its very simplicity marks the poem as not quite average.

I have tried to render "Awake!" into a form of English verse that approximates the original as closely as possible. To do this, I translate verse by verse, breaking at the caesura in cases where, as is usual, the diction of the original poem also pauses at that point. This produces two lines of English text for every line in Brajbhāṣā.[43] Often one needs the extra space that the more ample English format provides, since the translation must spell out grammatical connections that are left unstated in the original. For instance, one could interpret the second part of the first verse as meaning either "lotus sheaths blossom" or "lotuses blossom from their sheaths," and if the latter seems best, then the ablative idea requires the supplying of an English preposition ("from") that is unexpressed in Brajbhāṣā. Because the poet intends to make a comparison between the behavior of these lotuses and that of the lotuses he will mention in the phrase immediately following ("lotuses hide their faces"), I have in fact chosen this somewhat wordier option.

The comparison between two categories of lotus causes us to introduce a few more words, as well. Sūr—the ascribed author, as we have said, not necessarily the biological person—has a vast range of words from which to select in naming the flowers upon which he will focus. From that huge treasury he picks three separate words for "lotus" for use in this poem: *kaṃval* (v. 1), *kumudini* (v. 2), and *ambuj* (v. 6). Indeed, some hearers of the original may find it makes a significant difference whether a lotus is called the generic *kaṃval* rather than, say, *paṅ kaj* ("mud-born") or, as later in this composition, *ambuj* ("water-born"). The poet often exploits these possibilities, even if the flower to which his words refer is

43 Printed versions of the *Sūrsāgar* do usually adopt the verse-by-verse spacing I have displayed, but this never appears in early manuscripts. There the scribe uses all available space, almost always beginning a new verse on the same line as the one just concluded. Only a vertical stroke (*virāma*), doubled for a couplet, marks the break.

exactly the same and the terms are understood by native speakers as being entirely or nearly synonymous. But even if Sūr does not seem to want to draw out different shades of tone or meaning from the words he employs, the aggregate record of the sixteenth-century *Sūrsāgar* makes one thing sure: he regards it as awkward to repeat a word unless he has a specific reason for doing so. In this, the early *Sūrsāgar* presents a considerable contrast to many *pads* added to the corpus at a later date, and to later versions of *pads* that appear in the present collection.

So, then, in "Awake!" Sūr uses three separate terms for lotuses. As it happens, they have three distinguishable denotations. *Kaṃval* and *kumudini* designate two mutually exclusive classes—respectively, the day-blooming and the night-blooming varieties—and their contrast to one another in this respect was sufficiently celebrated in poetry that the Mughal emperor Jahāngīr commented on it.[44] This may have been a familiar world to Jahāngīr, but it is not to most English readers today. To make the day/night contrast clear, our translation requires just the sort of additional verbiage— "lotuses of day . . . lotuses of night"—that the original can suitably avoid. Unfortunately, this makes the English rendition a bit stiffer than the Brajbhāṣā original, which connects these two lotuses more gracefully, both in the intrinsic meaning of the words the poet selects, and by sound. Both words the poet chooses for his day- and night-blooming lotuses begin with "k."

In fact, these two words form a part of a larger alliteration on "k" that dominates much of the poem's first verse and propels it into the second. The reader may therefore object that the poet's association of "k" with lotuses is not exclusive. This is quite right. Although one of the two "k" words remaining in the first line also refers to lotuses—*kos* denotes the sheath—this still fails to account for the word *kuṃvar*, meaning "son." The poet will ultimately meet this objection. By the time he has finished, Sūr will have drawn this "king's son," or prince, quite firmly into the orbit of lotuses. In the last phrase of the last verse, he "lotusizes" the waking Krishna by drawing attention to his "lotus hand."

This is a formulaic comparison in Indian poetry. The gently tapered shape of the lotus petal makes it an appropriate simile for all beautiful hands, and with Krishna there are additional considerations, especially color: blue for the back of his hands, and a reddish tint for the palm. Both hues are also to be

44 Rogers, trans., *Tūzuk-i Jahāngīri or Memoirs of Jahāngīr (1605–1624)*, revised and annotated by Beveridge, pp. 412–413. In this passage, written in 1617, Jahāngīr refers to the poetry of Tānsen, which he had heard him sing at the court of his father Akbar. Quite probably a contemporary of Sūrdās, Tānsen also composed in Brajbhāṣā. I am grateful to Françoise "Nalini" Delvoye for having noticed the passage in the course of her extensive work on Tānsen. See Delvoye, "The Thematic Range of *Dhrupad* Songs Attributed to Tānsen, Foremost Court-Musician of the Mughal Emperor Akbar," especially pp. 414–415; and "Les Chants *dhrupad* en langue braj des poètes-musiciens de l'Inde moghole," especially pp. 174–179.

seen in lotuses. But Sūr does more than simply repeat a formula. He positions it at a crucial point in his composition—at the very end—and further mobilizes it as a tool to serve his aims by enlisting the element of sound, as well. The word he selects to designate Krishna's hand is *kar*—again, several others would have been possible—and *kar* is the only term after the poem's introductory salvo (verses 1–2a) that begins with "k." It is also the only one having to do with lotuses. Thus by the time he is done, Sūr manages to justify the "k" he used to identify Krishna (as "son") in his opening phrase. He shows how Krishna belongs to the "k" category otherwise entirely inhabited by lotuses, for Krishna too—by virtue of his hand—is a lotus. He too blooms, in response to the plea that is articulated in the *pad* as a whole. In this, he imitates the day-blooming lotus about which we hear in the title line itself.

Following the lead of Barbara Herrnstein Smith, I will be calling this phenomenon "closure" throughout my explanatory notes.[45] As Kenneth Bryant has explained, relating this vocabulary to *pads* attributed to Sūrdās, closure entails the completion of a contract established early in the poem, very often in the title line (*ṭek*).[46] In the present composition, the contract is that Krishna is bidden to awake, and in the last verse this contract is fulfilled: he does just that. At a subtler level, however—at the level of language—there is another contract, a contract in sound. In the opening verse the poet assays a "k" connection between the boy and the lotuses that begs for further confirmation; by the end of the poem, that confirmation is achieved. Hearers discover, as they listen to the *ṭek* again after the last verse, when it returns as a refrain, that the *ṭek* contains a logic of sound whose full meaning they could not have anticipated the first time they heard it.

As for the intervening verses, they do their part in working toward the ultimate contract by evolving a symmetrical structure that prepares and reinforces the special relation between the first and last lines. Like these framing verses, the second and second-to-last lines also bear a special connection. Both refer to the night in its relation to the day: in verse 2 "the lotuses of night hide"; in verse 5, "the moon is dimmed." And the remaining interior couplet (vv. 3–4) also takes its place in the picture. It deepens the poem's exploration of Krishna's environment by moving beyond flora to fauna—the birds and cattle.

This is quite relevant in that Krishna too is "fauna," and the mention of cows and calves resonates to the feelings expressed by the women of Braj—perhaps especially Yaśodā—as they see the child Krishna. Indeed, parental feeling is symbolized in Indian aesthetic and devotional theory by the "calf" emotion,

45 Smith, *Poetic Closure: A Study of How Poems End* (Chicago: University of Chicago Press, 1968).
46 Bryant, *Poems to the Child-God*, pp. 43–51, 66–68, *passim*.

which is called *vātsalya*. *Vātsalya* is based on the Sanskrit word *vatsa*, meaning "calf," and the poet actually uses a version of that word here, the vernacularized *bacharā* (v. 4). Thus upon entering the poem we gradually descend from child (v. 1a) to lotuses (vv. 1b–2a), to a mix of bees/birds and flower/trees (vv. 2b–3), and finally to cows and calves (v. 4). In the penultimate verse we are drawn back out by being asked to recall the contrast of day and night (v. 5a) that the poet had first associated with lotuses (vv. 1–2) and by integrating into the human world the old-to-young emotions he introduced through the lowing of cows (v. 4). Thus he works back toward his human subject as "the women of Braj sing" (v. 5b).

In other poems of the early *Sūrsāgar* this process of immersion and retrieval takes a variety of shapes. The "body" of the poem—the part following the initial contract but preceding its final confirmation or closure—may expand from a single interior couplet to six verses or more. Particularly in *pads* of eight verses, there may be a significant shift midway—after the fourth verse—so that the two halves of the poem in some way match (e.g., §§1, 65; cf. §300). Such a poem is thus symmetrical in a certain sense, but it must still be asymmetrical in another. It must be cumulative: the poet must anticipate at the beginning, and finish at the end.

Pads offer two major means of signaling closure. The first emerges from the simple requirement that the name of the poet be announced before the poem is complete. This usually occurs in the last line, and very frequently in the word that starts that verse; hence the signature tells the audience the *pad* is about to end. In doing so, it often effects a slight change of register. This is easiest to detect in poems that are in the nature of "quotations," as are most in the *Sūrsāgar* corpus. Such compositions seem naturally to emerge from the mouth of someone who belongs to the dramatic realm of Krishna (or Rām or Rādhā), so when the poet inserts his name, it is a voice from another world. In the poem at hand this change of register is quite marked. When we shift from the speech of a cowherd woman (*gopī*), perhaps Yaśodā, to that of a more neutrally positioned narrator, the shift is more than momentary. The mention of the poet's own name at the beginning of this verse suggests that we are hearing his voice from then until the poem concludes. Most listeners unhesitatingly conflate the identity of the potentially neutral narrator with the voice of the poet whose name has just been uttered. For them it is not "And then [Sūr] the blessed cowherd stirs . . ." but rather "And then, says Sūr, the blessed cowherd stirs . . . ." Hence the translation we have offered.

In "Awake!" Sūr goes one step further in making this change of register clear. At the end of the penultimate verse he makes reference to how "the women of Braj sing" (v. 5). We realize that the little boy is being urged to hear the very singing we have been hearing all along. At one level, at least, Yaśodā's words *are* this song—up to the final verse, that is. Sūr strengthens this suggestion by repeating the word "Braj" from the first verse, making these two "Brajes" function almost like quotation marks. It closes the quote that began in the title line. There "Braj" is a word away from the first in the verse (*jāgau braj*); here it is a word away form the last (*braj nārī*). Since a *pad* is normally heard rather than read, all such signals must be encoded into the language of the poem itself. But even when a *pad* appears in written form on a manuscript page, it lacks the word boundaries, capital letters, and punctuation marks that help clarify such transitions in modern European languages. The poet's rhetoric substitutes, and he often takes advantage of the *pad*'s relative plasticity in developing his own structures.[47]

A permanent shift into the voice of the narrator-poet, such as we have here, is distinctly exceptional in the early *Sūrsāgar*. Usually after "signing" his *pad* and thereby signaling its impending closure, Sūr goes on to preserve the dramatic integrity of his composition by returning us immediately to Krishna's world, to the voice we have been hearing all along—in this case, Yaśodā's. Sometimes the last verse is structured in such a way that audience can have it both ways, understanding that verse to have been spoken not only by the character in question but also by the poet himself. Yet the stricter, more "correct" construction—one that Sūr almost always makes possible—is to revert to the dramatic voice that makes sense within Krishna's own narrative world. Certain later variants of "Awake!" actually convert the poem to this more standard form through the simple expedient of transforming the perfect indicative verb *uṭhe* ("arose" > "stirs") into the imperative *uṭhau* ("arise"), though it is doubtful that the act of conversion was a conscious one. Here are the results, as revealed in the Nāgarīpracāraṇī Sabhā edition, where other words change as well:

6 *sūr syām prāta uṭhau / ambuja-kara-dhārī*
Sūr's Dark One, it's morning. Arise!—
you with the lotuslike hands.

In this apparently more recent version of the poem, only the mention of the poet's name suggests that we have departed momentarily from the level of diction with which we began—the voice we have supposed to be Yaśodā's. Yet the insertion of the poet's "seal" still has its effect. Once it has been heard, the poem is a bit more embracing: the poet's name reaches out from Krishna's world toward ours. In another way, simultaneously, it is more specific: the speech we have been hearing is now associated with the persona of a particular poet. Often

47 Bryant, *Poems to the Child-God*, p. 138.

Sūr plays with these possibilities, making his signature contribute to closure not just in a formal way but also by creatively altering the tone of the *pad*.

The second major way in which the poet signals impending closure is through his use of the penultimate line. We have already hinted at that fact in what we have observed about the construction of quotation in "Awake!," but there is more to be said. Each *pad* requires a signature, normally in the final verse, but in the line preceding it the poet has a freer hand. Nothing about its structure is actually mandated by the form of the *pad* per se. The broader milieu in which the poet works, however, does suggest what might be generally appropriate, and we frequently find Sūr adopting a technique that has an analogue in music. This practice is called *tihāī* ("thirds"), and it loosely parallels the discursive convention called *trivacan* ("three sayings"), indicating a declaration that threefold repetition makes binding, as in an oath. A musical performer uses *tihāī* to build a cadence that comes to its resolution just after a rhythmic phrase has been sounded a third time. The musician's target is the *sam*, the first beat in whatever rhythmic cycle governs a composition. The *tihāī*'s "thirds" strain forward to that *sam* as a chord progression or cadenza might prepare for the return of the tonic in Western music. The analogous resolution in a *pad* happens in the last line, and is often heralded by the announcing of the poet's signature as it starts.[48]

Since the normal structure of a *pad* is bipartite—with the caesura punctuating the sound and meaning of every verse—the division of the penultimate line into three parts rather than two represents an acceleration of pace. In more extreme instances, it can create a new rhythmic pattern that challenges the caesura itself by spanning it (e.g., §42), but it may also simply integrate an additional, third element of meaning into the preexisting caesura structure. This almost always happens in the first segment of the line, as in "Awake!" So instead of hearing the single phrase "Cows produce their sweet, lowing sound" as in the preceding verse (v. 4), we meet two shorter ones in the same space: "The moon is dimmed, the sun shines bright" (v. 5). The contrast between moon and sun makes the quickening tempo hard to miss, and practiced hearers know that closure is imminent. Following the musical analogue, I often call this technique "stretto." It creates a sense of heightened tension that is released in the final

48 It is worth underscoring that these correspondences between musical performance and the final two verses of a *pad* are meaningful only at the level of analogy. In modern performances of a *pad*'s final verse, the *sam* is often heard many more times than once, and only rarely coincides with the first syllable of the line. See Snell, "Metrical Forms in Braj Bhāṣā Verse: The *Caurāsī Pada* in Performance," pp. 363–364. Moreover, as we shall see, there is no way of knowing for sure what conventions of performance were dominant in the sixteenth century. Yet it is significant that the basic form of the *tihāī* is found in both folk and classical genres of north Indian music, and in the south as well. The analogy is proposed only at such a level of generality.

verse—frequently with a sense of relaxation that follows from the acknowledgment, through his signature, of the poet's own presence in the poem.

Relaxation is not invariably present, however. Kenneth Bryant has highlighted several examples of *pads* from the *Sūrsāgar* that conclude with a surprise, even a shock. The force of such poems is apt to depend in a particularly direct way on the ability of the "knowing audience" to marshal information that is not given in the poem itself, since it is the business of the poem precisely to hide the secret.[49] Yet it is also possible for Sūr to enlist the audience's "omniscience" in the cause of strengthening—surprisingly—a closure that would seem to have been adequately clinched by other means.

Some of this happens in the closing words of "Awake!" We have already seen several ways in which the poet establishes the conclusiveness, the "contractuality," of Krishna's awakening in verse 6. To this we could add the obvious fact that Sūr implicitly likens Krishna's stirring to the rising of the sun, which he mentions in verse 5. But he strengthens the closure by another means too, and this one depends on his audience's knowledge of how very young children behave—in this instance, how infants often relax their hands from a clenched position when first they emerge from sleep. This contributes to the poet's full meaning when he concludes by speaking of Krishna's "lotus hands." He may well expect his listeners to imagine that these hands open upon awakening, like lotuses blossoming from their sheaths (v. 1). Thus he takes advantage of our life experience in building the lotus-to-hand connection that lies at the center of his purpose.

Yet even life experience is not quite enough. One needs theological or devotional experience too, and the language of the poem nudges us toward this final dimension. As Rupert Snell has observed, the participle *dhārī* ("bearing") does not customarily take an "internal" object—say, a body part. Something more distinct from the subject would be the rule.[50] So there is something unusual in thinking of Krishna's lotus hands as the object he bears; the lotus is fine, but not the hands. Is it possible, then, that we are actually supposed to visualize the child as holding a lotus? Shrivatsa Goswami once suggested that one could achieve this effect without disrupting the scene by imagining Krishna as propping a "lotus"—his fresh, round face—on upraised palms, a familiar childhood pose. But perhaps we should move beyond lotus hands and lotus faces and recall that in standard four-armed representations of Vishnu, the god does indeed hold an actual lotus. If that is what the poet has in mind, the phrase "he who

49 For example, Bryant, *Poems to the Child-God*, pp. 51, 66–68.

50 Snell, e-mail communications, December 6–7, 2008, and in regard to other aspects of the poem, December 20–22.

bears the lotus in his hand" would serve as a cue that we have here something more than normally meets the eye—not by giving us a literal, physical lotus but by suggesting a cosmic dimension that might transvalue this otherwise cozy scene. Is this sleeping child really Vishnu recumbent upon the primordial milk ocean? Is he the awesome deity whose act of rousing himself from slumber will mean the dawning of the universe as we know it? What a way to fulfill the contract implied by the word "awake"—with the dawning of all creation!

It is hard to know exactly what the poet intended when first he uttered these words, but we can say with confidence on the basis of other poems that ambiguity is often his ally. Multiple layers of meaning contribute importantly to the richness of the early *Sūrsāgar*. Yet sometimes there can be too many meanings, and they are likely to arise in connection with enigmatic passages just like this. In such instances the manuscript variants tend to offer us readings that are either too simple or too far-fetched. The Nagarīpracāriṇī Sabhā's version, which we have mentioned earlier, gives us an example of the former, reducing *uṭhe* to *uṭhau*, while the oldest manuscript in which the poem appears, B2, does the opposite. Its reading of the last verse is *sūradāsa prabhu sovata uṭhe / karuṇā ambuja dhārī*, which one could translate either as

6 The Lord of Sūrdās arose from sleep,
bearer of compassion and the lotus.

or alternatively,

6 The Lord of Sūrdās arose from sleep,
bearer of the lotus of compassion.

The variant is obviously weak: why should compassion (*karuṇā*) enter the picture? We seem to have slipped into the realm of some general, worshipful title for Krishna—something on the order of *karuṇā nidhi*, meaning "treasury of compassion." Yet the term "compassion" does inadvertently help to confirm the correctness of the critical version, since one could easily postulate a lost original—*kar*, "hand"—as the basis for B2's faulty *karuṇā*.

Other meanings could legitimately be extracted from this poem. Consider verse 3, for example, where I have translated the expression *ban rāī* (v. 3) as meaning "the very forest," with *rāī* representing the word *rāji*, a streak or line, and by extension a range of something—here, the entire wilderness or forest (*ban*). Others have interpreted the same phrase as meaning "king of the forest," however, with *rāī* representing the word *rāja*, as it usually does. This might mean that a lion or a peacock was adding its voice to the din of "roosters and birds,"[51] but to me it seems likely that the poet wants to indicate groves so full of birds calling at dawn that one feels the very trees are speaking—or perhaps just one large tree, as the meaning of *ban rāī* also allows.

It is a shame to obscure the acts of choice that are occasioned by ambiguities such as these. Here lies much of the pleasure of a poem, and alas, most of it disappears in translation. In the following verse, for example, when "cows ruminate (*dhāī*) on their calves," they may also—on a derivation from a different verb—be "running toward their calves in their minds" (*cita dhāī*), but who would know it from the translation? The opposite loss can also occur, where translation obscures an element of clarity that is present in the original. Indeed, if English readers had only my translation of verse 3 to go by, they would never guess that the poet has bridged his caesura with acts of hearing *(sunata)* and speaking *(bolata)* that echo one another directly. No wonder "it seems the very forest is speaking!"

Finally let me mention the matter of rhyme, which contributes to the structure of every *pad*. On the face of it, it might seem logical to expect that an English translation would echo that rhyme in a corresponding way, yet I have held back, feeling that the consistent use of rhyme would seem as artificial to readers of modern English as its absence would be jarring in Brajbhāṣā. There are times when I use rhyme to respond to a poem in which sonority is a particularly vital element of Sūr's strategy, but on the whole I have taken a more conservative approach, hoping that a few reminders of rhyme will serve to suggest the ambience of the original. In "Awake!" these appear in the verse-end resonances that make sequences of the words "sheaths > bees > speaking" and " din > sound > sing > hand."

Obviously this sort of full-dress analysis is not possible for each of the poems translated in this book. But I hope that by digging this deep in one exemplary instance, readers can glimpse what makes so many of these poems seem classic to their intended audiences. One of the purposes of the explanatory notes is to keep that sense alive as we proceed to the collection as a whole.

The Poems That Follow

By now, I have referred many times to Kenneth Bryant's edition of the *Sūrsāgar*, which forms the basis for my translations. Interested readers may consult it in volume 2 of our jointly authored *Sūr's Ocean* (New York: Oxford University

51 This interpretation is preferred by a number of commentators: Bāharī and Varmā, *Sūr Śabd-Sāgar*, p. 382; Ṭaṇḍan, *Brajbhāṣā Sūr-Koś*, pp. 1187–1188; and Sūrdās, *Sūr-Granthāvalī*, edited by Caturvedī, vol. 1, pp. 141–142, 158–159.

Press, forthcoming). In volume 1, along with the translations themselves, I include the full history of attempts to edit the *Sūrsāgar* and describe what sets the Bryant edition apart from all earlier efforts, including that of the Nāgarīpracāriṇī Sabhā.

This is no place to recapitulate that large and complex subject. Suffice it to say that no other edition pays rigorous attention to the full array of dated manuscripts closely relevant to the reconstruction of the *Sūrsāgar* as it was known in the sixteenth century, when the Sūr tradition was just beginning to form. From that critical process emerge 433 poems. We can be sure that 239 of them circulated in some form in the poet's own century, since they are included in the oldest dated manuscript (J1), which was written at Fatehpur, northwest of present-day Jaipur, in 1582 C.E.[52] In fact, the Fatehpur manuscript appears to be a compilation of three earlier collections, so it sinks its roots even farther back into the sixteenth century.[53] As for the rest, a comparative analysis of somewhat later manuscripts, dating almost entirely to the seventeenth century, strongly suggests—on the basis of their dispersal and other factors—that they contain an additional 194 poems that must also have been in circulation before the end of the sixteenth century.[54] Obviously this is an arbitrary cutting-off point for an edition of the *Sūrsāgar;* the very adoption of that title, which first emerges to view only in 1640, helps signify that fact. But it is the best we can do, and it certainly sets to rest any idea that other works attributed to Sūrdās—the *Sūrsārāvalī,* for example, or the *Nal Daman*—belong in anything like the same league. The manuscripts associated with these texts come along only much later.[55]

In the end, we cannot tell what the "original" Sūrdās wrote. In fact, if we think in those terms, we are almost certainly missing the boat. In the Sūr tradition, with its complexly interwoven oral and written strands, we do not actually know whether Sūrdās wrote a word. We can think of him confidently as a literate but ultimately oral poet—a singer—but there too we come up against our limitations: there is no true way of knowing the musical vocabulary in which he worked. It is often assumed that Sūr sang in the *dhrupad* style, a formal diction that is kept alive in many temple traditions that flourish in Braj today. But

52 The manuscript is published in a facsimile edition: Bahura and Bryant, eds., *Pad Sūrdāsjī kā / The Padas of Sūrdās.*

53 For details see Hawley, *Three Bhakti Voices,* chapter 15, pp. 280–286.

54 See Hawley, *Sūr's Ocean,* vol. 1, "The Editorial Context," pp. 99–111; Bryant, *Sūr's Ocean,* vol. 2, introduction.

55 See Hawley, *Sūr Dās,* p. 25, note 48; also McGregor, *Hindi Literature from Its Beginnings to the Nineteenth Century,* pp. 152, 157, 185. The earliest manuscript that has yet come to light for this set of texts is the *Nal Daman,* for which we have an illustrated *nastālīq* manuscript housed in the Prince of Wales Museum, Mumbai, and dating to the final decade of the seventeenth century. Information in the text itself dates its composition to Lucknow in 1657, so it is clear on all grounds that the Sūrdās who was its author cannot be the same as the poet to whom the *Sūrsāgar* is ascribed. See Vāsudev Śaraṇ Agravāl and Daulatrām Juyāl, eds., *Nal Daman,* pp. 1–2, 6–7.

this assumption, like so many others, turns out to rest on shaky foundations. Certain basic features of *dhrupad* style as apparently performed in the sixteenth century—the absence of a *ṭek* and *dhrupad*'s unmistakable preference for *pads* that divide clearly into four parts (four verses, usually)—make it dubious that this was Sūr's habitual mode.[56] The uncertainties do not stop there. Even the ragas he might have used are in dispute: manuscripts regularly assign different ones to a single poem.[57] In all this haze it is lucky, as we have seen, that *pads* attributed to Sūrdās bear structural features that make it possible to appreciate them in isolation from their musical, performative context. Still, anyone who has heard these poems performed knows how much is lost when we reduce them to a thing of the page.

The present collection of poems contains about a third of the number that can be found in our two-volume *Sūr's Ocean.* I have selected them with several considerations in mind: the range of style and subject matter they represent, their sequencing, and their cogency in Brajbhāṣā and in translation. These are, by and large, poems about Krishna and his world—samples of the most influential collection of vernacular Krishna poetry to be found in all of north India. They often take a great deal for granted, being addressed to audiences already deeply familiar with the mythology of Krishna. The poet's job is not to lay out the contours of that mythology but, if anything, to review and even subvert it—to surprise his audiences with new perspectives on a narrative they think they already know.[58]

Of course, not all readers possess this familiarity, so I have been fairly liberal in supplying explanatory notes keyed to particular moments in the poems. Still more information and interpretive commentary may be found in the complete Oxford *Sūr's Ocean.* I have also taken the liberty of supplying short titles for each of the poems included in this volume. As we have seen, the practice of titling is not entirely foreign to the *pad:* often the *ṭek,* or refrain, effectively fills that role. But in the original there is no external title floating above the language of the poem itself. In supplying one—and I often borrow from the *ṭek* in doing so—my purpose is merely to provide a convenient term of reference for English readers. One final innovation is the headings under which I group these poems. Some earlier editions and anthologies, going way back to the seventeenth century, have also applied such rubrics, principally with the

56 See Sanyal and Widdess, *Dhrupad: Tradition and Performance in Indian Music,* pp. 49–51; Prem Lata Sharma, *Sahasarasa: Nāyak Bakhśū ke Drupadoṅ kā Saṅgrah;* also Sharma, "Sahasarasa," *Indian Music Journal* 8–10 (1972–1974), pp. 41–48.

57 See Hawley, *Sūr's Ocean,* vol. 1, introduction, chapter 2, "Performance, Past and Present."

58 This is broadly the theme of Bryant, *Poems to the Child-God,* chapter 2, pp. 43–71, and appears elsewhere in the book, as well. It will be encountered repeatedly in the explanatory notes accompanying this volume.

object of grouping the poems in such a way that they could be easily associated with successive stages in the life of Krishna. Many of my headings echo theirs, but not all. So far as I know, there is no precedent for concluding an anthology of Sūrdās poems with hymns to the sacred rivers, as I have done in hopes that this would help the collection flow together at the end.

Each poem is keyed to its original in the Bryant edition (signified by the symbol §) and to the standard Nāgarīpracāriṇī Sabhā (NPS) listing. Readers will notice that these numbering systems do not always run parallel. Principally this occurs because the Nāgarīpracāriṇī Sabhā editors followed the Vallabhite predilection and placed Sūr's *vinaya* poetry—petition and praise—before his Krishna poems. But no old manuscript takes this approach and neither do we. Like several of the old manuscripts, Bryant and I begin with Krishna's birth and move on from there.

One last word: it concerns, again, the thorny matter of translation. In the notes I sometimes mention particular opportunities that the original provides in this regard, but more numerous, to be sure, are the problems. Particular instances do figure in the notes, but in the background, unmentioned, stands a series of hurdles that must constantly be vaulted as we move from sixteenth-century Brajbhāṣā to the sort of English that is spoken and read in the twenty-first century. In Chapter 4 of my introduction to *Sūr's Ocean*, I comment further on the general task of trying to bridge this gap.

There is an old story about how the Mughal emperor Akbar fell in love with Sūr's poetry. Akbar offered to pay a substantial fee for every genuine poem of Sūr's that he could get his hands on, with the intent of adding it to the royal collection. Having done so, he was faced with the task of determining which of the many poems attributed to Sūrdās actually emerged from the master's mouth. A certain Pundit Kavīśvar, whose artificial-sounding name contains a familiar Mughal title meaning "lord among poets," attempted to put one over on the emperor by composing a *pad* of his own and then "stamping" it with Sūr's signature. But there was no fooling Akbar. He commanded that a genuine poem be brought as a standard of measure, and then submerged both it and Kavīśvar's forgery in water. The one survived undampened, while the other was ruined.[59] I hope the translations that follow—admittedly a soggy lot—will help readers imagine the crisp, well-shaped originals that have inspired many literary connoisseurs like Akbar to praise the poems of Sūrdās.

59 Parīkh, ed., *Caurāsī Vaiṣṇavan kī Vārtā*, chapter 4, pp. 418–419. Sheldon Pollock offers a glimpse of the wider genre of tales of trial-by-drowning to which this story belongs in *The Language of the Gods in the World of Men*, pp. 313–316.

The Memory of Love

A few paragraphs back I confessed to artificially partitioning "Sūr's Ocean" into eight segments in an effort to make its contents tell the story that many early editors regarded as its principal subject—the story of Krishna's life and of the vibrant world he inhabited. Largely speaking, this was a world of love, enacted on the stage of eternal youth. Sūrdās remembers this world—typically through the protests and recollections of characters actually on the scene, especially the women among them. They too have memories of Krishna and find it hard to shake them off. Yet when Sūrdās steps into the *gopīs'* shoes, he is not just retreating into nostalgia. To the contrary, he is piping into a stream of thought that never loses its currency, and the tradition tells us that part of the reason for this fact is that memory itself is ever active. Far from representing a retreat from present reality, it is the force that gives the present its shape. Poems are memory's special minions, its foot-soldiers, its dancers.

The Sanskrit language, which Sūrdās almost certainly knew to some extent, goes a step further in conceptualizing this process. It recognizes an intrinsic connection not just between memory and poetry but also between memory and love. Indeed one word, *smara,* sometimes designates both realities. Of course, there is a good bit more in *Sūr's Ocean* than can be captured in a single name, but if one has to choose—books do require titles—then perhaps the two registers of this single word *smara* will do. Most of the poems attributed to Sūrdās have deeply to do with *the memory of love,* even when Krishna is not involved.[60]

The prospect of remembering, enacting, and recreating the world of Krishna is understood by devotees to be the central purpose of life. Sūrdās has come to be regarded as an icon of this act. When Sūrdās is pictured calling Krishna to mind, visualizing him with his miraculously unblinded eyes and serenading him in the process, a claim is made about how active these poems can be in present time. Krishna listens, entranced. This moment—the special chemistry that is unleashed when a Sūrdās poem is recited—is remembered as being classic, something no other poet was ever quite able to achieve. In that way it is well and truly past. Yet in each new performance—perhaps even a performance filtered through the veil of translation—it is also potentially present. We all have loves to remember. With luck, through the words of Sūrdās, we may find Krishna in them all.

60 A striking instance is provided by §369, where the very phrase "the memory of love" swims to the surface in the course of translation. This poem concerns Sītā and Rām, not Rādhā and Krishna, and it contains a Brajbhāṣā double meaning that is not unlike what we find in the Sanskrit word *smara.*

Poems from *Sūr's Ocean*

I
Krishna Growing Up

The night he was born (§1, NPS 629)

"This night in the month of Bhādoṅ, this dark night—
Soldiers have closed the streets, dear, they've shut the doors,
   and the fear of Kaṃs is heavy everywhere.
The clouds are rumbling. Now it's started to pour.
   The Jamunā's waves are high, its waters black,
And the only thought in every heart is this:
   how to keep the child's bright face obscured?
Husband, why did I heed your words that day?
   Better I'd been slaughtered there and then,
For look at this child, and tell me how a mother
   could live if torn from such a son."
Devakī's wail was heard by the One
   who pities the poor and removes his servants' pain:
The chains were loosed, says Sūr, the gates undone.
   He gave her his wisdom and banished her distress.

Celebrating the birth (§3, NPS 642)

"Braj has been blessed with a headman's son"—
  and when the news traveled to everyone
How they were filled with joy!
  The worthy astrologers of Gokul,
Seeing that all the merits of the family's past
  had planted in the earth an unshakable pillar,
Searched pairings of planets, the powers of the stars,
  and chanted the sounds of the Veda.
When the Braj women heard, they all came running,
  dressed in their natural way,
Yet decking themselves with their newest clothes
  and applying mascara to their eyes.
Their forehead marks all set in place,
  blouses on bosoms, necklaces on breasts,
With braceleted hands braced to hold
  auspicious golden offering plates,
Group by group they left their houses
  in a lovely way, lovely to see,
Looking like a line of red *muni* birds
  that had broken free from their cages.
Friends gathered in clusters—five or ten—
  and sang their songs of blessing
Like early morning's lotus blossoms
  blooming at the sight of sun.
They didn't know—or care—that the breeze
  had blown their scarlet saris from their breasts.
On their faces and limbs was spread red powder,
  vermilion was daubed in the parts of their hair,
Earrings dangled in tandem from their ears,
  their hair was tied in loosely fastened braids,
And their exertion made sweat appear on their brows
  like droplets sprinkling from clouds.
The first to arrive at the darling baby's door
  was overcome with joy:
She called the others inside.
  They bowed, touching the feet of the child,

And when the veil was lifted from Hari's face
they showered out their blessings:
"Long live the one who fulfills
every wish of Yaśodā and Nanda!
Praise this day! Praise this night!
Praise this watch, this hour!
Praise the womb of this mother,
so full of wifely fortune
To have given birth to such a son—
the ripened fruits of joy!
In him the whole clan has found a foundation.
From every heart the spear of pain is gone."
Hearing the news, the cowherds urged their boys
to herd home the cows.
They threaded garlands of *guñjā* berries,
found chalk in the forest to rub on their limbs,
And with pots of curd and butter on their heads
they sang new songs as they went,
Making their way to Nanda's house
with cymbals and drums.
One of them danced an uproarious dance,
spattering the others with turmeric curd
As if rains in the month of Bhādoṅ
had flooded the rivers with milk and *ghī*.
Wherever their minds might take them,
it seemed there was marvel there,
And they gave no thought to anyone else,
so utterly absorbed were they in joy.
One of them rushed to Nanda,
repeatedly touching his feet;
One of them laughed and laughed to himself,
then fell into an embrace;
One of them stripped off his clothes
and cheerfully gave them away;
Another took a blade of *dūb* grass,
daubing every head with cow-powder and curd.
Then Nanda bathed and reappeared
with *kuśa* grass in his hand,
To honor his ancestors with the *nandīmukh* rite
so that every inner worry would be gone.

He chose his priest for the ritual and gave out clothes
to him and the other Brahmins—whatever they might wish—
And in doing so, with hands together in honor,
he touched their feet. He was moved with love.
Cows, there were countless cows—
young cows, mother cows with fine big calves,
The kind of cows that give double the milk
from grazing on the Jamunā's shores,
Gilt-horned cows with silver on their hooves
and backs all covered with copper—
These cows he gave to numerous Brahmins,
who joyfully responded with words of blessing.
Others crowded into the house and its courtyard—
minstrels, genealogists, and bards:
They sang out all the family's names,
forgetting none whom they held dear.
King Nanda gave cheerfully to anyone who begged,
gave to overflowing,
So from that moment all who'd ever begged
now would beg no more.
Then laughing, he summoned those near to him—
clan, friends, all his kin—
And marked their foreheads with a paste he prepared
from musk and saffron and camphor.
With wildflower garlands he draped their breasts
and gave them clothes of various colors,
Making it seem as if the rains of Āṣāḍh
had brought to life the peacocks and frogs.
Then he had masses of saris brought,
saris of beautiful colors,
And gave them out to the womenfolk.
They took whatever caught their eye.
Happy, so happy, those cowherds, made rich,
returned to the houses from which they had come,
Dispensing blessings as they went on their way,
distributing however they pleased.
From house to house you could hear the drums—
bheri, mṛdaṅg, paṭah, nisān—
Garlands of special leaves were strung above doors
there were celebratory pots and flags,

And ever since that day those folk have lacked nothing,
neither happiness nor wealth.
So says Sūr: that will also be the fate
of all who fall in praise at Hari's feet.

He loves butter (∫7, NPS 717)

How radiant!—fresh butter in his hand,
Crawling on his knees, his body adorned with dust,
  face all smeared with curd,
Cheeks so winsome, eyes so supple,
  a cow-powder mark on his head,
Curls swinging to and fro like swarms of bees
  besotted by drinking drafts of honey,
At his neck an infant's necklace, and on his lovely chest
  the glint of a diamond and a tiger-nail amulet.
Blessed, says Sūr, is one instant of this joy.
  Why live a hundred eons more?

Crawling (§8, NPS 720)

What pleasure to my heart, his innocent childish games!
He scrambles on his knees, carefree, across the floor
   to capture the reflection of his nails;
He calls for his butter, Nanda's little boy,
   by silently signaling a milkmaid with his eyes;
He marshals his sounds in an effort to speak
   but the words still won't emerge,
And the brilliance of millions of bits of the universe,
   in his infancy he obscures.
As for the people of Braj, the Master of Sūr
   brings fruition to the longing of their eyes.

Teaching him to walk (§9, NPS 733)

Mother Yaśodā is teaching him to walk.
He wobbles a little, so she gives him her hand;
  he sways, and puts his foot back on the ground.
Sometimes she sharply summons Balarām:
  "Play here in the courtyard, you two!"
Sometimes she prays to the household gods:
  "Let little Kānh, my son, live long!"
Sometimes she stands there just staring at his face,
  so that any harm to her heart's beguiler
    would rest on her instead.
The Lord of Sūrdās is the giver of all happiness,
  and King Nanda reaps the utmost joy.

His fabulous feet (§10, NPS 749)

Hari—how I love, love my little Mādhav.
He clambers over a threshold and tumbles, tumbles,
  but grasps with his lotus-petal palm and crawls on.
He has come to Yaśodā on account of love
  and placed his feet upon this earth, the ground–
The feet that he used to outwit King Bali,
  the feet from which the Ganges flowed
    as the merest sweat from beneath the toenails,
The feet whose visage captivated Brahmā and the gods,
  generating millions of moons and suns:
Those feet, says Sūrdās, inspired me to offer,
  offer,
    offer up my all.

Growing too slow (∫15, NPS 792)

"If you drink the milk of the black cow, Gopāl,
 you'll see your black braid grow.
Little son, listen, among all the little boys
 you'll be the finest, most splendid one.
Look at the other lads in Braj and see:
 it's milk that brought them their strength.
So drink: the fires daily burn in the bellies
 of your foes—Kaṃs and Keśī and the crane."
He takes a little bit and tugs his hair a little bit
 to see if his mother's telling lies.
Sūr says, Yaśodā looks at his face and laughs
 when he tries to coax his curls beyond his ear.

Topknot (∫16, NPS 793)

Yaśodā, when will my topknot grow?
How many times have you made me drink my milk?—
  and still it's so little, so small.
You keep saying sometime it'll be thick and long—
  longer than brother Balarām's;
Comb it and braid it and wash it, you say,
  and it'll slither to the ground like a big black snake;
But all the while you're after me with milk, milk, milk—
  you never give me bread and butter."
Sūr says, a taste of the childhood of these two—
  Hari and his brother, the Bearer of the Plow—
    is enough to make the three worlds reel.

Feeding his reflection (§17, NPS 796)

Today, my friend, at the first moments of dawn
  restless, I rose to start churning curd:
I filled up a vessel, put it down near a polished pillar,
  and set the churning rope running through my hands.
Such a sweet sound! Hearing it, Hari too
  stirred awake and scampered to the scene.
His quick and flickering movements captured my mind—
  my gaze froze, my mind glazed—
And I quite forgot my body as he studied his reflection;
  my heart was cooled with every kind of joy.
I saw him take both hands and halve a lump of butter.
  He offered it to the face he saw, and smiled.
Sūrdās says, the way that boy behaves
  is more than my heart can contain:
These childish antics of the God of every mercy
  entrance me, and cause my eyes to dance.

Awake! (§19, NPS 820)

"Prince of Braj, awake!
  The lotuses of day blossom from their sheaths
And the lotuses of night hide their faces.
  Vines swing, heavy with bees.
Roosters and birds make such a din
  that it seems the very forest is speaking.
Cows produce their sweet, lowing sound
  as they ruminate on their calves.
The moon is dimmed, the sun shines bright,
  and the women of Braj sing."
And then, says Sūr, the blessed Cowherd stirs,
  he who bears the lotus in his hand.

At dawn (∫20, NPS 821)

Nanda arose at the break of dawn,
  he gazed at the face of his sleeping son
And was so overcome he couldn't stay still,
  though his eyes still battled away the night.
That face shone forth from its clean, pure bed:
  the darkness disappeared, the lethargy fled
As if the gods were churning the Ocean of Milk
  and the moon emerged, parting the foam.
Sūr says, all the cowherds and herder girls heard
  and ran to the spot—clever, willful *cakor* birds
Who forgot their bodies as their minds held fast
  to the drinking of moonbeam pollen.

Butter thief (∫22, NPS 901)

"Gopāl is furtively eating butter.
Look, my friend, what a bright shimmer streams
  from the dusk-toned body of Śyām,
With drop after drop that was churned from curd
  trickling down his face to his chest
As if the moon rained lovely bits of nectar
  on lovers approaching from below.
His hand lends grace to the face beside it
  and flashes forth as if
The lotus had dropped its feud with the moon
  and come forth bearing gifts.
Look how he's risen to peer from his lair,
  to look around on every side;
With wary eye he scans the scene, and then
  he cheerfully feeds his friends."
Seeing Sūr's Lord in his boyish fun,
  the maidens start, weakened,
Until their hearts are lost to speech—
  thought after thought after thought.

The gopis complain (§23, NPS 909)

Why don't you reprimand that boy?
What can I say? Every day it happens.
  I haven't the strength to endure:
He swallows the butter, spills milk on the floor,
  smears his body with curd,
Then chases after the children left at home,
  spraying them with butter-whey.
If ever I hide a thing, even in places
  far-off and secret, he knows where.
What to do? Defeated, undone,
  I'm driven to despair by your son.
His thefts are so clever—that wish-fulfilling jewel!—
  that their tale cannot be told,
And so, to get a hold on him, says Sūr,
  all of Braj is flowing,
    dashing here and there.

Yaśodā answers (∫24, NPS 913)

Dark One, stop, don't go away.
I'm doing it for you, my cowherd boy—
  listen to me, my lovely little lad—
    I'm filling the vessels full as they'll go
      with all six tastes of food.
Why go off where others live?
  Why make such elaborate plans
    to get the milk and curd and *ghī*
      and butter they too have to give?
They hardly seem to find it a crime,
  to come and rehearse it a thousand times—
    that endlessly shameless company
      of newly married brides.
Big, uncouth Braj cowherd girls!
  Out in the streets they hawk their goods,
    shouting their taunts carelessly,
      always picking quarrels.
I've listened to them till I'm thin and ill.
  How much longer can I live with such bile?
    It's only guile, says Sūr: they want
      to see that dear, dark face.

Better mothers than Yaśodā (∫28, NPS 968)

Take a hard look at Hari's face and body.
How could such a little bit of curd, Yaśodā,
provoke in you such wrath?
His eyes look with fear at the stick you're holding;
they tremble and shimmer with tears
As if a bee had settled on a blue lotus petal
and made the dewdrops shiver.
It seems indeed as if a lotus—sheath and stem—
has been bent by a brisk morning breeze,
For his face and lips are similarly lowered,
speaking through their shame some sullen pique.
How much cow's wealth could you possibly have lost
to justify berating him so?
The tiny fear-erect hairs of Sūr's Lord
should suffice to make you sacrifice
both body and breath.

Aviary (§31, NPS 984)

How could you have become so angry with Kānh
That you took a stick in that harsh hand of yours
  and let it touch his soft, tender frame?
Look at how those tears drip down from his eyes
  and glisten as they settle on his breast,
As if a wagtail wanted to gather many pearls
  in a beak too small to hold them all inside.
Those eyes shuttle back and forth in such terror—
  look into his face and listen to what I say—
That it seems, says Sūr, two birds have seen the bow
  of a hunter, and are desperate to fly.

Back from the woods (§33, NPS 1094)

Look, my friend, as Nanda's Joy
  returns to Braj from the woods, bedecked—
On his head are peacock plumes; in his hand, his flute;
  a sandalwood mark on his forehead.
The curls in his hair swing down across his face
  with a restless motion, showering great joy,
As if a pair of wagtails had flown into a lotus
  and there had been snared in a trap.
When he sings his lilting, intoxicating sounds
  his teeth shine forth—and his deep red lips—
As if pearls had been placed in a sapphire setting
  and sprinkled with vermilion powder.
Destroyer of the wicked, this Lord in cowherd's clothes
  herds cows in a cowherders' clan,
And that, says Sūrdās, is the glory described
  when the Vedas chant,
    "He is not this, not that."

The dust of Brindavan (§34, NPS 1107)

If only we'd been fashioned as the dust of Brindavan!—
The dust that is trod by Nandanandan's feet
  when he goes grove to grove to herd the cows.
What have we gained by being born as gods?
  What's the point in gaining some elevated place
When the Merciful One, out of mercy for all beings,
  can inundate the world in a flash?
How much more blessed are the trees and blades of grass,
  the children and calves, the flutes and the horns,
For Sūr says, he laughs, talks, and plays with all of them,
  roams about and churns and drinks the foam.

Dancing on the snake (∫36, NPS 1193)

All Braj is gathered at edge of the Jamunā
To see Saṅkarṣaṇ's brother dance
  on the head of Kāliya the snake:
With his feet—*thei thei*—he sounds out the rhythm
  of the deep mridangam drum
And the heavens fill with chariots—courtiers and musicians
  whose love and delight make them sing.
Before him stand the wives of the snake,
  their eyes pouring streams of tears:
"Beautiful Dark One, grant us a boon.
  Let our husband be released."
Emerging from the water, his dark body flashed
  with the brilliance of his jewels and clothes.
Sūrdās says, joy overcame the herdsmen
  as they welcomed him with an embrace.

Forest fire (§37, NPS 1233)

"Come to our rescue now, Gopāl—
Now is the time: in all ten directions
  there's sprung up a fearsome forest fire!
Bamboos pop and bristle, the *kāṃs* grass crackles,
  palms and *tamāl* trees dangle to the side,
Sparks and cinders ricochet in air, fruits burst,
  tongues of flame lunge ruthlessly at us,
A great haze of smoke envelopes the earth
  and a net of firebrands glitters in the sky.
Does, pigs, peacocks, parrots, the *sāras*-crane—
  the life in them incinerates. Disaster!"
"Don't be scared. You all just close your eyes"—
  so spoke Nanda's lad with a laugh.
Sūr says, he poured the fire down his own mouth
  and left the boys of Braj unafraid.

The color of dusk (§38, NPS 1234)

That Beguiler-of-the-Mind is the color of dusk.
Look how he looks, my friend, the handsome son of Nanda
as he wends his way back from the woods:
Peacock-feather moons make, on Kānh, a shining crown
and from his mouth the simple sounds of Muralī have charm.
The lilt of his earrings, the luster on his cheek,
the honey in his speech—all beyond describing.
The little curls of hair against the beauty of his face
make a garland of honey-drinking bees
And the slow, broken rhythms of his smiles are thunderclouds
flashing secret, intermittent lightning in the sky.
A *tilak* stroke has been marked on his head,
set between his eyebrows, his brow, and his eyes
As if the sense of loveliness had gotten to be so strong
that it leapt across propriety's sober, modest line.
Sūr says, his lips, with their matchless redness
radiate their glory beneath the portals of his nose
Like ripe and brilliant *bimba* fruit sheltered by a parrot
who readies his beak to peck at them and taste.

A mass of delight (§42, NPS 1245)

Look, friend: look what a mass of delight—
For my *cātak*-bird mind, a cloud dark with love;
  a moon for my *cakor*-bird eyes.
His earrings coil in the hollows of his neck,
  gladdening his tender cheeks,
As crocodiles might play on a nectar pond
  and make the moonlight shudder in their wake.
A wealth of elixir, his mouth and lips,
  and little Muralī perched in his hands
Seems to be filling that pair of lotus vessels
  with still more of that immortal liquid.
His deep-toned body, sheathed in brilliant silk,
  glitters with a garland of basil leaves
As if a coalition of lightning and cloud
  had been ringed by parrots in flight.
Thick locks of hair; a lovely, easy laugh;
  eyebrows arched to a curve—
To gaze upon the splendor of the Lord of Sūr
  is to make one's wishes lame.

Muralī's kingdom (§45, NPS 1271)

1 These days Muralī has become so proud
she refuses to speak to a soul,
2 As if she'd found in the land of his lotus mouth
a kingdom to supply her every joy.
3 Insolent girl—his hands are her throne,
his lips her parasol,
4 His hair her whisk as she reigns, my friend,
over a court of cows.
5 There she decrees that the waters of the Jamunā
stop on their course to the sea,
6 And as for the gods in the city of the gods,
she summons their chariots to earth.
7 Stable things move and moving things are still—
both are triumphs for her
8 As she cancels the way the Creator set things up
to institute her own design.
9 That bamboo flute rules all, says Sūr—
god, sage, man, and snake:
10 Even Śrī's Lord—he forgets his Śrī,
obsessed with his newfound love.

Muralī makes him dance (§46, NPS 1273)

Even so, Muralī delights Gopāl,
Even though—listen, friend—she takes Nanda's Darling
  and makes him dance so many ways.
She makes him stand on a single foot
  to show the extent of her command,
Burdens his tender limbs with her decrees,
  turns him crooked at the waist,
And seeing him utterly submissive and servile
  bows the Mountain Lifter's neck.
She bounds on the bed that his lips provide,
  demands a massage from his flower-petal hands,
Furrows his brows, and makes his eyes and nostrils
  tremble with rage against us.
Let him think her happy for a instant, says Sūr,
  and she rolls her head on his torso—"No!"

Muralī transfixes (§47, NPS 1276)

Muralī adorns Balarām's brother's lips.
Just one sound and all the women are transfixed;
  clothes slip unnoticed from their breasts.
Birds close their eyes, motionless as yogis
  intent on a night of meditation.
No vine rustles or sways on its tree,
  so weary and sluggish the breeze;
Cows and deer have abandoned their grass;
  calves disdain their milk.
Sūr says, on hearing that beguiling sound,
  the waters of the Jamunā stand still.

Hero of the cow-clan (§55, NPS 1481)

Hero of the cow-clan, come and protect us!
The cows, the calves, the cowherds drip with rain—
  drenching rains: Raindrops sting like arrows
That Indra's thundercloud commander unleashes
  in pestle-torrents of battering battalions.
These unbearable torments! Who, son of Nanda,
  could vanquish them but you?
You tamed the great snake, tore open the heron's face,
  destroyed the heron woman, gave every happiness.
Who, says Sūr, could anyone ever fear—
  anyone who counts on constant succor from you?

Great crowds of clouds (∫56, NPS 1487)

"Today great crowds of clouds circle over Braj—
Brother Kānh, protect us now!
  All of us look to you!"
Hearing these few words, the Delight of Yaśodā
  glanced at the mass of Govardhan
And determined to lift that fine mountain:
  he held it, plucked it from the earth.
At that, clouds of the Great Flood were dispatched.
  Above Braj they set up their camp.
Five hundred sixty million clouds mounted up,
  so many the day turned dark.
Seven days long the clouds rained, then they ceased.
  They accepted their defeat, they turned about-face,
And thanks to the help of Śrī's husband, Sūr's Lord,
  not a drop came near—not even one.

We marvel at your arms (§58, NPS 1584)

"Dark One, we marvel at your arms.
How could such tender hands have been so strong
as to hold up a mountain?" they all ask.
"Indra was so angry that he sent his rains on Braj,
but, in the end, he failed"—
So say his cowherd pals as they hug their brother—
"It's you who rescued us all."
Excited, Yaśodā brings an offering plate
with betel leaves, *dūb* grass, curd, and grains of rice,
And marks his forehead, and bows to the dust of his feet
like a pauper finding a pot of gold.
Smiles come to the lovely women of Braj
as they gaze and gaze on his lotuslike hands,
Which serve as their excuse for looking again and again
with their unending thirst for love.
Sūrdās says, the timid captain of the gods
brings in all the cows and says,
"You—you're fathomless, impassable, indelible,
and I've not found the secret of how."

2
The Pangs and Politics of Love

The onslaught of love (§60, NPS 1744)

Rādhā is lost to the onslaught of love.
She weeps from tree to tree and finally succumbs,
searching through the forests and groves.
Her braid—a peacock grasps it, taking it for a snake;
her lotus feet attract the bees;
Her voice with its honey makes the crow in the *kadamb* tree
think her a cuckoo, and caw her away;
Her hands—the tender leaves of blossom-bringing spring:
thinking so, parrots come to peck;
And thinking her face to be the moon on a full-moon night,
the *cakor* bird drinks the water from her eyes.
Desperate at thinking perhaps she'd been dismembered,
the Joy of the Yadus appears in the nick of time:
Sūrdās's Lord takes that seedbud of new birth
and cradles it, a newborn in his arms.

Circle dance (∫62, NPS 1757)

See how Hari has arranged his circle dance—
Who has ever heard,
    ever seen such a thing?
        Where has this taste been secreted away?
First he conjured up a fine magic spell
    and spread it everywhere—
        no one was spared.
Then with one fine shot of an arrow
    he struck everything that moves or does not move.
        Who knows the recipe for such love?
Seeing his eyes' aesthetics,
    tasting the lilt of his voice,
        a welter of murmurs rippled through the army
Of Kāma, says Sūr, who could not control his bow.
    He turned his hands palm-up, that Bodiless One,
        and then began to dance.

Filling her pots (§64, not in NPS)

"On the banks of the River Jamunā,
In a secluded spot, alone,
  I was filling my pots with water
    when Kānh caught hold of my hair.
I placed the pitchers on my head, but the path
  was winding, and he was garbed all in yellow,
And the more I looked, the lovelier he seemed;
  his little waist-bells so fine."
The milkmaid's touch of embarrassment
  told how that warrior had won the battle—
Sūrdās's Cowherd: he'd taken her in his arms
  and given her golden pitchers their reward.

Black storm clouds (§65, NPS 1806)

Black storm clouds have risen in the sky,
  pierced by herons in an eerie row.
Please, Kānh, look: a rainbow—such beauty!—
  bearer of all colors,
    bow for the arrows of the gods.
Lightning flashes forth and strikes here and there
  like an eager, restless woman
Whose lover is outside, while her husband is still at home:
  she moves away, returns, helpless,
    burned by the God of Love.
Peacocks and crested cuckoos cry out in the woods,
  dispatched as messenger girls by the trees,
And just so the vines, love-deprived women,
  paragons of amorous anger and pride,
    break their vow of silence
      with another kind of poetry:
They mate with every tree they meet
  in a web of darkened groves.
Kāma, the expert, awakens to the wish
  of Sūr's dark Śyām: he lifts his own hand
    to decorate a bower as a home.

Serpent and vine (§67, NPS 1814)

A beguiling vine is draped on Hari's chest,
Grasped by a serpent that rests upon it,
  and then a full moon shines.
Strands in a rope, her golden upper arms
  cinch tight and braid with one of his,
Which resembles a snake upending a golden pot
  to reach the honey inside.
That lovely girl lifts the top of her sari
  to conceal it, but the shape shows through.
Lord of Sūrdās, it seems encountering you
  has caused pomegranate seeds to sprout—
    and smile.

Lost (∫72, NPS 1989)

Lost, lost, lost to Mohan's captivating image!
  Lost to his earrings,
    lost to his eyes so vast,
Lost to his eyebrows, lost to his splendid forehead mark,
  lost to Muralī, his flute,
    lost to her fluid sound,
Lost to the locks of his hair, lost to his splendid turban,
  lost to his cheeks,
    lost to the wildflower garland on his chest,
Lost to the vision that captivated Brahmā and the gods,
  lost to the shawl on the shoulders
    of that lovely Mountain-Lifter,
Lost to those arms, around the necks of his friends:
  lost to the way that beautiful Śyām
    walks with his clan,
Lost to the yellow cloth he's cinched around his thighs—
  Sūrdās says, I'm lost to Madan Gopāl,
    that intoxicating cowherd lad.

Flutist (§73, NPS 1995)

A beautiful flute glistens on his lotus mouth.
Mohan is playing and singing his ragas
  as he comes back from grazing the cows.
His curly, tousled hair is so lovely as to seem
  like the maneuvers of a militia of bees
Who resent that Muralī alone drinks his honey
  and want to capture some of their own.
His eyebrows arch as if Kāma too had come,
  charming bow in hand, to give them aid,
For the nectar of the lips of the Lord of Sūrdās
  has bred in them a deep unease.

Radiance (§74, NPS 1998)

The radiance of Mādhav's face:
His tangled hair—like honey-drinking bees
  hungry for the liquid of the lotus;
His eyebrows—lovely, playful fish
  drawn close to that fresh new flower;
His crown and earrings—the sun and sunbeams
  that touched it and brought it to bloom.
The dust of the cows, its pollen;
  Muralī's sound, the buzz of bees entranced;
And the band of boys around him are like ganders
  bewitched by that lovely lotus on the pond.
His teeth—lightning cast against the shade
  like light near a rain-bearing cloud:
If the Vedas can only say of truth, "not that, not this,"
  how can Sūrijdās say more?

The elements (∫81, NPS 2286)

I'm going off with one who's colored dusk.
Whatever is to happen, let it happen now—
  fame or infamy—I don't care what people say.
Let them rage against me. What difference does it make?
  Suppose they try to stop me—
    then and there I'll give my life,
But even with this body gone, I'll keep alive my vow,
  sowing the seeds of love for Hari once again:
Sūr, I'll make my flesh blend with the ageless earth;
  as ether, I'll suffuse myself throughout my dear one's home;
As air, I'll be his fan;
  as water, the pools where he plays;
    and as light, the shine in his mirror—
      thus I'll capture every joy.

In Rādhā's dress (§83, NPS 2298)

Exoteric

In Rādhā's dress,
  the dark jewel, Śyām,
Whom she saw as the moon, the Radiant One,
  a play of bright reflection,
    and knew in Hari the Radiant One, Desire,
      and turned into Passion, his mate.
Sūr says, the Lord is well-behaved
  but artful in love,
    so with his arm he drew her close,
      he drew her to his left-hand side,
And drank from her lips the nectar
  of life, and drank it well,
    and if any afterward remained,
      he kissed again—his seal.

Esoteric

In Rādhā's dress,
  the dark jewel, Śyām.
Her face was the radiant moon,
  a play of bright reflection:
    Hari, knowing radiant desire,
      came to her with passion.
He penetrated well, Sūr says,
  for the Lord is artful in love,
    and with his arm he drew her close,
      took her in the left-handed way,
Drank her nectar of life—
  he drank it well—
    and if any then remained,
      he gave it his seal.

Similes lost their nerve (§86, NPS 2374)

Similes, seeing his beauty, lost their nerve:
Love-gods by the thousands yielded up their strength;
  the brilliance of his earrings
    made the sun conceal itself.
Wagtails, lotuses, moons, bees, lightning,
  and clouds of rain, humiliated,
    found some corner to hide
As false poets made them metaphors for Hari.
  We may be embarrassed,
    but not poets such as these!
Even diamonds and pinnacle-gems felt shame
  seeing the glint of his teeth
    shine from a brilliant red.
Sūrdās says, when at his will he wore this body,
  he wiped all other metaphors
    away.

Krishna, the Ganges (§87, NPS 2376)

A necklace of pearls to captivate the mind
Glistens on the beautiful chest of Śyām—
  a Ganges descending from Himalayan heights to earth.
Its banks are his biceps; its whirlpools, Bhṛgu's scar;
  and its oh so lovely waves, his sandal-paste designs.
Fish shimmer brightly in the sparkle of his jewels:
  they've left their lakes to come and join
    his earring-crocodiles.
Sūr says, a lovely sacred thread flows down his chest
  as if within the stream there were
    a yet more splendid stream,
And the conch, disk, club, and lotus in his hands
  are ganders come to rest on his lovely lotus pond.

The gaze (§88, NPS 2379)

When Rādhā turns her mindful gaze
  to the one who is practiced in passion
It's a brilliant spray of eyes and faces—
  two moons, four *cakor* birds.
And bees—each hungers for the other's nectar.
  There, in fact, a pair of pair of bees sways
And they never slake their thirst:
  they bribe the eyelids not to close.
Night comes riding that chariot of the mind, desire,
  but morning comes and magnifies pain,
Bringing on the fate of Sūrdās's Lord:
  day, the thief that steals
    the couple's wealth, the heart.

Ignorant eyes (∫90, NPS 2401)

How ignorant my eyes!
They gazed on a single part of Hari
  and then turned away for more
Confused, like a thief in a house full of treasures
  who ends up taking none.
In the blinking of an eye the morning dawned:
  they grieved, but had to flee,
And so the happiness they once owned
  remains still unfulfilled.
Sūr, by hoarding the power they had
  they've magnified anew their need.

The deer in his face (§93, NPS 2415)

Look, my friend, look at Harī's nimble eyes.
How could the shimmer of lotuses and fish,
  even of darting wagtails,
    compare in charm with this?
When for a brilliant blink of time his hand
  and face and eyes bow down to Muralī—
    all four become as one—
It seems the lotus no longer wars with the moon:
  together they sound a note to soothe
    those lunar steeds, the deer.
Look at those beautiful, mind-entrancing curls,
  how they ramble uncontrolled
    over eyebrows just below
And startle the deer, it seems: they flee their chariot
  till the moon with a tremor of worry
    moves to tighten its reins, the brows.
Hari is a mirror that cleanses all desire.
  For him the women of Braj are offering
    their wealth—that is, their life.
They look at the face of Sūr's Dark Lord, absorbed.
  With him to fill their thoughts, their minds
    have nowhere else to roam.

Gopāl has stolen my heart (§102, NPS 2490)

Gopāl has stolen my heart, my friend.
He stole through my eyes and invaded my breast
  simply by looking—who knows how he did it?
Mother, father, husband, brothers, others
  crowded the courtyard, filled my world,
And society and scripture monitored the door—
  but nothing was enough to guard my heart.
Duty, sobriety, family honor:
  using these three keys I'd locked it away
Behind eyelid gates and inside hardened breasts.
  Nothing could prevail against efforts such as these.
Intellect, power of discretion, wit:
  an immoveable treasure, never once dislodged.
And then, says Sūr, he'd stolen it—
  with a thought and a laugh and a look—
    and my body was scorched with remorse.

Nothing I could do (§103, NPS 2498)

Nothing—there was nothing I could do
When Hari appeared; I could only stare
  like a woman captured in art
And flush with joy that my heart's lotus home
  should be offered as a flower, as his throne.
The upper end of my sari made its offering,
  and water from my eyes, a torrential oblation.
Now the great shame of it sprouts within my mind
  when I sense what my soul has done:
How my blouse tore open, baring the pitchers of my breasts
  as my bodice-string snapped with the strain.
Modesty to elders made me shrink from saying a word
  but listen to my wisdom, friend:
This stunning dumbness, this numbness, says Sūr—
  my Lord has reckoned it my luck.

His and hers (∫105, NPS 2522)

The Dark One and his dear one—what a lovely pair!
At the tying of their happy knot, Rādhā is pleased:
  she smiles a knowing smile, she turns her head away.
He is the bee; she, a *campā* bud.
  He is urbane; she, a simple girl.
Teach them, then, how to show each other love;
  steal them away from their fathers and mothers.
He is a sapphire daubed with sandal, and she—
  she is fair-skinned, like a golden vine.
Nanda's youthful lad is newly clever, and she—
  she's a clever girl newly blossomed into youth.
An emerald on a golden chain, lightning in dark clouds—
  similes like these cannot suffice.
Sūrdās says, for them, one has just *them*.
  To search for metaphors is vain.

Rādhā disbelieves (∫110, NPS 2741)

She's found him, she has, but Rādhā disbelieves.
Even though her eyes behold her master's moonlike face
  and she has the joy of seeing him.
As her gaze is fixed, her mind is glazed,
  her eyes refuse to close,
And her intellect wages a raging debate:
  Is it a dream? Or is this her true Lord?
Her eyes fill and fill with beauty's high pleasure
  and hide it away in her breast,
Yet with wits wild with longing, her eyes race off
  in all ten directions, like bees to gather honey.
Sometimes she musters her various thoughts—she wonders:
  "Who is this Hari? Who does he find alluring?"
For love, says Sūr, is an awkward thing.
  It ripples the mind with waves.

Slammed the door (§137, NPS 3150)

I became so aggrieved at Hari
When he came in lazy from another woman's love
   that I simply slammed the door to my room,
And with my own hands I took the huge chain
   and wound it, wound it, locked it tight,
But I looked: and there on the bed, his lovely image!
   My heart trembled with rage.
I bent, I recoiled, I raced to the courtyard,
   writhed, as with a seizure, on the floor,
And what can I say? There was nothing I could say,
   for there, now, I saw another Govind.
I forgot all my anger, forgot all his faults,
   as Desire beguiled my mind again
And Sūrdās's Lord, so deft in every limb,
   slyly sipped the nectar from my lips.

Red in the morning (§148, NPS 3299)

Today, Nanda's boy, you've some other sort of charm:
To look in your direction is to feel
  a pleasurable mixture of pleasure and anger.
Someone's serrated bracelet is etched on your back
  and a necklace, now stringless, shines on your chest;
Both your yellow garments are now a shining red,
  mascara is on your lips, betel at your eyes,
And from head to toe your jewelry's gone askew
  as if you'd gotten it by robbing someone else.
You parade yourself around before everyone, blossoming,
  boldly dispensing your smiles as bribes:
To hear of it is hard, or to speak, and for poets
  to describe this confluence of child and youth is cruel.
Things like this—an unspeakable surprise:
  to see the sun, Sūr, eclipsed before the dawn!

The tyranny of love (§163, NPS 3393)

Rādhā, justice no longer reigns in Braj.
With Kāma as king, and Kānh as his vizier,
 a strange, harsh polity has emerged:
Crooked curls and eyebrows in league with lovely eyes
 swarm around his ears as partners,
And with convoluted glances they spy out secrets,
 spreading false rumors from anything you say.
Low-minded slanderers, slimy bandit-sycophants—
 the master has no body, and the ministers, no fear!
Friend, unless you deal with them, nothing gets done.
 That's the plague that's settled
  on this harsh, despotic realm.
His mouth's gentle laugh
 and his speech's gentle charm
  and the gentle moves of his feet engender love,
Until every aspect of his body, head to toe,
 becomes a thief to your heart—
  minions mimic kings!
Since your body stores such a wealth of talent and beauty,
 and since handsome Śyām has heard your fame,
You should act to guard your honor, says Sūr,
 lest he forge his victory with force.

Only this mantra (§165, NPS 3399)

Ever since your name has entered Harī's ear
It's been "Rādhā, oh Rādhā," only this mantra,
  a formula chanted to a secret string of beads.
Nightly he stays by the Jamunā, in a grove
  far from his friends and his happiness and home.
He yearns for you. Like a great yogi
  he is constantly wakeful through hours that are ages.
Sometimes he spreads himself a bed of tender leaves;
  sometimes he chants your treasurehouse of fames;
Sometimes he closes his eyes in utter silence
  and meditates on every pleasure of your frame—
His eyes the libation, his heart the fire-oblation,
  his mutterings and lapses, food for a Brahmin feast.
So has Śyām's whole body wasted away.
  Says Sūr, let him see you. Fulfill his desire.

Proper hospitality (§170, NPS 3440)

Rādhikā, Hari is your guest.
At dinnertime the Lord of Love visits your house:
  rise and welcome him, we say.
For his seat, move aside and give him half your bed.
  Delight in touching and washing his feet.
Rejoice in offering the liquid of endless life
  with the flow from your lovely, languid eyes.
Overwhelm him instantly with the incense of your fragrance.
  Light a lamp with a smile to captivate his mind.
Serve him the rare flavor of love's sweetness—
  well-turned phrases and curved eyebrows and limbs.
For pungent flavor, give him properly pungent loveplay;
  for bitter, cast off your clothes, which could embitter;
    for sour, reverse love's roles—force him to your breast;
Then offer him the salty taste of nail wounds and hair tugs,
  and as *ghī* for the meal, your most delicious kisses.
With spice from little bites and with the nectar of your lips
  spread the scented pleasure of your full-moon face.
Satisfy the Dark One well, says Sūr,
  and great will be the merits of your ritual,
    your vow.

Exact whatever punishment (∫171, NPS 3441)

Do with me now what you think I deserve.
Listen to me, Rādhikā—so says Mādhav—
  exact whatever punishment you will.
Crush my breast with yours.
  Bind me with your arms.
    Find some tender flesh to gore with your arrow-nails.
Lift your eyebrows—string those bows.
  Grind your angry teeth.
    Gorge yourself on the nectar of my lips.
Tangle me in your limbs.
  Squeeze with such anger
    that my body sweats passion,
Then take your many traits,
  braid them in a secret knot,
    and soak that knot in sweat till it won't slacken.
Lovely friend, I touch your feet,
  begging you to listen:
    from so much bitterness, great passion thins.
Sūr says, the good life lasts but a few short days,
  so tame your enmity
    and let the world live.

Brindavan's splendor (§172, NPS 3465)

"Behold Brindavan's splendor,
lotus-eyed one,
Where Love has come
to pay his tribute of fine traits.
Fresh-petaled flowers
—a new battalion of many hues—
Crowd together
on every lovely vine:
Bows are in their hands,
and quivers at their waists
Like the bodies of warriors
arrayed in battle armor.
Cuckoos are the elephant ranks;
geese and peacocks, cavalry;
Mountain cliffs are the chariots;
cakors, the infantry.
Banana trees and palms
become poles and battle flags;
Waterfalls are herald drums,
and bees that buzz there, kettledrums.
Wise lieutenants proffer
sandal-breeze advice
And the forest, pleased,
titters with rustling leaves.
Beauty's cavalcade comes
galloping in so swiftly
That the horsemen's garments
flutter like flags."
Sūrdās says,
this is the girl's plea:
"Here is Kāma cowering
as at the time of Shiva's anger,
Imploring
with vast, quick-moving eyes:
Calm him now, Gopāl,
with a gesture of your hand."

Holi (§173, NPS 3471)

Lord of Braj, to see these woods today
  is to feel great stirrings of passion,
As if beguiling Love had joined with Spring
  in the game that's played at Phālgun time.
In among the trees the *palās* panicles
  rise like flames in a fire
As if they'd all gleefully ignited their houses
  to make a great Holi blaze.
Crickets sound like cymbals;
  waterfalls are *ḍaph* and herald drums;
    the droning buzz of bees, kettledrums—
As if sylvan retreats
  had been turned to city streets
    by the troupe of that beguiler, Love.
Peacocks, crows, cuckoos, and all the other birds
  raise a great cacophony of sound
As if cowherd boys and girls had come together
  in a tournament of taunts and jeers.
Wherever the bees see flowers blooming
  on the vines, they hasten there
Like the lecherous rogue who spies a crowd of courtesans
  and has to get his hands on every one.
In grove after grove the cuckoos raise
  their sweet, pure sound—and very loud—
Like well-bred girls who shed their family decorum
  to climb to the housetops and sing.
The flowers rule through multiple hues and patterns
  and trees are clad in their finery, as if Spring,
King of the seasons, smiled to rule over courtiers
  coming from everywhere, dressed in many shades.
Treasury of mercy, how can I find words
  to name the company that fills your basil woods?
For Lord of Sūrdās, every pleasure thrives
  when the kingdom, oh Krishna, is yours.

3
Krishna Departs for Mathura, Never to Return

Mathura the bride (§183, NPS 3640)

Mathura has decked herself out today
Like a bride, oh Hari, when her husband comes:
  she's dressed in finery.
Curtains embroidered with coral and quartz
  are parted from latticed oriels
As if her eyes had forgotten how to close
  at the prospect of beholding you.
The charm of umbrellas arrayed on high rooftops
  makes her seem to flower as she gazes out,
Revealing breasts that look like golden jars
  as in happiness her bodice slips away.
Her ramparts are a waistband of tinkling bells;
  her gardens, garments of manifold hues;
And ornaments fashioned of glorious palaces
  lend splendor to her beautiful limbs.
A thicket of deep-toned gongs
  make anklets that sound at her feet,
And the wandering, fluttering upper end of her sari
  is found in the flags the houses fly.
Hero of Braj, look closely. Consider
  how matchless, how entrancing her form.
Lord of Sūrdās, conquer Kaṃs!
  Become this city's king!

Kaṃs he killed (§186, NPS 3705)

The people of Mathura felt great joy
When Nanda's Delight, dressed like a fine actor,
  arrived with Akrūr at his side.
First the Mind-Beguiler killed the washerman,
  awarding the clothes to his cowherd band,
Then he broke the bow—a sophisticated act,
  made a mere toy of the elephant,
And came on stage slapping his thighs with his mighty arms
  as a challenge to Muṣṭik and Cānur.
The women of the city cursed King Kaṃs
  for mounting such an unfair match;
Bass drums, kettle drums, conches, and reeds
  sounded *rāg māru*, the strains of war;
And godlings, heavenly musicians, and gods
  no less eagerly filled the skies.
Kaṃs he killed: he accomplished his aim,
  he gladdened the heart of Ugrasen,
And when he released his parents from their bonds,
  says Sūr, they sang their fill of his great fame.

Daddy, Daddy (ʃ187, NPS 3734)

"Master Gopāl, I won't desert your feet and go.
If I leave you here in Mathura, my Mohan,
  what will I take with me to Braj?
For twelve years we mistreated you, and why?
  We didn't know the glory of who you really were.
Now, though, it's clear: you're the son of Vasudev.
  Yes, Garg's words have proven true.
Still, what kind of answer can I give Yaśodā
  when she rises and runs to meet me?
Who will she, as mother, rising from sleep at dawn,
  take in her arms when he awakes?
Whose will be the face that gives her life by day?
  Who will she stay near at night, to cradle to sleep?
And if, despite your absence, fate somehow keeps her alive,
  who, at day's end, will she laughingly feed?
What was your purpose in killing our great foes?
  Why did you destroy our destitution?
When you held the mountain in your lotus hand,
  why didn't you drop it and crush us to death?
And now: May you reign a thousand ages
  and in doing so burn away your parents' sorrow,
But come to our cowherd town Gokul once again
  and call me 'Daddy, Daddy.'"
With that he sighed, his feet refused to move,
  and his eyes could no longer hold their tears.
Sūr says, the tragedy of Nanda's taking leave
  is more than I can say.

A boor from Braj (§191, NPS 3797)

If you still have any memory of me,
Then let me just once see Mohan's face—
his fascinating image.
You are the wife of Vasudev, a queen,
and I'm just a boor from Braj,
But it's time to send me my darling boy
and put this joke to an end.
It was fine for him to kill Kaṃs and the rest,
doing the work of all the gods,
But the worry that weighs so heavy on my heart is:
who's to herd these cows?
You can ply him with thousands of royal delights—
handsome clothes and the finest food and drink—
But nothing more, says Sūr, than a bowl of butter
delights my little cowherd Kānh.

Disastrous leaves (§192, NPS 3807)

That's the way my days are now.
What am I to do, friend? It's really no one's fault
  what's happened since Hari turned his loving eyes away.
The musk, the sandal, the camphor, the saffron—
  all of them, always, like servants to me—
And the lazy breeze, the moon and tender flowers:
  now they have a harsh and vengeful look.
The koels, peacocks, and crested cuckoos
  to whom I've given shelter in my garden
Babble night and day as they please.
  I forbid it, but they pay no heed.
The saplings I've nurtured with my own hands—watered,
  watered into full-grown trees:
Tell them, Sūr, they obscure my line of vision
  by sprouting disastrous leaves.

The dark Jamunā's blackened (§193, NPS 3809)

Wayfarer, see how the dark Jamunā's blackened.
Carry to that Hari of yours the word
  that she's scorched in a fever of longing.
From her couch she seems to have fainted to the earth,
  writhing with waves, her weight too great to lift.
By means of her banks, as if by a poultice,
  her torrent is channeled into rivulets of sweat.
Her disheveled hair: the grass and reeds in the sand;
  the mud: her kohl-black sari.
She flails about like aimless, restless bees,
  turning side to side, horrid and forlorn,
Babbling like a sheldrake night and day,
  subsisting on a diet of foam.
Sūrdās says, Lord, the state of the Jamunā
  is not hers alone: it's also our own.

The fever of being apart (§196, NPS 3815)

It all seems something else these days—
Now that our enchanting Cowherd has gone,
   everything in Braj has changed.
Our homes have turned to caverns, lions' lairs,
   and the beast is panting for its prey.
You know how they say, friend, that moonbeams are cool
   and soothing, but we've been scalded instead,
And no matter how much we women shower each other
   with water mixed with *kumkum* and sandalwood powder
And musk from the deer, it all comes to naught
   in face of the fever of being apart.
We've heard that love is a life-giving vine,
   but now, without Sūr's Lord, it bears a poison fruit,
And deprived of the light from Hari's lunar face
   the lotus of our hearts declines to bloom.

The memory of that passion (§197, NPS 3821)

Lord of Braj, the memory of that passion does not fade:
How stubbornly I acted, how silent and hurt
  as I played with you so happily—we two.
You saw you were lost, but your penitence I spurned
  as you laughed and touched your hand to my feet.
Then you feigned sleep. You turned your face away.
  You curled up and covered it with your shawl.
But love's a restless thing. You couldn't stay away
  when you saw the night was passing fruitlessly—
That great long night. Then it cheated me of you,
  as I learned, Sūr's Śyām,
    when I heard the songs of dawn.

Begging bowl (∫201, NPS 3844)

If I knew where to find Gopāl, I'd go—
Go with horn, earring, begging bowl in hand
  and wearing the clothes that yogi women do;
I'd don a patchwork cloak, slather ashes on my skin,
  and bind my hair in a unkempt mound.
If I thought I could meet Hari, I'd rouse old Gorakh
  by carrying on like Shiva, that great god.
I'd burn my mind and body and cover myself with dust—
  the sort of thing gurus tell lonely women to do—
For without Sūr's Dark One, all Braj is empty
  like a cobra that's lost the jewel in its crown.

Aflame at both ends (§206, NPS 4723)

How can a woman parted from her lover
  endure a sharp parting that cuts two ways?
Hari, I wonder if anyone else
  could make you understand what I mean:
When it's Rādhā she is, at her mouth is Mādhav—
  Mādhav, her constant refrain;
When it's Mādhav she becomes, her body burns
  with the pain of parting from Rādhā.
An insect in a log aflame at both ends
  only wants a cooling of the heat:
Lord of Sūrdās, that desperate woman,
  lost in separation,
    can nowhere find relief.

All my symptoms (§212, NPS 3880)

I thought, my friend, that Hari had come,
  but then I awoke and lamented,
    my friend.
Believe me, since then my body has been tossing
  like a fish out of water, on the shore,
    my friend.
This fine frame of mine, friend, burns with the fever of longing.
  It takes many tries to bring it to life,
    my friend.
What am I to do? I've strayed from the prescription.
  My sorrows are rising; my troubles, doubled,
    my friend,
So I've written all my symptoms and sent them with a traveler—
  the tortured mutterings of longing,
    my friend:
"Lord of Sūrdās, unless I somehow see you
  how will this harshness end?"
    —my friend.

Thoughts of him stalk me (§214, NPS 3886)

Thoughts of him stalk me, even in my dreams,
Now that he has gone; and oh, my friend, it hurts
  as hard as on the day that Nandanandan left.
Last night, in fact, that cowherd came to my house:
  he laughed his laugh and grasped me by the arm.
What am I to do? Sleep has turned my enemy:
  not another wink will she remain.
I've become like a sheldrake who sees her own reflection,
  takes it as the gladdening image of her mate,
And then, says Sūr, that menacing Creator
  masquerades as wind and brings ripples to the lake.

With love (∫217, NPS 3908)

With love there's never a thought that one might die.
With love the moth can be drawn into the flame
  and never flinch from the heat.
With love the turtle dove will mount the skies
  until it falls to earth, with not a care for its life.
With love the deer lusts for sound, and draws so near
  that it's doomed to the huntsman's arrow.
The thirsty cuckoo, in the rainy month of Śrāvaṇ,
  coos love, coos love—she shouts it out.
Sūrdās says, what has such a one to fear?
  A lonely woman sets herself on fire.

Clogged with my letters (§219, NPS 3918)

Mathura's wells must be clogged with my letters.
Mohan, for his part, sends not a one,
  and mine are never returned.
Messengers traveling there from Braj
  seem to forget to search him out,
Or maybe Śyām silences them with some palaver,
  or maybe they perish halfway there.
Maybe a cloudburst has soaked all the paper,
  or all the ink has dried, or a forest fire
    has burned all the shoots that make the quills,
Or the scribes, says Sūr, have gone blind
  from all their writing:
    cataract-doors have blocked their eyes.

Elephant clouds (§220, NPS 3921)

In all directions the thickening clouds,
Like strong, lustful elephants of the Love-god,
  break the chains with which they are bound
And sprinkle passion from the temples of their fine
  dark bodies—they sprinkle little raindrops.
They run: they refuse to be turned aside
  by the goad of the wind, their mahout,
And all beyond control, they shatter the bounds of ponds
  with tusks that are rows of airborne herons.
Our tears, too, without shores to restrain them,
  overrun their bodice-banks, flood our breasts.
Once, in time long past, there was a moment when the Lord
  of Airāvat joined hands to submit to the Lord of Braj,
But now all has changed. Without Kānh, Sūr's dark lion,
  our bodies melt like hail upon the ground.

Maybe (§223, NPS 3928)

Maybe clouds don't thunder in places like that
Or maybe in his happiness Hari has muffled Indra
  or the snakes have eaten all the frogs
Or the herons have abandoned the road to where he is
  or the ladybugs can't find the earth
Or the peacocks and wagtails and cuckoos there
  have all been slaughtered by hunters
Or the women there don't like to swing
  and sing about their lovely land.
Travelers don't travel to the Lord of Sūr,
  so how can we let him know
    that the monsoon now has come?

The season of rains (§224, NPS 3935)

The season of rains has come
   but Hari is not to be found.
Thunder rumbles deep
   as lightning lights the dark sky;
Peacocks screech in the wood;
   the frogs are alert, alive;
Cuckoos send out a high piercing sound
   and I, friend, I could die.
Rainbows brandish arrows;
   they shoot, and full of ire
They loose their pointed raindrops
   at my body. I can't endure.
Quick, dispatch a letter
   by some traveler, then, says Sūr,
So that the Yādav king may know
   what torture I've been through.

Autumn alone (§230, NPS 3961)

The time is autumn—still, the Dark One has not come.
I cannot imagine what love-spells were exerted
  by some female foe to bar his way.
Skies are now spotless, and the *kāṃs* grass has flowered:
  its flowering means there's no more chance of rain.
The water in lakes, pools, and streams is clean,
  lotuses bring pleasure to the bees,
And great drops of pollen dispensed by the moon—
  why, they frighten my heart, they pour scorching poison
On a woman who is left without her lover's body to hold
  as she gathers moonbeam-flowers to be cooled by their dew.
A terrible frost blankets my empty bed
  with a measureless ocean of longing.
Sūrdās says, all hope of meeting him is gone.
  The Lord of Braj belongs to someone else.

Lines with her fingernails (§241, NPS 4023)

Hand on her cheeks, Mother, arm around her knees,
  she's writing lines with her fingernails.
She sits with her worries and thoughts, lovely woman,
  and contemplates his Love-god's mouth and clothes.
Her eyes fill with tears. She heaves a set of sighs.
  Herder girl, she damns the way so many days have passed
With the lotus-eyed one so far off in Mathura,
  whose virtues even thousand-hooded serpents do not know.
Kānh has made a lie of the time he said he'd come.
  If at night she sees more lightning, friend,
    how will she survive?
Sūrdās's Lord has come in a flash and gone,
  a dancing street performer—
    many costumes, many roles.

4
The Bee-messenger

Ūdho, go (§244, NPS 4045)

Ūdho, go to Braj as quickly as you can.
Sound out your message of Vedic revelation
  and quench the fire that inflames those lovelorn girls.
Passion is its blaze, their bodies are the wick,
  and their sighs apart from me,
    the wind that fans the flames.
Only the water that their eyes supply
  keeps them from turning to ash.
Up until today, somehow, in this way
  they've kept their bodies in health,
But even so, without some reassurance
  how can women patiently endure?
Listen, what more is there I can say?
  You're my trusted friend, and an expert.
Give the matter careful thought, says Sūr:
  how can fish survive without the sea?

Uncanny resemblance (§246, NPS 4077)

What's this uncanny resemblance?
Take a long, hard look, my friend,
  at the one who's coming from Mathura:
The crown and the earrings are just the same,
  so are his lovely yellow clothes,
And so is the way he talks to his charioteer,
  gesturing to show the way to Braj.
How long has it been since Hari left?
  It seems the world's four eons have passed.
Sūrdās says, forgotten in Braj
  we're like fish who exist without water.

A letter has arrived (∫248, NPS 4107)

A letter has arrived, sealed by the Lord of Braj,
And Ūdho's parading it around on his head.
  It's painful to hear him read it
For Nandanandan is acting in a strange new way
  that slaps the mark of hardship on every house.
Why should we take up the discipline of yoga,
  so unknowable, untellable, unmeasurable?
Why should we live with the smoldering knowledge
  that a hunchback woman tells him what to say?
Sūr says, tell us, which are the sins
  that have made us have to listen
    to a message such as this?

Such good advice (§253, NPS 4132)

Ūdho has come to give such good advice!
Come on, girls, let's all go hear
  this gentleman who sports the mark of fame.
He says to leave behind our clothes and jewels,
  also our love for family and home,
Let our hair grow wild, put ash on our skin,
  and study his tasteless no-trait path.
To my way of thinking, he's only spreading grief—
  love's pain—in the hearts of poor young maidens.
That's why his body's black: it's singed with his own curse,
  and still he lacks the wit to fear for his life.
No one who has a nature such as his
  cares if he brings good or ill.
Sūr says, he's like a snake: he bites and scurries off.
  And what's in his jaws? The juice of eternal life?

Clad with the sky (§261, NPS 4184)

Ever since the day we first saw Hari's face
Our eyes forget to blink: the pupils wander naked
  like those who are clad with the sky.
They've shaved their Brahmin's braid—their in-laws' teachings,
  burned up the sacred thread of decorum,
And left their veils—their homes—to mumble exposed
  through the forests, day and night, down the roads
In simple concentration. It's the way ascetics die.
  Their taste for beauty means they never waver
And anyone who tries to thwart their stare—
  husbands, cousins, fathers—fails.
So Ūdho, though we hear your words
  and in our minds we follow what you say,
These, says Sūrdās, brook no opposition:
  our fixed and stubborn haṭha-yoga eyes.

Peddling yoga (∫266, NPS 4208)

Those Mathura people, they're all of them frauds!
From living with them, friend, our beautiful Śyām
   has learned to use these tactics:
Ūdho, they say, has arrived in our midst
   to peddle his yoga to poor young maidens.
His postures, dispassion, his eyes turned within—
   friend, how can they cancel our distance from Śyām?
Of course, we're just herders, so how should we know
   the pleasures of mating with a hunchback girl?
But what kind of doctor, says Sūr, can this be
   who hands out prescriptions
      when he doesn't know the disease?

Lord of the Milkmaids (∫277, NPS 4265)

How can he call himself Lord of the Milkmaids?
If Śyām belongs to us, oh honeybee,
  then why does he avoid our cowherding town?
So he's come to think our meeting was only a dream—
  for a dream we're reaping all this slander!
Then fine: If a hunchback girl appeals to his lotus eyes,
  why doesn't he take his name from hers?
But no, he's like an elephant: two sets of teeth—
  one for real work, the other just for show.
Sūr says, to Śyām we're only for display.
  There's somebody else when it's really time to play.

Dirty trick (§278, NPS 4282)

It's a dirty trick, this yoga,
  and it won't sell in Braj.
Who is going to let her pearls
  be auctioned off for radish leaves?
Ūdho, that's the measure of success
  your tradesmanship will meet.
The person from whom you got this teaching—
  maybe he can stomach it,
But who will give up grapes to feed
  on fruit from the bitter *nīm* tree?
How could we leave the taste of Sūr's Dark Lord,
  and live on that insipid stuff of yours?

Working on ourselves (§283, NPS 4340)

Ūdho, we too work on ourselves
  both night and day to make our minds unyielding,
So you can lecture and lecture us, honeybee,
  but Nanda's Joy is the joy we have to have.
Your message in our ears makes tears flood our eyes,
  it makes our mouths want to speak of something else,
And our minds turn stern with many forms of concentration
  designed to cleanse the memory of everything but him.
Assessing the joy of every heavenly realm
  they find that next to Hari stands none.
Like birds who tire in trailing a ship to sea
  they circle and circle, calling out his praise,
And the more their inward thoughts trace patterns from the past,
  the more their hearts burn with fire.
So, says Sūr, they can't abandon their bodies:
  they long to be with him just one more time.

Turban of deceit (§287, NPS 4364)

Ūdho, you've ferreted out a secret liaison,
Taken the knowledge of what's in others' hearts,
  and wound it around your head in a turban of deceit.
The yellow strand—that flag is Hari's favorite color;
  the red's the flag of the hunchback whore;
The fine fame of Braj is bound up in the white;
  and your infamy, Ūdho—that one's black.
What? His love is holy, heart-absorbing?
  What? His righteousness hews to yogic vows?
No, says Sūr: False oaths and devious tricks—
  these two he has,
    and they're the two things Ūdho loves.

This bee—and that (∫288, NPS 4378)

How can you get trapped in sweet words like these?
This bee before you is that other one's friend—
 both are dark of body and agile of mind.
That one seduces the world with Muralī's sounds;
 this one makes the honeyed buzz
  that's heard when morning comes.
This one has six feet; that one, only two—
 but also four arms,
  so the brothers don't differ.
That one spends each night at a different woman's house;
 this one, inside some new lotus flower.
That one rises early to entice another heart;
 this one, to taste some other nectar.
Don't trust those who love what's virgin-fresh:
 experts in selfishness,
  they give the pain of parting.
That honeyed boy, this honeybee—
 neither, says Sūr, is
  less wicked than the other.

Dragged him from the blueing vat (§289, NPS 4380)

Don't take amiss what I say, my dear Ūdho,
But this Mathura of yours, what a soot-blackened oven!
  Whatever comes from there is black—
Bodies black, deeds black,
  black, even, the royal army!
And what can one say of Nandanandan?
  He is the shining jewel of all that
As if someone dragged him from the blueing vat
  and tried to launder him in the Jamunā.
Lotus-Eyes, I give up, I offer myself to you.
  How rare your traits, Dark Lord of Sūr!

The black (§290, NPS 4368)

Those dark ones, my friend, what would they know of love?
For how can one ever love—in what way?—
  if only one's own qualities matter?
Look at how these clouds behave:
  they favor others with nourishing rains
While *cātak* birds, ever their slaves,
  are tortured for something to drink.
Bumblebees, black bucks, crows, and koels—
  poets describe them as a very rotten lot.
Sūrdās says, you can give them all you have
  but the black will never thank you for the deed.

Ten-day trial (§300, NPS 4501)

Why not do it then—just for ourselves?
Let's give yoga a ten-day trial:
  We'll deck ourselves out and see if Hari comes.
We'll twist our hair into an unkempt mass,
  wear a quilt of patches, slather face and limbs with ash,
Take the staff and whistle and antelope skin,
  keep our eyes closed, abandon mascara,
And being enlightened, suffer arrows straight in the face:
  from now on, no flight, no release.
We're living in a land ruled by two hostile kings—
  yoga and love's longing—and we're dying of the pain.
Ūdho, here's the truth we see in what you've said:
  Yoga's fifth stage is thunder and it heralds murderous rains.
It's as when Sūr's Lord made us leave the Jamunā's waters:
  He took away our clothes and our bodies lost their shame.

Utterly soiled (§313, NPS 4690)

Bṛṣabhānu's daughter—so utterly soiled!
Hari's sweat is soaked into her clothes;
  her lust for it keeps her from changing that sari.
She hangs her head, she won't raise her eyes,
  like a haggard gambler who's lost his stake in the game.
Hair abandoned, face withered,
  she looks like a lotus bitten by the frost.
Hearing Hari's message has made her but a corpse:
  burned once by longing, burned again by the bee.
Why, says Sūrdās, should she live as one who longs—
  this paragon of Braj, Nanda's darling girl?

Overwrought (§315, NPS 1367)

Ūdho, when she heard your words
her eyes began to overflow.
She lost her sense of modesty,
became overwrought,
she couldn't retain her peace of mind,
She trembled in her breast,
her body shivered with sweat,
her mouth forgot how to speak.
Somehow she managed to stand there,
then she drooped
and fell to the ground in a faint.
Someone sent for something cooling,
or for lotuses or poultices;
someone ran to bring her water;
But nothing availed against the cruel bite
of that serpent,
the God of Love,
So she sent me, an experienced messenger girl,
without a word—
with a sign—
To ask, Sūr's Dark Lord,
how without even meeting her
you could give Rādhikā such pain.

Thank goodness he's come (§316, NPS 4721)

"Hari has come—thank goodness he's come!"
These were the words that tumbled from Rādhā
  as soon as she saw me: she wrapped herself in darkness.
Her body trembled in her great desperation.
  Wasted with worry, her heart beat hard.
As her feet moved forward into the lane,
  she fell,
    covered in a river of sweat,
And however hard they pulled, she wouldn't be moved.
  Her bangles broke, her hair flew loose,
    and her gossamer bodice tore,
Seeming to reveal two doves married for love,
  lost in reciting to one another their vows.
She appeared, O Ramāpati, bewildered as a snake
  when the guiding gem is pulled from its cobra crown.
Lord of Sūrdās, my words are at an end.
  I know nothing.
    It's as if I'd lost my mind.

River of tears (§319, NPS 4730)

Because she's away from you, Lord of Braj,
  a river has flooded her eyes
And risen to such a high-water mark
  that it overflows the eyelid-banks.
Glistening new boats—her eyes—cannot move:
  with the ropes that kept them moored, my friend,
    they're sunken, destroyed.
Upward gusts from her sighs fan the waves;
  their fury tears apart the *tilak*-mark tree.
Collyrium mud has mired the shores of the borders
  of her sari, and mired her lips and cheeks,
Stranding travelers wherever they might be—
  the hands and feet and speech.
Lord of Ramā, there is no other cure:
  How, unless she sees you, can she live?
Gokul is drowning in the river of her tears.
  Sūr says, rescue it: Reach out your hand.

Last rites? (∫321, NPS 4735)

Her heart has lost awareness.
Even though Rādhikā's friends—hear me, Śyām—
  labor to keep her conscious.
She communicates with signs.
  She tears wildflowers with her nails.
    Her ears cannot abide hearing even two words.
She shoos away the koel birds by rattling her bangles
  so that she'll avoid speaking their names.
Fearing that meshed windows might admit the moon at night,
  she mends any gaps in her clothes
And hides from whatever cool winds might waft her way
  by pulling the edge of her sari to her face.
If her body should touch sandalwood or musk
  it recoils—as if she'd drunk some heinous poison.
Sūr's Dark Lord, unless you meet her soon
  I cannot think she'll survive.

She's going mad (∬324, NPS 4764)

The way Rādhā talks, they can tell she's going mad,
And listen, Śyām, how her clever friends prevent her
from hearing that the monsoon season has arrived.
If she sees clouds, they deftly say it's mountains.
Thunder? It's the lions roaring in their caves.
No, that isn't lightning! It's a mountain forest fire:
Flames cascade upwards, driven by the winds.
No, not frogs and peacocks calling in the woods:
It's just the cowherds jeering at the birds.
No, not rain at all: It's only a waterfall—
the drops always spatter, even over here.
Sometimes a cuckoo will open its throat and speak:
"Bad bird!" they say, and hasten to clap it away.
Lord of Sūrdās, how can I explain
how terribly she suffers
till she meets with you again?

5
Lordly Encounters—and Others

A cataract of arrows (§325, NPS 4780)

It seemed that thickly knotted thunderclouds
Were raining passels of arrows on the army,
  gorging the great stream of battle—
Archer clouds of every hue
  with lightning daggers in their hands,
And a roar of kettledrums, conches, and battledrums
  screaming elephants and horses.
A dusty mist flew in all ten directions
  and a torrent of javelins and spears
As Vasudev's two sons showed themselves, hid themselves,
  brilliant moon and sun.
Flotsam of elephants littered the shore
  of a river flowing deep with blood—
Bows were its waves; chariot wheels, its whirlpools;
  its water creatures, the torsos of warriors;
Banners and standards and ropes to hoist the flags
  lay broken like trees uprooted on the banks,
But totally fearless in that river of conflict
  the hero of the Yādavs played.
Palaces were emptied as kings laid claim
  to the heavenly mansions that awaited them
In the instant that Hari, treasury of mercy,
  removed the griefs of earth.
Mathura's citizens were seized with happiness
  to see the city's siege undone,
For the Lord of Sūr had vanquished Jarāsandh
  and come to his rightful home.

Hari's chariot (§326, NPS 4782)

Today, my friend, let your eyes fill
  with the splendor of Hari's chariot.
The thirst to behold it makes people perform sacrifices,
  practice yoga and penance, and take on pilgrim vows.
See the fine paintings inlaid with wondrous jewels,
  the whisks and the banner fluttering in the wind
And the white umbrella, which rises above it
  like the moon in the east on a full-moon night.
The darkness of his body, his lovely golden clothes,
  the crown on his head, and the garland on his chest
Seem lightning and thunderclouds, sun and stars
  all assembled at a single time.
What beauty when he lifts the conch to his lips
  in sounds of heroic praise:
It seems like the lovely cry of a gander
  as it nestles in a circle of russet waterlilies.
The way his mother and father feel joy in their hearts
  on meeting Krishna brings pleasure to my soul.
Sūrdās says, for the citizens of Dvaraka
  the sight of Hari is happiness.

The lure of Dvaraka (§327, NPS 4783)

Day after day they come to see Dvaraka—
Nārad and Sanak and the others, all great sages:
  It lures them away from their dispassionate state.
Its structures are built of precious stones—
  coral, quartz, and emerald inlaid over gold—
And from every surface images rebound
  when men and women walk on them, and so also birds,
Displaying in complex ways rare hues of sea or land.
  To look on them brings mounting joy,
And even the cleverest cannot find the key
  that would tell if what they see is reality or art.
Among forests and glades, fruits, flowers, and lovely lakes,
  the mynahs, the parrots, the ganders and doves,
The wagtails, peacocks, *cakors*, and cuckoos speak
  as if reciting their lessons in a classroom taught by Love.
From house to house comes music as sensitive poets
  play on flutes and vinas, and drum their mridangams,
Making bodies thrill with the great joy of love
  wherever the fame of the Yādavs' Lord is sung.
Day and night, mounted on their chariots, all the gods
  hover in fascination, surrounded by their women,
For the spectacle of the sporting of Sūr's Dark Lord
  makes even immortals feel dissatisfied with home.

Wine in the red of his eyes (§332, NPS 4819)

Wine shows her strength in the red of his eyes:
  he roams through the forest finding pleasure
With the splendor of an elephant king in rut
  trailing a harem of mates.
Beautiful the visage of his free-flying hair
  and his lovely garments of blue;
A full golden bowl he holds in his hand:
  he drinks from it; he makes his girlfriends taste.
He laughs, he sputters anger. He beckons, sends away.
  He pinches his eyebrows in a scolding scowl,
Then weeps, exults, rises, and staggers
  as his mind fills with thoughts of his little brother.
His color is the moon's. His strength supports the earth.
  The darling girls of Braj adore him,
And nothing makes them flow with so much joy
  as to hear him sing the virtues of Sūr's Śyām.

Kālindī, do what I say (§333, NPS 4821)

Kālindī, do what I say.
Quick, come here where I'm sporting in the woods
  and bathe my body. I'm exhausted.
Stream, what makes you so obstinate of mind?
  Leave every speck of self-importance behind.
I'm the one who's always singing Hari's praises
  and always defending your honor and pride,
And you, now: Look how you act toward me!
  Spread out your whirlpools, your waves, your water course
And stop dismissing me—I swear by Gopāl—
  or I'll pull on my plough
    and I'll *make* your current flow.
Shiva, Brahmā, the gods, the snakes, the sages:
  They can say what they want
    but it won't make me change.
Here I am the brother of Śyām and Subhadrā,
  so idiot river, how could you think
    says Sūr, that I've had too much to drink?

Jarāsandh bound us (§335, NPS 4831)

"You who are mounted on Garuḍ, the bird—
  who can I call upon but you?
You're the friend of the dejected, an ocean of pity,
  shelter to the shelterless, truth, home of joy,
    commander of all knowledge, and master.
Jarāsandh, blind with drunkenness,
  battered our pride, bound us up
    for no cause at all, brought us here
And infuriated us by blocking us
  in a mountain cave, where we live like insects
    terrified of the *bhṛṅgi* bee.
Lord, we're unperturbed by how much wealth
  or earth we've lost, but the suffering
    he's caused is worse than death.
Because of the Magadhan king we all live
  lives of fear, and the gods
    are in a frenzy to control him.
You—you churned Madhu, Kaiṭabh, Mur;
  split apart Bhaum and Keśī; and removed
    the anguish of death from Kaṃs's clan.
But now that he recognizes the post to be used for sacrifice,
  the king, afraid, will take on just that mode
    and burden the earth with many sins."
Thus spoke the messenger of the kings, conveying
  the terror they felt in their hearts. When he heard,
    says Sūr, Hari sent for his charioteer.
In anger he climbed the chariot and answered,
  "Go spread happiness: I'm on my way.
    In fact, I'm almost there."

He conquered Jarāsandh (§336, NPS 4834)

He conquered Jarāsandh and set the captives free,
Opened wide their way by tearing down the pair
  of doors that so much effort had riveted in place.
Jarāsandh, like a fowler with a great, unwieldy net,
  had pulled a whole flock of kings to the ground,
But the Lord of the Yādavs hunted down the hunter
  and sundered the cavelike cage he had made.
They were out! So they sang as with a single voice
  to bless the virgin glories of the one who set them free,
Flying off like birds that flee to the open sky
  after someone cuts the snares that cruelly bind their feet—
Gone now their squabbles, the hubbub of bondage,
  quiet as the stillness after Holi's crackling fire.
Sūr says, no one can measure the greatness of my Lord.
  Whatever I might say would never be enough.

Dvaraka's so close (§337, NPS 4843)

There's still one thing I haven't been able to say
And it's this, oh Brahmin: Dvaraka's so close.
   Why don't you go to the Lord of the Yadus there?
Anyone who has a friend like handsome Śyām—
   Śrī's husband grants every happiness to him.
Considering he's there, why laze around here,
   my beloved, making your body weak and thin?
They say he's most compassionate, a treasury of mercy,
   father of all three worlds, knower of what's within,
Someone who provides for his devotees' every need,
   thrilled to have a *tulsī* leaf in exchange.
So leave your hesitation. Take some grains of rice,
   tie them in your garment, set off with the sun,
And let your eyes, my dear, reap the satisfaction
   of seeing his lotus face open to a smile.

His boyhood friend Śrīdāmā (∫338, NPS 4846)

Balarām's brother saw him from afar—
His boyhood friend Śrīdāmā, but his face had grown sad
  and his body was wasted away.
Seated on his couch in supreme contentment,
  fanned with a chowry by Rukmiṇī at his side,
He jumped up and ran in a frenzy of welcome
  and his eyes welled up with tears when they met.
Then, overjoyed, he sat him down on the throne
  and asked, "How are you? Relax, tell me all.
What have you brought me?" He laughed: "Let me have it.
  What are you hiding there in your clothes?"
Seeing and touching and coming together in love—
  it left his heart with not the slightest care.
Sūr says, the moment he started chewing the rice
  he remembered—
    and Kamalā gripped his hand in fear.

Homecoming (§339, NPS 4854)

He looked, the poor Brahmin, but it left him at a loss.
He couldn't quite remember and he didn't dare to ask:
  What had happened to his old familiar home?
He stood at a distance, dizzy-headed
  at the wondrous creation ahead:
A lofty mansion with jeweled, gilded walls
  and charming balconies.
"Have I been duped by some divine illusion
  or have I simply come to the wrong place?
Searching for wealth has made me lose even the shade
  of the straw I labored so hard to thatch!"
Then his beautiful wife, says Sūr, recognized her husband
  and descended from the house:
"Come, my dear, it's all from Hari's care.
  Come, set foot inside your home."

The wrong address (§340, NPS 4855)

The Brahmin got confused as he looked at his house:
Its style was wrong and it was built all wrong.
  He wondered, he wavered, he felt fear:
"Either someone's come and snatched away my place—
  some powerful person who chose to live here—
Or else I've simply come to the wrong address.
  This must be Kailāś, where they say Shiva lives!
There's a saying among the wise that fate attacks the weak—
  well, I'm the perfect example. I'm like the lotus
That left the wilderness to hide in open water
  and was burned by a golden sun, where once it had a jungle pond."
Just then the lady of the house descended:
  "Darling, enter the manse!" She lent him her hand.
"By the grace of Sūr's Dark Lord," she said,
  "a wishing tree's been planted at your door."

Inaccessible in Dvaraka (§347, NPS 4873)

How can I find a way to see him
In the land of Dvaraka—even if, traveler,
  I travel there with you?
Outside, there'll be a crowd of kings
  and I'll be too shy to ask for him.
Inside, he'll be dallying with his wives
  and what messenger can I find to send?
And suppose—by wit or force or fate or luck or work—
  I could place my body near that of my beloved,
How could I possibly speak of how it is—
  Braj, the woods, the Jamunā, the bowers—
    except to a connoisseur of love?
Suppose by trying hard, says Sūr, I got through to his majesty,
  suppose I even brought my mind to accept that this is he—
Without that strapping lad and Muralī at his mouth,
    what would I have to show these eyes?

Nothing now remains (§355, NPS 247)

"Nothing now remains.
Duhśāsan has dragged me into the court
  and he's even grabbed my clothes.
Land, wealth, happiness, palace—all lost:
  Every kind of sadness I've suffered.
Somewhere in my heart I wore the mantle of your mercy,
  but now their stares have burned it away—
"Govind!" she shouted, "Govind!
  Guard me at such a time!"
And then, says Sūr, the sea of compassion surged:
  its water, a current of cloth.

Mādhav, in anger (§356, NPS 273)

Mādhav, in anger, took the wheel in his hand.
Abandoning the word of the Veda, his own promise,
he did what would please his devotee.
He stepped from his chariot to earth, all astir,
and the moment his foot touched the ground he ran.
The earth could not endure the weight
and shuddered fearfully, as if deranged.
His upper garment slipped down his limbs
and as he lifted his vast, strong arm
It revealed a torso radiant with sweat and blood—
a thundercloud raining pearls and rubies.
Sūr says, when Brahmā saw that fine warrior
and the discus he held, called Fine Vision,
He fell into confusion, as if this were a new creation
and he a baby, lotus-born upon an umbilical stem.

The wheel in his hand (§357, NPS 279)

The way his yellow garments fluttered,
The wheel in his hand, how swiftly he ran—
   I'll never forget how he appeared
When he stepped from his chariot to earth, all astir.
   With bits of dust smeared through his hair he seemed
Like a lion emerging from a mountain lair
   on sensing some great, mad elephant.
The same Gopāl who fulfilled my vow,
   who brushed aside the Vedic sense of right—
This is the one who's coming to my aid:
   such a Lord, says Sūr, and yet so near.

Toward Badarī (§359, NPS 383)

What am I going to say to Hari?
Lord, inward knower, knower of all—
  when I hear these words, I worry and ponder.
You command me, "Go to the Badarī forest,"
  and if you say it, I should want to go,
But Treasury of Mercy, without will or mind
  and with my body numb and lifeless—
    how?
As I come to understand, Master, what I have done,
  why shouldn't I feel a stab of pain?
I used this knowledge of mine to mislead the women of Braj.
  Must I not take what once I gave?
The ache in my body manifests my sin.
  Sūr's Lord, where can I cling?
The fire of not discerning has settled in this breast
  and now as my deeds cook through to their effects,
    I burn.

Body like a flagstaff (§360, not in NPS)

Your word is not to be erased.
Lord of my life, most merciful one,
most insightful king of the Yadus,
You're sending me off to the Badarī retreat
to be instructed in secret wisdom,
And my will, though it falters, musters the courage,
but my feet refuse to budge.
This body is like a flagstaff—
I can move it along by force—
But what of my mind? Like the flag, it flutters
behind, in the direction of your feet.
All the aspects of this heart of mine,
Hari, consider how hard they must be
To hear the things you've said to me, says Sūr,
and not to have shattered into parts.

Dwarf at the door (§361, NPS 440)

"A Brahmin dwarf is standing at the door!"
Hearing him chant the Veda brought the king such joy
that he asked the scholar to come in.
He bathed his feet, drank the water from those feet,
and asked the Brahmin what he might desire.
"Just give me three and a half steps' worth of earth
for a fine little hut in which to dwell."
"But why," said the king, "would you ask for only that?
I'd give you many jewels, many towns."
Then the Lord of Sūrdās took what he had asked:
On the prostrate monarch's back
he placed his foot.

Scholar at your door (§362, NPS 441)

"King, there's a scholar standing at your door.
All four Vedas come tripping off his tongue
  and he bears the body of a dwarf.
He understands the language of animals—two legs,
  four legs, or none. His face glows like the sun.
He's dazzled the citizens of every city he's visited,
  yet all we know is that he scarcely eats."
Hearing the sound of the Vedas, the king sprang to his feet,
  forgetting his own unfinished sacrificial offerings,
And when he saw the Beguiling One's whole, fine form,
  he prostrated before him on the ground:
"Come, oh Brahmin, come to the altar—
  I beg you, I pray you, please.
Whatever you want, ask, and right away I'll give it—
  treasurehouses of diamonds and jewels."
"Please, king, listen: say no more,
  lest it be grounds for heavy reproach.
Give me just some earth—three and half steps' worth—
  to build myself a little place to stay."
Śukra intervened: "King Bali, listen,
  whatever you do, don't give land,
For that's no Brahmin. It's someone else—
  it's Murāri, who's arrived disguised."
"But what should I do?" the king replied.
  "The one who begs from me is the teacher of the world"
And with a water offering he stated his decision.
  The learned one, for his part, stretched his frame.
"Victory!" exclaimed the crowd as they saw
  that in three steps he had measured the world.
"Quick," said the Brahmin to the king, "A half-step more,
  or you'll lose your reputation for truth."
"I—why, I'll never waver from the truth.
  Here's my outstretched back. Measure it there."
Sūrdās says, he smiled and gave up all—
  and gained a whole new realm:
    a world beneath the world.

6
Rāmāyaṇa

This jungle (§366, NPS 507)

"Listen, my own little brother,
  so many aspects of this jungle
    conspire to steal Jānakī away,
Making my eyes encounter
  certain reminders
    of features she once had.
The lion has her waist;
  the koel bird, her voice;
    the moon, the brilliance of her face;
The luster in her eyes
  appears in a herd of deer—
    nothing is hidden from sight.
The *campā* bloom keeps her color in view;
  the lotus, her hands and feet;
    the pomegranate, her teeth;
The swan, the way she walks;
  the red *bandhūk*, her lips;
    and a snake, the matchless braid that binds her hair."
The deep pathos of the Raghus' Lord,
  the master,
    makes an instant expand to seem an age.
Overpowered—Sūr's Lord—by the love of the one he loves,
  he's forgotten
    what grandeur is his own.

The breaths (§367, NPS 536)

Now that you've seen me in such a state,
as you go, what more message need I send?
Listen, oh monkey: how much longer
can I keep my lifebreath under guard?
It's a very restless thing. It wants to depart.
It no longer thinks at all.
I only restrain it by calling, calling his name,
and thereby closing, closing the door of my mouth.
Hanumān, I fear to trouble you
with knowledge of so humble a thing,
But never has he heard such misery, says Sūr—
that mercy-loving husband of mine.

The memory of love (§369, NPS 545)

As for myself, I have only this request:
First sound my name and bow before his feet,
then put this jewel in Raghunāth's hand.
On the banks of the Mandākinī, on that crystal rock—
on remembering, the memory of love blocks my heart.
Monkey, how can I say it? If I say it, it'll be now—
how face met face to make a forehead mark.
You, Hanumān, are the son of the holy wind,
so fly to him. Tell him what I've described
And bring before these eyes, says Sūr, the image—
his image—that can take away
this awful flaw, this pain.

Rāvaṇ roars in battle (§370, NPS 574)

Rāvaṇ roars in battle, but only for so long
As arrows do not glisten forth in the hand
  of him who holds the Sāraṅg bow.
Yama, Kuber, and Indra, as they eagerly
  decorate the chariot of Rāvaṇ, are aware
That the light from the sun of the Lord of the Raghus
  is snuffing out its fleeing enemy, night.
Many drums sound at the moment when a woman
  follows her husband to the funeral pyre:
In such a way, says Sūr, that death-determined Demon
  shamelessly shouts the vanguard battle cry.

Today Rām is raging in battle (§372, NPS 602)

Today Rām is raging in battle,
And Brahmā and his company have mounted their chariots—
  gods come to witness the fray.
Rām has arrayed his cloud-dark body in godlike armor;
  he's set his bow, Sāraṅg, in his hand;
He's purified his arrows, straightened them all,
  and fastened his quiver to his waist.
Oceans rumble; Śeṣ's hood trembles;
  the wind is crippled to a hush;
Indra laughs, while Shiva smiles and weeps
  to see that what he's promised cannot be.
Earth and sky and the directions melt to one
  as arrows fill the air like so many rays of sun,
Announcing, as it were, the ending of the world,
  when at a single time the twelve suns rise.
Flags, flagpoles, parasols, and chariots break—
  bows, shields, swords, and armor;
Brilliant warriors burn, as in a forest fire
  trees are stripped of branches and leaves.
Splashes of blood spatter to the sky
  as arrows hit elephants and horses:
It looks like a city where suddenly a great fire
  leaps from the straw-carriers' houses.
Headless corpses rise and stagger about in fear,
  awakened by burns. They try to flee
While jackals circle, dig for heads from the heap,
  snatch them, and chase away.
The fury of Raghupati stokes the blaze,
  the sighs of Sītā are the breeze,
And Rāvaṇ's family, stubborn warriors all,
  like a forest of thick bamboo
Turns in a second to ash, as if someone
  had touched a flame to old, discarded clothes.
Sūrdās's Lord, with the power of his massive arms,
  has smashed them in an instant to ants.

The view from Ayodhya (§374, NPS 611)

"Look, there he is! The Lord of the Raghus is coming.
From afar it seems like a thin crescent moon"—
so the citizens describe his aerial chariot.
"With Sītā at his side that fine hero glistens;
at the sight of him our joy abounds.
Monkeys sit before him—heroes, great warriors,
looking like dark clouds blown across the sky."
When he senses the city is near, he descends to earth
and begins to tell about the place where he was born:
"These are my younger brothers," he explains to the monkeys.
"These are my beloved subjects.
This is Vasiṣṭha, our family preceptor.
Touch his feet in reverence," he teaches all his friends.
Then turning to Vasiṣṭha, he says, "Master, these
are Sugrīv and Vibhīṣaṇ, even dearer to me than Bharat,
For when the sons of Daśarath went into the forest
who knew what would happen? No news came.
But this is now the sum of it, the glory of it all:
What burned then is gone. Our hearts are whole.
Enemies are conquered, the work of the gods is done,
there's happiness and wealth, says Sūr—
and all, thanks to these."
Such is the sense of respect
that graces that Treasure of Grace:
As he enters his city,
he sings his servants' praise.

The worn-out world (§377, NPS Appendix I–205)

Hero of the Raghus, you who know from within,
Sea of compassion, wishing tree for ill-starred times,
  you understand your servants' pain.
When the terror of Bāli suffused his body
  as he wandered as an exile in the dreadful jungle,
You made Sugrīv the head of the monkey clan
  by destroying his fearsome arch-foe.
The unbearable ten-headed forest fire of rage,
  fed by the breeze from your sighs—
From its heat you rescued Vibhīṣaṇ, ablaze,
  with a sprinkling of water well drawn.
Hearing these ancient, well-renowned tales,
  the worn-out world has known your fame
And you have worked to make it new, Sūr's Lord,
  as Rāmacandra, firm in war.

7

The Poet's Petition and Praise

A bellyful (§384, NPS 52)

How many days have I lost ignoring Hari?
My tongue has tasted the slandering of others—
  seeds sown to weigh down future lives.
My wardrobe has been stocked with clean and lovely clothes;
  every part of my body massaged;
Forehead mark in place, I was a leader among men,
  but I made myself a slave to the senses.
Then it dawned on me. I shook with the fear of death.
  I even started whining to Brahmā and the gods.
Poor wretched Sūr! Where does it all lead?
  To a belly full,
    and once it's full,
      to sleep.

Mādhav, control that cow (§386, NPS 56)

Mādhav, please, control that cow.
Night and day she wanders over paths that are no paths,
  too elusive to be caught,
And starved, so starved—why can nothing fill her?
  She's stripped the Veda-tree of all its leaves.
From the eighteen jars she's drunk Purāṇa-water
  and still there's no slaking her thirst.
Place the six kinds of taste before her
  and she'll sniff around for more,
Eating what's unhealthy, food she shouldn't touch,
  things the tongue can scarcely describe.
Oceans, mountains, forests, heaven and earth—
  she forages through them all. They're not enough.
So every day she tramples down the fields of fourteen worlds
  and even there she cannot be contained.
Her hooves are dark blue; her belly, brilliant red;
  her horns, a pure and simple white;
Equipped with all three elements she challenges the world,
  impudent, fearless, unafraid.
She tames the demons with the power of nails and heart
  She tosses the gods off the top of her head,
Whose face and brows are decorated deftly:
  as she roams about she captivates the mind.
Nārad and the rest; Sanak, Śuk, and so forth—
  they've wearied themselves to no avail.
So tell me, says Sūr, how a bumbling fool like me
  can ever hope to herd someone like her.

In the birth canal (§389, NPS 77)

Who was with you then, that day?
  Who but Hari wished you well?
    Give it some thought, you miser-minded one.
      Remember, if you would. Reflect.
Think of the pain, the harsh karmic past
  that thrust you into the world that day
    and smeared you with that fetal blood
      as you came into the womb again.
It's a tortuous place, where no one can go,
  dreadful, daunting, dark,
    in every way repulsive,
      a mine of vile filth.
Earth, water, sky, wind, fire—
  the elements: these gave your body form,
    and mind and strength and clan were born.
      Where was your decorum then?
Oh the thrall of such disaster—
  the birth that kept you, fed you, bred you,
    and gifted you with that face of yours,
      your eyes, nose, hands, and feet:
Ingrate, listen, who do you think
  adopted you as a companion that day?
    The one you long ago forgot—
      that is, if ever you knew.
Even today he stays at your side,
  the one who was first to salvage your pride,
    always wanting your life to go well,
      and loving you as his own.
Sūr says, he's a jewel of a friend,
  foremost among the gods.
    And listen, fool, your lying, willful,
      cheating ways—don't let them stand.

Toiling like a dog (§390, NPS 103)

Master, my mind is drained of thought.
It's left your lotus feet, treasury of all delight,
  and taken to toiling like a dog,
Endlessly wandering, licking pots
  in barren houses and on burning pyres.
Can one ever satiate such greed?
  No, the soul never slakes its thirst.
Wherever it goes, it's in constant fear
  of stones and sticks and shoes.
How many insults has it suffered, poor dumb fool?
  How many slurs for a mouthful here and there?
Hari, most merciful, you guard the whole world;
  you yourself take charge of every heart.
Only a grand fool, says Sūr, a fool like me,
  would leave that home to scavenge with the lost.

The gift of your devotion (§391, NPS 106)

Give me the gift of your devotion, Lord.
Show me, if you will, the thousand things
  that one might crave. I don't desire them—
I'm stubborn as they come. Even the thought
  of dying doesn't move me,
For I've vowed that from now on I'll be sprawled
  on your ground, waiting at your door.
Ever since the day this world gave me birth—
  since then I've followed its ways,
Quaffing without fear the poisons of the senses,
  willfully doing ill.
Once there was a time when this lustful, awful age
  angrily hunted the cattle of truth,
Till their young, when they saw it, fled their homes,
  and even Indra grew afraid.
As for me, I've burned myself alive,
  leapt off mountains, severed my own head,
And the gods, when they saw my daring, felt shame
  that none of them was god enough to guard me.
Many times I went to the city of Death,
  plunging into the wells of hell,
Until Death's agents grew weary pulling me out,
  and then I'd go and do it all again.
Treasury of mercy, rage if you will,
  but it's useless: there's nothing green about me.
Lord of Sūr, I beg you, go ahead:
  Toss me out, drag me away.

Truth in advertising (§397, NPS 124)

What did I ever *not* do?
  Think of my actions one by one
And tell me how you can advertise yourself
  as Purifier of the Fallen.
Ever since I was born into the world
  and called a living being,
Aside from the evils and errors I've done,
  I've simply done nothing at all.
Those who are virtuous, obedient, pure—
  how can you help but be drawn toward them?
But to shield someone burdened with fear
  proves the lordliness of the Lord indeed.
Oh beautiful dark one, lotus-eyed,
  who knows us all inside,
What kind of prayer can be made to you by Sūr,
  who is cruel,
    who is crooked,
      who craves?

They say you're so giving (§399, NPS 135)

They say you're so giving, so self-denying, Rām,
That you offered Sudāmā the four goals of life
and to your guru you granted a son.
Vibhīṣaṇ: you gave him the land of Lanka
to honor his early devotion to you.
Rāvaṇ: his were the ten heads you severed
simply by reaching for your bow.
Prahlād: you justified the claim he made.
Indra, leader of the gods, you made a sage.
Sūrdās: how could you be so harsh with him—
leaving him without his very eyes?

Danced too much (§400, NPS 153)

Now I have danced too much, Gopāl,
Dressed in anger and lust, and garlanded
  with a necklace of passions at the throat.
Girded with ankle-bells of sham and delusion—
  how sweet their slanderous sound—
I am bound at the waist with a sash of illusion,
  and the vermilion of greed is daubed on my brow.
Cravings roar inside my body
  in a host of differing rhythms
And my mind, a drum pasted with the dough of confusion,
  sets my movements to a dissonant pulse.
I've marshaled and flaunted so many artful steps
  and filled my sinful net:
All this ignorance Sūrdās has learned—
  take it far away, Nandalāl.

So many other sinners (§402, NPS 158)

The way you've saved so many other sinners—
Who could utter the splendor of your merciful feet,
  the greatness of singing your praise, the joy?
You've rescued them all: the desperate elephant,
  the dissolute prostitute, the king in the well.
The Brahmin let out a cry for his son
  but you came instead, cutting loose his load of sin.
Hunter, vulture, monkey, Gautam's wife, the deer—
  which of them ever practiced vows to earn your favor?
Kaṃs, Keśī, Kuvalayāpīḍ, Muṣṭik—
  all these sinners left this life for a blissful home.
And what about the woman who smeared her breasts with poison
  and came to Braj a heron? What state did she attain?
Or the laundryman? Pralamba? Nalakūbar and his brother?
  You felled the trees that trapped them, and gave them joy.
Or King Śiśupāl, so obsessed with worldly thoughts
  that he couldn't tell a right time from a wrong?
Snake demon, bird demon, storm demon, ass demon—
  you grasped onto their good and cast away their bad.
And the daughter-in-law of Pāṇḍu? They stripped her clothes
  in public—or tried: You gave her endless reams of cloth.
In times of distress, wherever you're remembered
  you stir awake, you hasten to the scene.
Cows, cowherds, calves, all terrified of the rain:
  you held Mount Govardhan in your hand.
Constantly wretched, manifoldly wicked
  Sūr: how could you forget?

The master list (§409, NPS 193)

Those others with whom my heart sang out for help
Have been redeemed by you, Govind my master.
  You've taken them on as your own.
And this is how they served you: at some uncharted moment
  your name chanced to pass across their lips
And that would send you scurrying, merciful one,
  to summon each of them to your side.
Ajāmil—he's a great friend of mine.
  As he walked along, I talked with him,
And master, what can I say?
  He didn't whisper even a word of it to you.
Other names are also written on your list—
  hunter, harlot, vulture—and I've added another:
One more sinner so you'd have a Council of Five.
  But when the time came, you forgot this Sūr.
    The shame of it! I could die!

Overeager acrobat (∫412, NPS 292)

Life has stumbled, stumbled by.
I had sons, the power to rule, a flow of wealth—
  but no discrimination, so soon it ambled off
And got tangled in a noose of illusion so foolproof
  that now I cannot break it or slip it free.
Songs of the Lord, gatherings of the good—
  I left myself hanging in air without either,
Like an overeager acrobat who does just one more trick
  because his greed won't let him close the show.
What splendor, says Sūr, can you find in flaunting wealth
  when your husband, your lover, has gone?

Broken horoscope (§413, NPS 298)

Everyone has long stopped loving me.
Oh Gopāl! My body is gripped by age
  and I wither away inch by inch.
The horoscope that once structured my life—
  my zodiac, my lunar sign, my natal day and date—
These no longer signify a thing.
  The days are over when I tried to win the world.
Money, mansion, lineage, name,
  everything I worked so hard to make:
I see them now the way a dog looks at a face—
  motionless, staring from afar.
With all the days and years I've grown old.
  Soon they'll be writing my horoscope again,
And the thought of all that unabated fault, Lord of Sūr,
  makes me turn to you, Hari, for care.

Cooked like an eggplant (§416, NPS 320)

Now that you've returned, you've forgotten those days:
How you tasted the drug of mindless delusion,
  wandered about with your hair all wild,
Settled again in the belly of a woman—your new mother—
  and once again your troubles began.
The terror, the trauma: cooked like an eggplant
  and head-first thrust in filth!
Your intellect was weak, your body thin,
  every advantage was wrested from your hand:
Who was it, tell me, that stood beside you then,
  providing you with food and drink?
Give it some thought. The Lord was your father—
  the master who gives all living beings life—
But like the deer you endure the arrow, says Sūr,
  when the huntsman of the senses sings his song.

Sūr's twenty-five (§418, NPS 325)

Pledge your love to Mādhav, oh my mind.
Put every opposite emotion aside:
  lust, rage, greed, pride, and the ego's "I."
Bees feast on love, so they wander through the wilderness
  in search of fragrance. Their joy knows no bounds.
They drain the nectar from every blossom
  until the lotus catches them inside.
Listen to the limit a lover's love can know:
  how the crested cuckoo trains its eye afar
And suffers every ill in hopes of a raincloud,
  never begging elsewhere for drink.
The moth, not knowing that a flame brings pain,
  lets itself be taken by the fire:
But even as its body is singed in the blaze
  nothing dries the nectar from its soul.
On robbery, good folk and the holy books agree—
  every eye can see its horrors—
But thievery is something a thief will never leave,
  even at the cost of losing all.
A fish cannot suffer being parted from its water,
  yet the water never thinks to miss the fish;
That, you see, is the way things work with love—
  the body may go, but the passion doesn't lift.
Remember the tenacious obsession of the deer,
  how its ear became enraptured with the hunter's sound
And it held its ground, its back to the path of flight,
  and faced the arrow destined for its breast.
Look how that lifeless woman burns
  alongside the corpse of her mate:
Even a pyre cannot bleach the color
  from a heart that is dyed with love.
It's love that propels the turtle dove
  to soar aloft in the sky,
And soaring, look for its beloved, and seeing her,
  dive, even if it means he dies.

Look at the way of the lotus,
how it's bound by its love of the sun:
It may lose its life, but it never loses love
as it lets itself go dry along with the pond.
Love is the essence of every other essence,
and to the worldly man it's a game of dice:
He may lose body and mind, wealth and youth,
but never will he say he's lost the prize.
Now the jewel you've won is a jewel indeed—
but you can't seem to understand its worth;
Love is a tale you've heard told every day,
but even so you've yet to yield to shame.
The one who always stays with you, the one who is your own,
the one who breathes life into those who live—
That's the one you've so effortlessly forgotten:
Hari, the Blessed, the Lord,
The One who made you conscious by taking lifeless matter
and ordering its elements and traits,
Molding your feet, your hair, hands, and nails,
your eyes and ears and nose.
What a fearful place, that womb where you were
before any limb had taken form,
And listen, fool, the guardian of your life
refused to leave you there alone.
Day by day he held you and fed you,
wrapped you like a breast in a bodice,
Then pulled you out of that unhappy place,
grasped you and gave you milk to drink.
All kinds of food and clothes he gave you
whenever the need arose,
A mother and father and brothers to surround you—
new tastes, a new identity.
Your fine friendships grew, your house and your kin,
your sons and wife and wealth and home,
But these great worldly wiles made a worldly man of you
as desire started pulling at your mind.
Your happiness grew, your wealth grew too,
so did the lusts of your body,
Till in time, in the haze, as your eyesight slipped away
you no longer knew who'd befriended you,

And now it's gone: youth and life are spent
in the tastes of food and drink and clothes,
Like a rogue who beds down with someone else's wife,
then at dawn begins to feel the chill of fear.
Death knows all about it. And the whole world has heard:
the glory of your name has grown to matchless infamy
And no one is left to intervene
when the messengers of Death strike you down.
Who knows how many deaths like this you've died?
Bad thoughts make bad deaths.
Oh low-minded one, you set Hari's love aside
to satisfy yourself with fun.
The Lord is the companion who fulfills and purifies.
The Lord is the guardian of everything that lives.
More merciful than any, a treasury of giving—
life he holds in his hands.
It is he who is praised in all the Vedas and Purāṇas
and Smṛtis, and by gods and human beings:
Faced with the world's great wiles, its ego, its folly,
why did you not tend your tie to him?
Now I have searched through every place I know—
I've talked of moths and fish and birds and deer,
Whatever creatures there be on land or sea—
tell me, what can I say more?
If one speaks to a person who has no sense of shame,
what's the point in saying it a hundred times?
For never, not once, did you ever sing of Hari.
You're wasted, Sūr. You're a fool.

Turn away (§419, NPS 332)

Turn away, mind, from those who turn from Hari.
What's the good in giving cobras milk?
   Snakes never lose their venom.
Why waste camphor feeding it to crows
   or squander Ganges water washing dogs?
Why go plastering perfume on an ass
   or covering a monkey with jewels?
Empty your quiver, but arrows cannot pierce
   a stone that's fallen to the ground.
Sūrdās says, once a blanket's dyed black
   it never takes on a different hue.

Those feet, that lake (§420, NPS 337)

O *cakaī* bird, flee to those feet, that lake
   where love never suffers separation
And the dark, aimless night never comes—
   that ocean of joy, of union.
There Sanak swims with swans,
   the fish are Shiva and sages,
      and sunlight glints from the nails on those toes.
Where the lotuses bloom,
   never shrinking from the moon,
      there comes a constant hum, a Vedic fragrance,
And everywhere are lovely pearls of freedom.
   You should be drinking that pure water of good deeds.
You ignorant bird! Why are you here?
   Why ever abandon that perfect lake,
That place where he forever plays, with Śrī,
   his effortless game, while Sūrdās prays?
This puddle of existence, with its pleasures, seems so dry
   when one could hope instead for the sea.

Blind to the sun (§428, NPS 368)

Until you wake up to what you really are
You'll be like the man who searches the jungle
  for a jewel that hangs from his neck.
Oil, wick, and fire: if you mix them in a cruse
  won't they give bright light?
But how can you expect to dissipate the darkness
  simply by talking about lamps?
You're the sort of fool who sees your face
  fouled by inky filth in a mirror
And proceeds to try to erase the blackness
  by cleaning the reflection to a shine.
Sūrdās says, time to wise up now:
  Those days were futile, gone,
For who could comprehend the greatness of the sun
  by seeing without eyes—being blind?

An offering of lights (§429, NPS 371)

Hari has fashioned an offering of lights
Created in so utterly unusual a way
  that language can hardly give it measure.
A tortoise provides him with a throne unexcelled,
  while Śeṣ the snake makes a long, hooded handle
For its vessel, Island Earth; the seven seas are the butter-oil;
  and the wick is thick as a mountain.
The sun and the moon fill the world with their glow,
  vanquishing the darkness of night,
And sparks fly up like stars, undarkened by a sky
  spread black with the collyrium of clouds.
Shiva and Brahmā, Sanak, Prajāpati,
  and all the host of gods and anti-gods and men—
They rise and dance their dance of many parts,
  each in a rhythm of its own.
The times, the deeds, the character
  of those who love the Lord
    are creatures of his wisdom and will,
For Sūrdās's Lord has fashioned it all—
  substance and artifice—
    an offering unexcelled.

8
To the Holy Rivers

Jamunā (§431, NPS 4823)

Oh Kālindī, whom Keśav loves,
Grant to me your own special favor
  as the Dark One has already done.
Oh Jamunā, treasure of glory in all four ages,
  Yama's elder sister, mother of the world,
Never be angry at what I may have done.
  My nature, says Sūr, makes me as I am.

Ganges (§432, NPS 454)

From the lotus of those beloved feet, it is nectar
To divert the bee of a mind of impure thoughts
   from the dulling liquor of the senses.
It flows with less impurity than even ambrosia,
   the liquid of deathlessness. Its form is inner joy.
Its great cooling powers were known by Shiva
   when he bore it on his head, casting aside the moon
And caring nothing for mountains or snakes
   or the duel in which gods and anti-gods were bound.
In all three worlds, says Sūr, that River-of-the-Gods
   is immanent, immortal, and so free.

Confluence (§433, NPS 455)

Hail to Mādhav's Braid, the confluence of rivers
That he manifested for love of the world
  to open a way for those who'd lost the way.
It is as if Trivikram, the Triple-Victory Lord,
  knowing this Kali age to be a harsh, crooked king
Whose body is adorned with armies of evil,
  decided in anger to unsheathe his sword against him:
With Mount Meru for a hilt, glistening with great waters,
  and purchased at enormous cost
It's the Triple Confluence! The waves of its body glint,
  and the blade of its current is so very sharp
That the merest sight of it conquers Yama's soldiers:
  Greeks, Kāpālikas, Jains.
They make its name—one name—their boat and flee,
  leaving their hells for a fine peaceful realm.
Heavenly damsels observe that water war
  with lovely faces and lotus eyes,
Raise a great uproar among themselves, says Sūr,
  and with their hands bear garlands
    for the river of Nārāyaṇ.

Notes

Key: The notes that follow are enumerated according to the verse numberings appropriate to the Brajbhāṣā original. In English translation, a new Brajbhāṣā verse is indicated by the fact that it appears flush left on the page. Subsequent parts of the verse are indented.

I. KRISHNA GROWING UP

1.1 *Bhādoṅ* The month of Bhādoṅ (Skt. *bhādrapada*) corresponds to parts of August and September, when the monsoon is normally in full swing. Krishna is traditionally said to have been born on the eighth day in the waning or dark fortnight (*kṛṣṇa pakṣa*) of the month—in Mathura, at midnight.

1.2 *the fear of Kaṃs* Kaṃs, usually said to be Krishna's maternal uncle as the brother of his biological mother Devakī, is usurper to the throne of Mathura. Threatened by a prophecy that Devakī's eighth child will be his undoing, he has incarcerated Devakī and her husband Vasudev as the birth approaches, so as to kill the child upon his birth.

1.5 *your words that day* Kaṃs's warning had come on the day of Devakī's wedding, and he had threatened to kill Devakī on the spot. Vasudev, however, interceded: he dissuaded the king by promising to deliver all Devakī's offspring into his hands. Now the eighth child, Krishna, has been born, and when Devakī sees him and contemplates his fate, she wishes she had accepted death earlier. She implies that a father might be able to stand consigning such a luminous infant to the enemy in exchange for his own life, but not a mother.

1.7 *Devakī's wail* In remonstrating with Vasudev, Devakī calls him *pati* (1.5). The word means "husband," but it also means "lord," and Devakī's wail is answered by a lord other than her mate. This is "the One who pities the poor and removes his servants' pain" (*dīnadayāla dāsa duṣahārī*)—God himself, who is at the same time her own newborn baby. Krishna manifests himself in his supernal form at the very moment of his birth and reassures Devakī about all that has been and is to be.

1.8 *The chains were loosed* By means of his divine magic (*māyā*) Krishna makes possible his own escape, spreading a thick sleep over all of Mathura and enveloping the prison guards in it. He looses the fetters that bind his parents and opens the prison doors so that Vasudev can carry him across the river Jamunā to safety in the encampment of Nanda's clan on the other side. As for Devakī, she now has the wisdom (*sumati*, v. 8) that can remove her terror, for Krishna has shown her that the current moment is only a brief, stressful episode in a much larger story of salvation in which she has been a participant in former lives.

1.8 *distress* In the original this word is *bipati*, and it hides a pun. If heard as being derived from Skt. *vipatti*, it means "distress," but it could also be taken as meaning "one who is without [*bi*] a lord [*pati*]." When Devakī's true lord appears—her God, who is at the same time her son—her lordlessness is banished.

3.1 *headman's son* Formally speaking, Krishna is the adoptive son of Nanda, who is headman—even king (v. 47)—of the cowherding village of Gokul. Because of the amnesiac powers of *māyā*, however, everyone in Gokul receives the newborn infant as the actual son of Nanda and his wife Yaśodā–a son born to them miraculously in their old age. His birth is celebrated accordingly. This day is memorialized as *nandotsav* ("Nanda's festival"), and is observed on the day following Krishna's birthday (*kṛṣṇajanmāṣṭamī*). In some temples this Sūrdās poem is sung on *janmāṣṭamī* itself; in others, on *nandotsav*; in many, on both. On *nandotsav* parts of it are reenacted with great éclat, famously in the Vallabhite *havelī* in the town now known as Gokul, right down to the moment when pots of yogurt mixed with turmeric are dumped over the heads of male worshipers, as is described in verses 29–30.

3.4 *the Veda* "Wisdom": Collectively, Hinduism's most ancient sacred utterances.

3.10 *red muṇī birds* The *muṇī* bird is a familiar term of comparison for beautiful women because of its delicacy, and its red color is particularly appropriate for a happy celebration. So is the fact that *muṇīs* tend to fly about in great flocks.

3.14 *vermilion* Vermilion (*saindura*) is daubed in a woman's part as an emblem of her married status. The color red is generally auspicious.

3.19 *Hari* "The remover" (of distress or sin), a familiar title of Vishnu/Krishna.

3.26 *chalk* A "forest substance" (*bana dhātu*) that the cowherds use to draw designs on their bodies as a sign of celebration.

3.29 *turmeric curd* See §3.1. Turmeric colors yogurt yellow, which is, like red, an auspicious color.

3.30 *ghī* Clarified butter.

3.36 *dūb grass, cow-powder* *Rocan* (that is, *gorocan*) is a powder made from various products of the cow, yellow in color. *Dūb* grass, a familiar complement to traditional religious ceremonies, adds to the auspiciousness that yogurt and *gorocan* derive from their common source, the cow. A blade of *dūb* grass serves as an applicator when marks of yogurt and *gorocan* are placed on the forehead.

3.38 *the nandīmukh rite* A ceremony in the *śrāddh* group dedicated to generations past, but one that is specifically performed on a number of important occasions, especially those that have to do with the life cycle. It must be preceded by a bath, and in the case of childbirth it is ordained that this should be completed immediately, if possible even before the umbilical cord is cut. This done, Nanda, who had been childless, can for the first time honor his forefathers in good conscience, knowing that he has provided for their care in the future. Male offspring are the principal functionaries in these memorial rites.

3.44 *cows he gave to . . . Brahmins* The gift prescribed for Brahmins is that of a cow (*godān*). Other gifts follow similarly (vv. 53–55).

3.52 *Āṣāḍh* The month preceding Śrāvaṇ and Bhādoṅ. Āṣāḍh normally coincides with parts of June and July, which puts it at the very beginning of the rainy season. It "brings to life the peacocks and frogs" after a period of dormancy during the intense heat of the immediately preceding months.

3.57 *bheri, mṛdaṅg, paṭah, nisān* Among these four drums, the *nisān*, a kettle drum, is the largest. Its great resonance means that it is often used to herald public announcements. The *bheri* is similar, but not quite so large. The *mṛdaṅg* is an oblong drum with a deep sound that is frequently used as part of a musical ensemble and to accompany dance. The *paṭah* is a smaller instrument, more in the nature of a snare drum, usually hung from the neck and played with sticks.

7.1 *fresh butter* The deity depicted in this poem of *darśan* ("seeing") is one of Hinduism's most beloved icons. It is the infant Krishna lifting one hand to hold a ball of butter—soft, white, and freshly churned—as he uses the rest of his limbs to crawl across the floor. The iconographic type, in this exact form, can be traced back to a large eleventh-century soapstone image from Harnahadgalli in the state of Karnataka (see Hawley, *Krishna, The Butter Thief*, p. 361) but is more commonly seen in tiny bronze images that have proliferated throughout India between that time and the present day. In this poem, the poet brings that icon to life.

7.5 *infant's necklace . . . amulet* The "infant's necklace" (*kaṇṭhulā*, v. 5), diamond, and tiger-nail amulet are also to be expected in depictions of Krishna at this tender age. Like kohl, the *kaṇṭhulā*, a thick black thread, has the function of blackening the child's overall visage so that he will appear less attractive to anyone possessed of an evil eye. Paradoxically, however, the rough little necklace only contributes to Krishna's beauty, by suggesting a certain quality of rusticity that aligns him with every common child and by implication attracts them all to his divine aura.

8.3 *calls for his butter* A number of the favorite moments in Krishna's early childhood make their appearance here—playful amusements that are often labeled *līlās* but are here called *binoda* ("games," v. 1). Familiar though they are, each is given a little twist, so that it displays a novel aspect. The best known, undoubtedly, is Krishna's butter-stealing "game" (v. 3), which is here depicted as an act of charming self-confidence: lacking the ability to talk (v. 4), the child merely gives a signal and expects the butter to come his way. Also familiar is the motif of Krishna's gleeful crawling, but it is combined with another childhood staple: his fascination with his own reflection, which he sees as he looks down at his father's brightly polished floor (v. 2). This delight is the obverse of the disquiet he feels when he passes a shiny pillar and discovers that a little boy who looks just like him has been observing him as he steals butter (the *maṇikhambh līlā*), so verse 2 is subtly related to verse 3, where Krishna's appetite for butter is first mentioned. On the *maṇikhambh līlā*, see §17 and Hawley, *Krishna, the Butter Thief*, pp. 142–143, 238–248.

9.3–5 *Sometimes* Kenneth Bryant comments on Sūr's use—here and elsewhere—of the word "sometimes" (*kabahuṅka*) to induce a mood of nostalgic dreaminess in his audience: *Poems to the Child-God*, p. 74. Such a mood is particularly appropriate to the parental *vātsalya bhāv* ("cow-to-calf sentiment") that this poem cultivates.

9.4 *little Kānh* Kānh, Kanhāī, and Kanhaiyā are all vernacular derivatives of the standard Krishna (Skt. *kṛṣṇa*), meaning black or dark. All three are translated Kānh in this book. Kanhaiyā, which appears here, and its shortened form Kanhāī have a particularly familiar—even diminutive—ring.

9.6 *giver of all happiness* A certain closure is reached at the end of verse 5, where Yaśodā's maternal role, announced in the first verse, becomes fully focused on herself. This gives the poet freedom to range a bit more widely after he announces his signature at the beginning of the sixth verse. Heretofore Sūr has always spoken of Yaśodā as the one who is constantly giving; now he turns the tables and calls Krishna "the giver of all happiness" (*saba suṣadātā*). Heretofore Yaśodā's emotions have been Sūr's entire concern; now Sūr also draws attention to those of Krishna's foster-father Nanda. By making these two quick shifts, he suggests the full range of *vātsalya bhāv*. It characterizes the emotions of both parents, not just those of the "cow," and it designates not only what a parent may feel for a child but also the complete emotional field that is established thereby, in which the child's relation to and feelings for the parent also play an important part.

10.3 *on account of love* The word translated as "love" is *bhakti*.

10.3–6 *his feet* Like a number of other poems of Krishna's childhood, this one exposits the ironic contrast between Krishna as child and as deity. Its focus is Krishna's feet. They are the appendage through which Krishna, the child, makes contact with the earth (v. 3), even if he cannot always stand up on them himself (v. 2). But at the same time, as divine feet, they are the vehicle whose touch gives mortals access to a power that goes beyond this earth (v. 6).

10.4 *King Bali . . . Ganges* To prepare his listeners to join him in embracing Krishna's wondrous feet at the conclusion of the poem, Sūr describes the role they have played in several mythological episodes. He begins by referring to the story in which Vishnu/Krishna expanded from the size of a dwarf to overcome King Bali (v. 4). The boon the dwarf requested of the magnanimous king was a mere three steps, but their collective range proved stupendous (for details, see §§361, 362). The next reference (v. 4) is to the story of the descent of the Ganges. That river is said to emerge from the heavenly toe of Vishnu and plunge to earth from there (cf. §433).

10.6 *offer, offer, offer* In the original, the first-person pronoun (*maiṅ*) is uttered three times and the verb (*bali*) twice: *maiṅ bali maiṅ bali maiṅ gaiyā* (cf. §70). In translation, the threefold recurrence is retained, but transferred to the verb. In

Brajbhāṣā such a trio (*trivacan*) is emphatic, constituting an oath. The pun between *bali* as sacrifice or self-offering and the name of King Bali is also, actually, an evocation of that King's self-sacrificing action, on which see §§361, 362.

15.1 *black cow* Every Indian mother wants a nice plump baby, so Yaśodā attempts to convince Krishna that milk from a black cow, a much rarer species among Indian cattle than the white, will have the effect of lengthening his hair, which is also black. Until the twentieth century, upper-caste boys living in Braj were customarily encouraged to let their hair grow long until the ceremony of tonsure, which was typically performed in an odd-numbered year up to the age of seven. Hence the poet visualizes Krishna's locks as being fastened in a braid. As with Samson, long hair symbolizes virility, and in other poems Krishna laments that his braid is not as well developed as that of his older brother (cf. §16).

15.4 *Keśī and the crane* The horse-demon Keśī ("the hairy one") attacked Krishna as a child. He responded by jamming his elbow into the horse's mouth, breaking his jaw and, in some depictions, exploding his entire body. The crane-demon (*baka*) attacked Krishna with his huge beak, but the child grasped its upper and lower parts and pulled them asunder.

16.1 *topknot* The speaker is Krishna, who unfavorably compares his own short topknot (*coṭī*, v. 1) to the longer, thicker braid possessed by his older brother Balarām. The *coṭī* is the uncut tuft of hair traditionally maintained by upper-caste boys at the crown of the head even after tonsure. As we have seen in §16, it may be braided; and if tonsure is delayed, of course, that braid may be quite luxuriant indeed.

16.4 *big black snake* When the poet chooses the image of a "big black snake" (*nāgini*) by means of which Yaśodā may assure Krishna that all will soon be well, he makes her display a characteristic naiveté. For in truth there is an intimate association between Balarām and the serpent world that makes his long, snakelike braid a natural attribute for him in a way that it can never be for Krishna. Unbeknownst to Yaśodā, Balarām is an incarnation of Śeṣ, the great snake that is Vishnu's primordial companion. The earthshaking impact of cosmic associations such as these may be lost on her, but they are sensed in the rest of the universe, as is hinted in the final line.

16.6 *Bearer of the Plow* The plow is Balarām's characteristic emblem (cf. §333.6).

17.5 *he studied his reflection* This poem, recording one *gopī*'s experience of Krishna to another, belongs to the *maṇikhambh* genre, in which the child Krishna sees his reflection in a shiny pillar as he pilfers butter (cf. §8). Part of the episode's charm is that Krishna is not the only one to be mesmerized by his reflection; so is the *gopī* who watches him—and it. The poet can succeed in sketching the central episode of the *maṇikhambh līlā* so briefly—he uses a mere couplet (vv. 5–6)—because he assumes that his hearers already know the story. It may be touching and visually fascinating for the *gopī* in question (and by extension her friend and us as well) to see Krishna offer butter to a likeness of himself, but it becomes considerably more fascinating if one knows more than the few words of this poem actually convey. Then the *gopī*'s report calls up memories of how Krishna feared his thievery was being discovered and tried to buy off the spy with an equal part of the spoils. This makes full sense of what he is said to do in verse 6.

19.1 *awake!* This poem treats a theme that is frequently sung in temples and in other performance settings, such as *rās līlās*, where Krishna's daily life is celebrated. As we have seen in the Introduction, it is consummately simple in both construction and content, yet with an intriguing twist at the end.

19.6 *he who bears the lotus* In the Introduction we considered several possible interpretations of the phrase *ambuja kara*. If we regard it as a compound—the most common understanding—the translation might run as follows:

And then, says Sūr, the blessed Cowherd stirs,
  the one with lotuslike hands.

If we adopt Shrivatsa Goswami's suggestion and regard the words *ambuj kar* as denoting two independent entites—envisioning a child who places his elbows on some surface (the floor, perhaps, or a bed), rests his head on his palms, and looks out thoughtfully at the world—the translation would be:

And then, says Sūr, the blessed Cowherd wakes,
  holding a lotus in his hands.

As the Introduction explains, the translation chosen in the main text makes room for a third possibility

20.4 *churning the Ocean of Milk* The imagery throughout this poem is consistent. Krishna's bright, awakening face is implicitly likened to the moon (v. 4)—a complement to the rising sun (v. 1)—and the herdspeople gather to catch sight of it with the same attention that *cakor* birds lavish on moonbeams (vv. 5–6), since that is said to be their entire subsistence. When so bright a moon appears, it seems its own kind of dawn, and the poet compares that moment to the one in which the moon first emerged onto the stage of cosmic history. It was churned forth when gods and demons cooperated for a brief moment because of their common hope of extracting the liquid of immortality (*amṛt*) from the primeval Milk Ocean. The moon is the vessel of this *amṛt*, the liquid of immortality, which explains its beautiful glow.

22.4 *the moon rained lovely bits of nectar* This nectar is *amṛt*, on which see §20.4.

22.4 *feud with the moon* When the *gopī* makes reference to a "feud" (*baira*, v. 6) between the moon and the lotus, she is thinking of the fact that most lotuses bloom by day and retreat into themselves at night (cf. §§19, 93). But by the time we complete verse 6, we know that there is to be no attack. These lotus lovers "approach" (*āgama*, v. 4), bearing tribute.

23.7 *that wish-fulfilling jewel* When the *gopīs* call Krishna a "wish-fulfilling jewel" (*cintāmaṇi*, v. 7) in this poem of complaint addressed to Yaśodā, they speak with heavy irony. They wish to convey the sense that Krishna has robbed them of something rather than offering them anything, though many commentators have judged that the real purpose of their visit to Yaśodā was less to complain of Krishna's crimes than to get a glimpse of the culprit. They too, after all, are "dashing here and there" (v. 8; cf. §24.4–6).

24.2 *all six tastes* Yaśodā tries hard to keep Krishna at home by offering him foods of every description. The "six tastes" (*sarasa chahūṅ*) mentioned here provide the standard taxonomy for all possible flavors: sweet, pungent, bitter, astringent, sour, and salty. Yaśodā's efforts are in vain, however. Krishna seems to prefer the shorter, simpler list of milk products that is given in verse 3.

28.1 *cow's wealth* In this poem the *gopīs* find Yaśodā threatening Krishna with a stick, and respond to his pitiful, cowering condition with words of reproach. Krishna is being punished for having stolen milk products (*gorasa*, v. 7: "cow's wealth," literally "cow's juice") or specifically curd (*dadhi*, v. 2).

31.4 *wagtail* The voice we hear in this poem is that of a *gopī* who comes upon Yaśodā threatening Krishna with a stick, presumably in answer to one of his butter-stealing episodes. She appeals to Krishna's mother in terms of a single, developing metaphor that affords the hearer a vision of the tearful child. When she chooses to compare Krishna's eyes to the wagtail bird (*ṣañjana*), she selects a species that is usually drawn into poetry because of the gay and sprightly darting of its eyes. This is intrinsically an accusation, then, since in this case the tremulousness of Krishna's eyes has anything but gaity as its cause. There may be a suggestion of the child's thievish instincts in the *gopī's* mention of the bird's appetite for pearls (which are normally the food of a different bird, the *haṃs*), but by the time the speaker is done the focus has definitely shifted from any undue expansiveness in the past to its radical inhibition in the present.

33.1 *Nanda's Joy Nandanandana*, that is, Krishna. The poet portrays him as he looks in the beloved moment when he returns to Gokul with his cows at evening. The description is entirely standard except in one respect: Krishna is depicted not only as a rustic flutist (v. 2) but as a singer (*gāvata*, v. 5), too.

33.4 The reference to wagtails (*ṣañjana*) might be puzzling for the uninitiated, since the poet does not specify the feature of Krishna's physiognomy to which they are being compared, but any practiced listener immediately identifies these birds as Krishna's ever-active eyes. The lotus trap into which they have flown is, of course, his face, and his hair constitutes the strings that make it work. Probably the poet is thinking that the trap could be laid out from both sides of the face, with curls falling lazily toward each eye like a noose left slack, yet ready to be pulled tight if the wagtails happen to come within the grasp of a stray wisp of hair.

33.7 *Destroyer of the wicked* Beginning with the penultimate line, it is not entirely clear whose voice we are hearing. The poet may still be speaking through the persona of a *gopī*, who shifts at this point to a more general level of reflection on what she has been seeing. Alternatively, we may sense that at this point the poet begins to speak on his own behalf. Either way, his purpose in verse 7 is to sum up the scene by stating its subject explicitly. With a phrase that employs the word cow (*go*) in three separate connections, he tells us very clearly that we have been gazing at a simple cowherd. But he also tells us that this cowherd has a magisterial aspect: he is the Lord (*prabhu*), the "destroyer of the wicked" (*duṣṭa nikandana*). The wondersome tension between the supremacy and accessibility of Krishna creates a new way of understanding the well-known Upanishadic—and therefore Vedic (*śruti*, v. 8)—dictum that ultimate reality is "not this, not that" (*neti neti*, v. 8).

33.8 *not this, not that* The phrase *neti neti* is usually interpreted as meaning that the ultimate is simply beyond the reach of language or of anything to which we have access through the senses; it is *nirguṇ*, "without attributes." That may well be the conclusion here, too, but the method of approach is different: through very vivid attributes that seem to stand in a contradictory relation to one another. Krishna is on the one hand a lowly cowherd and on the other, the supreme Lord. If he can be both these things, then he seems in reality to be neither: "He is not this, not that" (*neti neti*, v. 8). Or at least, according to Sūrdās, that is the conclusion to which the seers who composed Vedic verses (*śruti chandana*, v. 8) were driven. It flies in the face of Advaitan orthodoxy to say so, but Sūr seems to be suggesting that a *saguṇ* ("with attributes") approach to *nirguṇ* reality—working through contrasts and contradictions, and through music, poetry, and the emotions—gives a truer view than the abstract, even languageless via negativa often cultivated by philosophical exponents of the *nirguṇ* school.

34.1 *dust of Brindavan* Brindavan is Krishna's pastoral home—roughly equivalent to Gokul in the broad sweep of Puranic literature but nowadays, like Gokul, associated with a particular town. Literally spreaking, Brindavan is the basil-tree or wildflower (*brindā* < *vṛndā*) forest (*ban, van*) where Krishna herded his cows. The dust of Brindavan earns the special reverence that is accorded it by virtue of having received the imprint of Krishna's feet. Many pilgrims touch their foreheads to the earth as their first act upon entering Brindavan's sacred but intentionally commonplace precincts. Some swallow bits of dust as acts of piety.

34.2 *Nandanandan* Nanda's joy, i.e., Krishna (cf. §33.1).

34.3 *born as gods* Only at this point in the poem do we learn that we are hearing the speech of the gods. In an inversion of commonly accepted herarchies they lament their distance from the feet of Krishna (cf. §10).

36.2 *Saṅkarṣaṇ . . . Kāliya* This poem relates in outline the story of how Krishna subdued the serpent Kāliya ("the black one") and received a petition from the snake's wives that the life of their husband be spared. Their request is granted—Krishna banishes Kāliya to the sea rather than killing him—but the poet stops short of actually narrating that event here. Implicitly, perhaps, this result is assumed, since Krishna takes no further action after the women make their plea. Saṅkarṣaṇ, "the attractive one" (v. 2), is an alternate name for Balarām, whose connection both iconographically and mythologically to snake-deities (*nāgas*) helps explain his important presence in most tellings of the Kāliya story.

36.3 *mridangam* The *mṛdaṅg* (v. 3) is the classical drum of the Braj area, a long instrument typically held between the knees and played on both ends. Krishna's dance on Kāliya's heads, with its regular slaps of the feet (*thei thei*, v. 3), sounds out the sort of rhythmic pattern (*tāla*, v. 3) one expects from a *mṛdaṅg*.

36.6 *Dark One* Clearly Kāliya's wives, the *nāginīs*, are addressing themselves to Krishna, but there is irony in the fact that they address him with a title (*sundara syāma sarīra*, "one who possesses a beautiful, dark body") that is also appropriate to their husband.

37.1 *our rescue* As so often in the genre of the *pad*, audiences for this poem derive part of their pleasure from answering the implicit question, "Who is speaking?" The poet does not divulge the answer until the final verse—after Krishna himself has spoken words of reassurance.

38.1 *Beguiler-of-the-Mind* "Beguiler-of-the-Mind" translates the term *manmohan* (v. 1), a title of Krishna.

38.1 *the color of dusk* In the original, the first word of the poem is *sāṅvarau* ("dusk"). It clearly situates the poem as to time of day, but also introduces a distinctive palette of colors associated with the rainy season. It also bears close associations with Krishna, one of whose most common names, Śyām ("the dark one"), refers to just this range of hues. *Sāṅvarau* is a close relative of *śyām*. There is a long tradition of viewing Krishna at precisely the moment when he emerges from the wilderness after having herded the cows all day. The monsoon and the time immediately afterward have long been celebrated as the season in which such a vision is at its best, since the colors are so clear (cf. BhP 10.21.1–9).

38.10 *bimba fruit* The final couplet (vv. 9–10) begins with standard comparisons between the nose and the parrot on the one hand and the lips and the *bimba* fruit on the other. The *bimba* derives its likeness to the lips from its red color, its oblong shape, and its size: it grows to be about two inches long when ripe. The poet orchestrates this familiar set of similes into a little drama of brightness and shadow, with the parrot trying unsuccessfully to peck at the fruit he shelters beneath his beak. For all its activity, with nostrils flaring and collapsing as Krishna breathes to play his flute, the nose never reaches his mouth.

42.1 *Look, friend* One *gopī* speaks to another, introducing a *darśan* poem.

42.1 *mass of delight* This "mass of delight" (*ānanda kanda*)—the mass of Krishna's beauty—takes shape as the poem progresses. Several meanings of word *kand* ("mass") are relevant to this poem. Its usual sense is to denote something round and bulbous—a head of garlic, an elaborate knot, a tuber or root. That circular shape begins to emerge as our *gopī* describes the coiled earrings of verse 3 and the hollow of the cheeks against which they are reflected, and other circular forms appear all the way up to the "curve" or "bend" (*bhaṅg*) of the penultimate line. The second meaning of *kand* is "cloud," and as Nadine Berardi has pointed out (conversation, 1988), that too is present throughout the poem. This is largely possible because of the darkness of Krishna's skin, to which Sūr refers in verse 2 when the *gopī* says that he is "a cloud dark with love." The crowning touch is added by a third dimension of *kand*, and this one Sūr saves for the very last word in the poem. This third meaning is medical, for *kand* may also designate a lump or swelling, the sort of thing that reminds one of the gnarled roots or knotted trunks of certain trees. Thus when Sūr's *gopī* acknowledges that her wishes have gone lame at the sight of Krishna's colors and curves, this sense of her own deformation (*kand*) also comes to mind. It is a comparative thing: one can scarcely see Krishna without sensing how one's own form pales. Or to put it as Sūr does, the fulfillment offered by the sight of Krishna is so intense that desire itself is crippled. For a more extended treatment of these intricacies, see Chapter 2 of the Introduction to Hawley, *Sūr's Ocean*, vol. 1.

42.2 *cātak-bird* The *cakravāk* or *cātak* bird is said to eschew every form of nourishment other than rainwater that falls under the *svāti* asterism, which appears only at the end of the monsoon season.

42.2 *cakor-bird* See the note on §20.4, which is also relevant to the elixir (*amṛt*) that figures in verses 5–6.

42.6 *pair of lotus vessels* Krishna's mouth and lips are both familiarly compared to lotuses—the mouth because of its luscious pink opening and the moistness it holds, like the nectar held in the lotus's pericarp; the lips because their beautifully tapered shape matches that of a lotus leaf.

42.7 *brilliant silk* Mention of this material explains the special flash of Krishna's yellow *dhotī*, which is likened to lightning in the next verse.

42.7 *a garland of basil leaves* On first hearing, one might expect the phrase *tulasī māl* ("basil garland") to refer to a necklace of brown *tulsī* beads, sacred to Vishnu/ Krishna. Yet Sūr apparently constructs his *tulsī* garland not of beads but of leaves, as the subsequent comparison to green parrots suggests. The comparison is apt. Parrots do indeed fly in great arching rows, and are particularly striking in the monsoon season, when dark clouds serve as their background.

45.6 *she summons their chariots* Krishna's music-making is so irresistible that even heavenly beings descend to earth to hear what it portends, as they are sometimes said to gather for the purpose of witnessing Krishna's *rās* dance.

45.8–10 *the Creator . . . Śrī's Lord* The class of beings mentioned in verse 9 covers the entire range that the universe provides, beginning with the gods, seated in heaven, and ending with the snakes, who rule the netherworld. Their Creator is the god Brahmā, a figure more comparable to the Gnostic demiurge than to the biblical Creator-God. Above him—and above them all—is Vishnu, who reigns in Vaikunṭh, the heaven above the heavens, with his consort Śrī, whose name means "auspiciousness." Thanks to Muralī, this Vishnu, who is also Krishna, has forgotten the consort who signifies his royal power. He has succumbed to the infatuation spread abroad by his own flute; and with his submission the entire universe, by extension, is hers. Because it challenges their own claim to Krishna's affections, the *gopīs* are jealous of this infatuation. It is they who speak the poem.

46.3 *makes him stand on a single foot* This poem provides a novel interpretation of Krishna's classical *tribhaṅg* pose, according to which he is "triply bent"—once at the knees (v. 3), once at the waist (v. 4), and once at the neck (v. 5). Speaking through the envious *gopī* who gives voice to the poem, Sūrdās shows how it is really not Krishna who plays Muralī, as the standard image would have it, but she who "plays" him. For a detailed exposition, see Bryant, *Poems to the Child-God*, pp. 95–99.

46.5 *Mountain-Lifter* Krishna as the lifter of Mount Govardhan: see §§55, 56, 58.

47.1 *Balarām's brother* The title *balabīr* is unusual in that it can designate either Balarām or Krishna. It is a question of which way the compound is understood. As Bal the hero (*bīr*), this is Balarām. As the brother (*bīr*) of Bal, it is Krishna. Clearly the latter is meant in this poem.

55.1 *cow-clan* "Cow-clan" gives a literal translation of *gokul*, but as we have seen (§3.1–2), the word is also one of the names used to designate the place in which Krishna's herdspeople live.

55.2 *cows . . . drip with rain* In this poem the people of Braj petition for Krishna's help in reversing the consequences of an act that he himself has urged them to take. Krishna argued that they should direct their worship to Mount Govardhan, the symbolic center of Braj and emblem of its inherent abundance, rather than to the unpredictable forces over which Indra rules as king of the ancient Vedic pantheon. Every Hindu knows the outcome of the cowherders' plea: Krishna lifts the mountain itself to shelter them and their herds from Indra's ravaging revenge.

55.5 *great snake . . . heron woman* The three victories to which the herder folk appeal are all miraculous encounters in which the child Krishna defeated demons sent upon him by Kaṃs. The snake Agh opened its mouth so wide that Krishna and his playmates wandered in, thinking it a cave, but Krishna expanded his size until the snake burst. The heron demon Bak (cf. §15.4) attempted to swallow Krishna in its huge beaks, but the child responded by "defacing" him (*badana bidārana*), that is, wrenching the beaks totally apart. The demoness Pūtanā flew into Braj in the form of a heron (*bakī*), then transformed herself into a woman with poisoned breasts and attempted to suckle Krishna. She succeeded, but the infant was unaffected and proceeded to suck the very life out of her. In each case, says the *Bhāgavata Purāṇa*, the touch of the Lord communicated to his enemy not only defeat, but simultaneous salvation: he "gave every happiness."

56.5 *Great Flood* The reference is to *pralaya*, the dissolution of the universe into the same watery mass from which it periodically emerges, thanks to the power of Vishnu. The power of dissolution also belongs by rights to Vishnu, so there is something especially fearful about the fact that to the residents of Braj it now seems that Indra is in control.

56.8 *Śrī's husband* Vishnu/Krishna: cf. §45.10.

58.5–6 *an offering plate* Yaśodā brings a circular plate (*thāla*) on which she has set out the substances that are traditionally used to welcome an honored guest or celebrate an auspicious arrival: betel, yogurt, unbroken grains of rice, and *dūb*, a sort of grass that has been used in Indian rituals since Vedic times (cf. §3.36).

58.9 *the timid captain of the gods* Rather than naming him directly, Sūr refers to Indra as "the captain of the gods" (*surapati*), and says that he "brings in all the cows" (*saba surabhi saṅga lai āe*). The sense seems to be that Indra hides himself among the cattle of Braj to become a sort of spy, rather than announcing himself with cloud-warrior heralds and his accustomed mount, the great elephant Airāvat. Far from assuming his Vedic flamboyancy and releasing a group of pent-up cattle that stand for cosmic forces of water and light (*Rig Veda* 3.31), he gathers a mundane herd and takes them home to Krishna. As if to simulate Indra's new-found diffidence (*saṅkita*), Sūr supplies a long alliteration as verbal camouflage (*sūradāsa saṅkita surapati saba surabhi saṅga*, v. 9), concealing this erstwhile "captain of the gods" (*surapati*) somewhere in the middle. Thus when Indra cannot keep himself from bursting out with an exclamation, his words have unusual force. Here is the head of the Vedic pantheon confessing bewilderment at the incommensurable secret of a small boy!

2. THE PANGS AND POLITICS OF LOVE

60.1 *onslought of love* The title line of this poem announces its subject as *anurāg*, a word that means love or passion in a general sense but carries quite specific connotations in the *rasa* (MSH *ras*) school of Sanskrit poetics. The great theorist of Sūr's time was the poet-theologian Rūp Gosvāmī, who worked with elements of the earlier *ras* tradition, such as the *Rasārṇava-sudhākara* of Siṅgabhūpāl (14th century?) and elaborated a theory of the devotional sentiments that placed *anurāg* as the seventh of eight stages of amorous love (*madhurati*). These, he held, were best exemplified by Rādhā. For Rūp, the special characteristic of *anurāg* is that it manifests continual freshness (*nava navatva*), despite the fact that it is by no means the first blush of love. (Rūp Gosvāmī, *Ujjvalanīlamaṇi*, verse 14.146, p. 143.) Rūp goes on to say that among the aspects especially associated with *anurāg* is *aprāṇī-janma*, a desire for "[re]birth [even] as inanimate matter," if that form of existence would succeed in placing the lover in proximity to the beloved. In the present composition of Sūrdās, we appear to have a meditation on Rādhā's *anurāg* that is relevant to exactly this conception. Exhausted by searching through the woods for Krishna (v. 2), Rādhā finds her body melting into the scenery, or so it seems to the forest creatures who surround her (vv. 3–6). Not all the elements into which she seems to merge are inanimate (*aprāṇī*)—they comprise both flora and fauna—but they do resonate to Rūp's idea: her total identification with the place she associates with Krishna, namely, his forest. Ultimately Krishna worries about death by dismemberment (*vikal*, v. 7) and causes Rādhā to emerge as "a seedbud of new life." This new birth is anything but inanimate (*aprāṇī-janma*): in Krishna's arms she becomes a living child.

60.4 *crow and cuckoo* The crow begins cawing because it mistakes Rādhā's sweet voice for the call of the cuckoo—or to be precise, the koel (*pika*), which is said to leave its eggs in the crow's nest with the expectation that the crow will do the hard work of hatching the egg.

62.1 *circle dance* The subject here is Krishna's *rās* dance, which is so named in the title line. The word *rās* is translated as "circle" because of the shape according to which this dance had come to be visualized in the sixteenth century, but the term actually bears no intrinsic relation to a circle and earlier representations show it in various configurations. The etymology of *rās* is uncertain, but the close aural resemblance between *rās* and *ras*—the important aesthetic term meaning "flavor," "taste," and by extension "mood," "emotion," or "flow" (e.g., §31)—has often caused the two words to be closely associated. This happens in the current composition, where the word *ras* appears twice. We encounter it in the second verse as an independent term ("taste"), then later it recurs as part of the phrase *ras rīti* (v. 5), meaning roughly "aesthetics."

62.3–4 *fine magic spell . . . fine shot* One way of interpreting *sumāyā*, "fine magic" (v. 3) is to understand it as referring to the spell cast over Braj by Vishnu/Krishna through his agent *yogamāyā*. The effect was that no *gopī* called to participate in the *rās* dance was missed at home, since a double was put in her place. Another interpretation would take this "fine magic" as simply indicating the power of the flute by means of which Krishna announces his dance. The "fine blow" (*sumāra*, v. 4) it administers is enough to transfix all beings. In one group of manuscripts that blow is struck purely by sound (*sura*); in another group, as reflected in the present translation, the vowel changes and the metaphor of an arrow (*sara*) is introduced.

62.6 *Kāma* It is often said in Braj that the *rās* dance represents the victory of one sort of love over another. In the *rās*, the sort of love in which a person offers herself to her beloved unconditionally and without hope of gain is shown to be victorious over the sort of love that produces a fruit beneficial to the lover. The former love is designated by the concept *prem*, while the latter is *kām*, often personified as the god Kāma, as here (cf. Hawley, *At Play with Krishna*, pp. 186–187). The poem comes to its climax when Kāma becomes so disoriented by the love Krishna has generated—and so moved by it—that he is unable to maintain his warrior's posture. He too begins to dance, perhaps turning his hand palm-down and then palm-upward (*ulaṭi*, v. 6: "upside-down") in one of the gestures that often accompany Indian dance as a way for singers to keep track of the beat.

62.6 *Bodiless One* *Anaṅg*, a title Kāma earned when he challenged Shiva's ascetic rigor and failed; the great god reduced him to ash with the power of his third eye, where that rigor was stored. In this poem, however, Sūr implies that Kāma actually lost his body in a different battle, one he waged not against yogic asceticism but against a competing form of love. Kāma—passion, lust—is transfigured, "disembodied," and enabled to join in a dance where *prem* sets the tune. The logic of this is that erotic love (*kām*) is not excluded by love's higher form (*prem*), but subordinated and transformed.

64.2 *filling my pots* This poem depicts a type of episode usually referred to as the *paṅghat līlā*, in which Krishna encounters one or another *gopī* as she fills her pots with water at the riverbank. It is a perfect setting for romance. The spot is secluded (v. 2), the path perhaps somewhat overgrown, and the motion she makes as she carries the shining metal waterpots (*gagarī*, v. 3) on her head is graceful and alluring. Krishna, wearing his simple yellow *dhotī* decorated at its sash with little bells (v. 4), is no less attractive than she, and before long their union is achieved (vv. 5–6).

64.6 *golden pitchers* The *gopī*'s other "pots," the gold ones shaped by her breasts, were, as the original says, "made to bear good fruit" (*suphala kiye*, v. 6): they both received and bestowed their reward. And not just the breasts but the *gopī*'s entire body, for the word describing them as pitchers or pots (*ghaṭa*, v. 6)—the last word in the poem—is frequently used to refer to the body as a whole. When the poet tells us that these pitchers were golden (*kañcana*, v. 6), he gives us a hint that the heretofore anonymous *gopī* may have been Rādhā herself, since Rādhā's skin is renowned for displaying exactly that hue. Sūr hides her identity until the last phrase in the poem, making her modesty in earlier verses all the more affecting.

65.4 *God of Love* The sounds of peacocks and crested cuckoos (*cātaka*, v. 5) are especially associated with the rains—*cātaks* are said to exist solely on raindrops—and so, of course, are mating and fecundity in general. It therefore makes sense that Kāma, "the God of Love," plays a leading role here. He appears at the poem's halfway point (*madana*, v. 4) and again at the end (*kāma*, v. 8). In verse 4 he is mentioned in connection with a woman torn between husband and lover—there his effect is a devastating burn. But in verse 8 we find him closely paired with Krishna, and this time the imagery is all flowers. Apparently the woman's description of what she sees—in the first half of the poem, the drama of the sky; in the second half, of the forest—arouses Krishna's desire, and Kāma responds (v. 8). Thus we move from devastation to satisfaction. This is not really so surprising. Ever since our heroine noticed a line of herons cutting across an arc of black clouds (v. 1), the motif of bow and arrow has been hovering over this scene. These are Kāma's accoutrements. In seeing them, she has been invoking his presence since the beginning. The bower the vines create (v. 8)—the archetypal trysting place—heralds more to come.

65.6 *vow of silence* The vines generate "another kind of poetry" (*bacana racana*) that is parallel to the language of the birds, breaking a vow (*brata ṭārī*) in order to do so. The poet does not tell us what kind of vow this is, but we have guessed he has in mind a vow of silence, as a way of referring to the bare, almost ascetical appearance that vines assume in the hot season, just before the monsoon breaks in. An alternate interpretation would be to consider that the vow they break is the wedding vow (*pativrat*). In that case Sūr would be describing the way in which these vines put out fresh tentacles, reaching for new branches and trees, as if it bespoke the profligacy of love-starved women who decide to abandon marital chastity. If so, he would be returning in a new way to the scene he depicts in verse 4, this time stressing the manner in which these "restless women" (v. 4) are *virahiṇīs* ("love-deprived women," *biṣa birahinī*, v. 6). Since the vow being broken is no longer, on this hypothesis, a vow of silence, perhaps we might understand the vines to be responding to the poetry of the birds rather than generating their own:

> And just so the vines, love-deprived women,
> paragons of amorous anger and pride,
> hearing such poetry,
> break their marriage vow.

67.1 *beguiling vine* As soon as the title line of this poem has been uttered, the practiced listener knows that an encounter between Hari and one of the *gopīs* is being described, for it is often said that Krishna's women wind themselves around him as vines cling to a tree (cf. §65). Once the color gold (*cāmīkara*, v. 3) is mentioned, we know conclusively that the *gopī* in question is Rādhā (cf. §64.6); the darker shade, of course, is his.

67.2 *grasped by a serpent* The dark color we usually associate with a snake suggests that this is Krishna's arm resting on Rādhā's—that is, Rādhā's "vine."

67.2 *full moon* This may refer either to Rādhā's face or to Krishna's, for both would appear luminous in their encounter with one another. As in painting, the two lovers are shown intertwined to such an extent that it is sometimes difficult to tell exactly who is who. In English translation one is almost forced to abandon the full extent of this ambiguity, supplying "his" and "her" when necessary. In the original, however, these possessive adjectives are absent: listeners must find their own way.

67.6 *pomegranate seeds* The reference is to Rādhā's white, almost translucent teeth. They emerge from a fruit—a face—so ripe that it opens naturally, as if sprouting to reveal her smile.

72.1 *Lost, lost, lost* This composition belongs to the genre of praise-poems in which the primary effect is achieved through repetition (cf. §10). The repeated element in this poem is the noun *bali*, literally "sacrifice," which serves as a shortened form of the expression *bali jānā*, "to sacrifice oneself." It conveys a general sense of self-emptying that is here translated with the word "lost," and that corresponds to English expressions such as being "swept away" or "blown away." One may well assume that the subject is the poet himself and that he finds he has lost himself to an image (*mūrati*, v. 1; *darasa*, v. 4) of Krishna herding cows with his friends. Alternatively one can think of Sūrdās speaking through a *gopī*, someone who beholds this image as the actual person of Krishna. Whichever interpretation one prefers, the speaker begins with the threefold repetition (*trivacan*) that is tantamount to an oath (*bali bali bali*, v. 1). The repetitions that frame the remainder of the poem further intensify this oath, which testifies that everything has been offered and is gone.

72.1, 6 *Mohan . . . Madan Gopāl* In verse 1, *mohan* is rendered as both "Mohan" and "captivating"; in verse 6, *madan gupāl* is both "Madan Gopāl" and "that intoxicating cowherd lad." In both cases the second translation attempts to convey the adjectival force associated with these titles in the original. *Mohan* can be heard as an adjective modifying *mūrati* ("image," v. 1), and the first word in the name Madan Gopāl may be heard as modifying the second ("intoxicating Gopāl" or "intoxicating cowherd lad," v. 6).

73.3 *militia of bees* As Krishna strides home with the cows, his curls swing to and fro and are blown by the breeze in such a way that they stray into the vicinity of his mouth. This makes it appear that they are invading an area of the face that does not belong to them. It is as if they were a swarm of bees hungry for the honey of Krishna's lips.

74.8 *not that, not this* As in poem 33, Sūr throws up his hands and despairs of saying anything, justifying his silence by saying that the Vedas themselves found no way of describing ultimate truth except to say "It isn't thus" (*neti*, v. 8). In its most familiar form that Upanishadic formula includes a repetition—*neti neti*—hence the translation "not that, not this." It is noteworthy that until the final line there is not a single independent, finite verb in the entire poem, and when one does appear, in this last line, it is merely to question the possibility of meaningful speech: "how can Sūrijdās say more?" Faced with "the radiance of Mādhav's face" (v. 1), the vaunted resources of verbal rationality pale—especially in a poet whose name make him slave (*dās*) to the sun (*sūrij*).

81.5 *ether* At first hearing of the original, the last two verses of this poem may seem dreamy, as if the *gopī* who speaks were ready to waft herself to heaven like a *satī* in pursuit of her departed husband. The word *akāsa* (Skt. *ākāśa*) in verse 5 does mean "heaven," and if we construe *vijana* in the final verse as meaning an uninhabited forest, then a translation something like the following emerges for verses 5–6:

> Sūr, I will keep this earthly body ever young
>   and once in heaven I'll settle in my dear one's home;
> Its breezes, its forests, its pools with their water play—
>   I'll make myself a mirror to refract all that joy.

Closer inspection, however, reveals a more intricate set of meanings. *Akāsa* is not just "heaven" but "ether," and *vijana* can mean not only "forest" (Skt. *vijana*) but "fan" (Skt. *vyajana*) Once these substitutions have been made, the final couplet shapes itself around the five elements—earth (*avanī*, v. 5), ether (*akāsa*, v. 5), air (*bāya*, v. 6), water (*jala*, v. 6), and light (the fiery brilliance *teja*, v. 6). We see how these elements would appear if recast in the crucible of love. Thus the earthly body (*dehau*, v. 4) is indeed left behind and a new one constructed in its place, but this process of deliberate reconstitution is very different from wandering off into some naive sphere of eternal romance. Here is no dreamy heaven, but the elements of earth itself.

83.2 *the Radiant One* This poem explores the manifold ambiguities of the term *sāraṅg* ("possessed of color, radiance, or emotion") and may have been sufficiently influential to inspire a number of other "riddle poems" (*kūṭ kāvya*) on *sāraṅg* that came into the *Sūrsāgar* at a later date (cf. *Sūr's Ocean* §125). In this composition the term is used twice, both times in verse 2 ("the Radiant One"). In its first occurrence the reference is clearly the moon, a familiar metaphor for Krishna's face, but not long afterward the same word denotes Kāma, who is known as "the Radiant One" because all things blossom as he comes near. When Rādhā sees Kāma in Krishna, she gives forth passion (*rati kīnhī*, v. 2), but in so doing she herself becomes Passion (*rati*), Kāma's wife. Thus the peculiar intimacy suggested by Krishna's fondness for disguising himself in Rādhā's dress is fulfilled in her amorous response to him as he does so. This close interplay has made the icon of Rādhā and Krishna as a single figure—a "dual divinity"—a favorite one among some Vaishnavas, and crossdressing is a major theme in Brajbhāṣā dramas depicting the couple's adventures. In the first half of our poem Rādhā is the active partner, at least insofar as she is active in perceiving Krishna. In the second half Krishna takes over.

83.3 *left-hand side* Drawing Rādhā to his left-hand side, Krishna puts her in the position that a wife or consort would normally occupy in relation to her mate, so he reciprocates the conjugal gesture she has made in the preceding line, behaving as if she were Krishna's mate.

83.4 *nectar of life* The word used is *sudhā*, that is, *amṛt*, the immortal elixir Indians imagine as the substance that gives the moon its brightness. Krishna drinks this nectar—implicitly, from Rādhā's moonlike face (cf. Krishna's, §20.3–4)—by kissing her.

83b.1–4 *esoteric* The foregoing interpretation, which sees the topic of this poem as crossdressing, is not the only approach to understanding its concise diction. Another interpretation is possible—a more fully sexual one. According to this second interpretation the "dark jewel" (*śyām maṇi*) mentioned at the outset—perhaps it is specifically the sapphire (*nīlamaṇi*), with which Krishna is often associated—would represent not just Krishna's face but his entire body, observed as it emerges from Rādhā's garments, which he had entered in embrace. The interplay of faces remains in the first half of verse 2, but in the second half one can see Hari, not Rādhā, as the lover who takes the active role. He "does Rati" (*rati kīnhī*)—he initiates lovemaking—when he recognizes Kāma (*sāraṅga*, "desire") in her.

Another reversal—this time in the opposite direction—may be detected in verse 3. The change pivots on one's understanding of what is meant by "the left-hand side" (*vāma taṭa*, v. 3). In Indian culture left is not only a married woman's proper place in relation to her husband (*vāmāṅginī*); in a contrasting way it is also the indicator of anything unusual or forbidden, as in tantric practice. If the poet intends this, he may also have in mind a second meaning for the term *subedha* (v. 3), which he employs in the first half of the same verse. The "right-handed" translation given above renders this word as "well-behaved," deriving it from the root *vith/vidh* and the resultant Sanskrit adjective *vedh/vedhas*, meaning "pious, kind, virtuous." A "left-handed" translation, however, might take it as deriving from the root *vyadh*, which denotes the act of piercing and also produces the word *vedh*—this time a noun conveying the sense of piercing or breaking through. We would then have a reference to sexual penetration.

As for the drinking of fluids in the last line, there is nothing in the original that forces us to associate this action with a lip-to-lip kiss, though at first it seems natural to do so. Again there is a second option. In tantric ritual the culminating act—the "seal" (*mudrā*, v. 4), so to speak—comes when the male participant drinks the menstrual blood of the woman who acts as his partner.

86.1–5 *similes* Many readers will already have a sense for the comparisons evoked by the similes listed in verses 2–3 and 5, but a summary follows. The Love-god (Kāma, here called Madan, v. 2) is a general term of comparison when Krishna's powers of amorous attraction are being stressed. The sparkle of his earrings is frequently said to be so bright that it rivals the brilliance of the sun (v. 2). The darting wagtails are similes for his quick-moving eyes; the lotuses, for his hands; the bees, for his masses of curly black hair; the moon, for his lovely face; lightning, for its shine; rainclouds, for his dark complexion (v. 3). Precious jewels serve as the culminating entries in this list of similes (v. 5). Diamonds serve as a standard comparison for Krishna's brilliant teeth, and they are joined by the reddish-white *śikhar* gem, which is often said to resemble a pomegranate seed and whose very name means "pinnacle."

86.4 *false poets* Sūrdās uses this same device—"bad poets"—at the same point in §68 of *Sūr's Ocean*, also a six-verse composition. On that occasion, however, he actually replicates their speech.

86.6 *this body* In saying that Krishna has taken on his current form as a result of his own wish or whim, the poet seems to suggests that Krishna, the unmanifest divinity, has decorated himself with a garment—a body (*bapu*, v. 6)—that would serve as an appropriate indication of his true nature. If Krishna's body is his own metaphor for the ultimate in truth and beauty, then it is no wonder that any metaphor someone else might contrive to depict that body will necessarily seem insipid in comparison. As a familiar phrase has it, "Rām is like Rām" (*rām jaise rām*), or in more formal prosodic discourse, *ananvayopamā* or *upameyopamā*, where the thing to be compared is its own term of comparison (cf. §105.8).

87.2 *Bhṛgu's scar* The dark tuft of hair (*śrīvats*) that grew up on the spot in the middle of Vishnu's (and by extension Krishna's) chest where the supreme Lord absorbed the undeserved anger of the sage Bhṛgu. This *śrīvats* is represented in a number of ways, but many of them involve circles or curls, and that is what makes the comparison with the whirling eddies of the Ganges apt.

87.3 *sandal-paste designs* The poet goes beyond the general, cooling salve with which Krishna might be adorned, and alludes by means of the word *citra* ("painting," here "designs," v. 3) to the twelve sandalwood marks that figure in the iconography of Vishnu, adorning various limbs.

87.6 *conch, disk, club, and lotus* These are the four implements distributed to each hand of standard four-armed images of Vishnu: three weapons and a flower. Sūrdās treats them inventively when he compares them to ganders (*haṃsani*), for *haṃs* birds are not implied by his controlling metaphor, the Ganges. Its waters cease to flow when the poem comes to its conclusion—in a pond.

88.3 *pair of pair of bees* The poet adopts the image of bees to describe the eyes of Rādhā and Krishna, as they watch one another intently. This "pair of pair of bees" drones back and forth—the poet says they "sway" (*ḍola*)—with each pair hoping to drink the nectar held by the other. And drink they do (v. 4).

88.6 The classification "heart thievery" (*man haraṇ*), as in manuscripts J3 and J4, normally refers to the effect that Krishna's wiles have on the *gopīs,* so we can imagine what fun the poet must have had in making a change this time. Here he transforms the person who is usually the thief into the victim. The role of "thief of hearts" goes instead to the figure of day, for it is day that separates Krishna from his mate and thereby "steals the couple's wealth, the heart" (*dampati bita cita cora*).

90.3 *thief* In this poem, as frequently elsewhere (e.g., *Sūr's Ocean* §125), Sūr has one of the *gopīs* complain that she has been betrayed by her eyes. In many such poems the eyes enlist in the service of the one whom they see, Krishna, rather than remaining loyal to their owner. From the point of view of the woman who speaks, this makes thieves of these turncoats, since they steal away something she herself owns—her faculty of sight—rather than acquiring in any permanent way the vision she seeks. Here, however, the situation is altered: as thieves, these eyes are not traitors but naifs (v. 1). When they find themselves in the presence of such an embarrassment of visual riches, they cannot decide what to steal first. Thus the night speeds past, and with it the chance to do any thieving. For all they manage to acquire for this *gopī,* they might as well have been Krishna's confederates, like the eye-thieves we meet elsewhere.

93.4 *lotus . . . wars with the moon* As we have seen, Krishna's face is familiarly compared with the moon, and his hands are lotuslike: these are the most standard images possible. The enmity of which Sūr speaks is caused by the fact that most lotuses open by day and close at nightfall, when the moon appears.

93.4 *note to soothe those lunar steeds, the deer* In Indian mythology the moon is frequently envisioned as a chariot pulled by deer. In other contexts the normally fleet-footed deer are said to have a weakness for certain musical tones that cause them to stop and listen, even if their lives are put in danger (cf. §§217.4, 416.8, 418.13–14). The eyes with which they stare under such circumstances are proverbial for their size and beauty. By introducing deer in this multifaceted way, the poet establishes the network of connections one needs before being able to interpret his extension of the "lunar steed" metaphor in verses 5 and 6. He further exploits the relation between moon and deer, and suggests an image in which Krishna's eyebrows, which are notorious for arching and bending in response to the music of his flute (e.g., §73.5), serve as the intermediary link between face and eyes. They are the reins by means of which the moon-charioteer (Krishna's face) controls—or fails to control—his deer (the eyes). The identification of reins and eyebrows is supplied in the translation (v. 6) but must be deduced in the original, where the eyebrows are mentioned in one verse (v. 5) and the reins in the next.

102.1 *stolen my heart* For a sense of the position occupied by this poem in the wider landscape of poetry depicting Krishna as a thief, see Hawley, *Krishna, the Butter Thief*, pp. 147–150.

103.4 *sari made its offering* In their early manuscript versions, verses 4–6 of this poem describe a woman unable to restain her bodily reactions as her eyes survey the reality of Krishna. The upper end of her sari slips from her shoulder, setting in motion a chain reaction that reveals her breasts. At some point in the eighteenth century or after, this became a very different poem. It came to be understood as definitively registering the speech of Rādhā, rather than conceivably belonging to any of her companions among the *gopīs*, and that seems to have accompanied a wholesale alteration of its meaning. A number of existing phrases changed and several short words were introduced, each bearing a negative force, and the poem that emerged bore almost exactly the opposite meaning from what we read in the translation given here. (For details, see Hawley, *Sūr Dās*, pp. 67–71, 183.) This later version is much quoted as evidence that Sūr conceived Rādhā, especially in her maturity, to be a woman distinguished by great strength of character. Far from vulnerable to the heady winds of infatuation, she displays a sense of noble self-restraint under difficult circumstances. As published in the Nāgarīpracāriṇī Sabhā edition, the poem is given a much later place in the corpus (NPS 4911). It is grouped with compositions celebrating the moment when Krishna met Rādhā and other Brajbāsīs at Kurukṣetra, long after he had married and assumed the throne of Dvaraka (cf. *Sūr's Ocean* §352). In this later version, the poem might be translated as follows:

Nothing, today there was nothing I could do.
When Hari appeared I was stunned
  like a woman captured in art.
I held back my heart, though it flushed at the thought
  he might make it his throne, his lotus home.
My chest bowed low, but my eyes refused
  to release the torrential oblation they held,
And though my breasts, round pitchers, heaved in my blouse,
  never did my bodice-string snap at the strain.
Now great shame has sprouted in my mind
  as I sense what I have done;
At the sight of his face how strange I have become—
  how lacking in wisdom, friend.
Even so, says Sūr, this numbness, this dumbness—
    I reckon it as my luck.

105.2 *their happy knot* Early on, Rādhā muses over the "happy knot" (*saguna gāṇhi*) that has been tied between her and Krishna. Apparently the knot to which she refers is marriage, for in Hindu practice the bride and groom knot their garments together before circling the solemn marriage fire. Yet according to most devotees Rādhā's marriage to Krishna is not the sort observed in polite society. There has been no formal ceremony: this is a marriage of love, of poetry. So the job of tying the knot falls to the poet, and he accomplishes it by presenting a series of contrasting entities joined together by an overarching bond. First he generates a set of equally weighted contrasts—"his and hers"—held in balance by a larger frame. In verse 3, his frame is the half-verse. In verse 4, the frame enlarges to become the verse as a whole, with the two contrasting parts balanced at the caesura. In verse 5, however, he takes the major step of moving away from this familiar, well-balanced formula. He defies the caesura, thrusting the pronoun *yah*—"she," referring to Rādhā—into the first section of the verse, where Krishna resides. Clearly this tightens the knot between the two halves of the amorous couple. He repeats this device in verse 6, but cinches the knot a little tighter this time by adding the element of chiasmus (*kisora navala nāgara . . . nāgari navala kisorī:* "youth . . . clever . . . clever . . . youth").

105.3–8 *he . . . she . . . them* On a number of occasions it becomes clear that to the person who frames the poem, the more familiar member of the dyad is Rādhā. In the original, Krishna is called "that one" (*vai*, twice in v. 3), while Rādhā is repeatedly referred to as "this one" (*yaha*, vv. 3, 5, 6), although the word comes across in translation merely as "she." Such a perspective would be natural if the narrator were female—one of Rādhā's friends or perhaps an older figure among the women of Braj such as Paurṇamāsī, the kindly matchmaker imagined in Rūp Gosvāmī's *Vidagdhamādhava*. The demonstrative pronouns *vai* and *yah*—both singular in intent if not always in form—govern the discourse in this distributive way until the last verse, when we meet the plural demonstrative *in* ("these"). At that point we are seeing the conjunction of Rādhā and Krishna as a single unit (cf. *ananvayopamā*, §86.6), as forecast in the penultimate line, where her brilliant golden color mixes with his darker, emeraldlike hue.

110.1 *found him . . . disbelieves* This poem is a fine example of the genre in which the intensity of love is celebrated by showing that the lover longs for the beloved not only under conditions in which he is absent but also when he is near (vv. 1–2, 5–6). Here one has separation-in-union (*premavaicittya*, "love's confusion"), which manifests itself in a debate between reality and hallucination (v. 4). The ins and outs of this debate are appropriately likened to waves (v. 8), which ripple the surface of a mind that really ought to be satisfied and clear. Krishna may be Rādhā's answer, but her mind cannot rest from questions: "Who is this Hari?" Who does he find alluring?" (v. 7). She has him, but she cannot help thinking there might be someone else.

110.6 *ten directions* The "ten directions" (*duhū diśi*) are a standard way to refer to every direction. They comprise the four points of the compass and the points halfway between them (northeast and so forth), plus up and down.

137.1 *aggrieved* This poem celebrates the anger (*mān*) of a woman cheated by her lover—and says so clearly in the first line: the *gopī* who speaks declares that she has become "aggrieved" (*māna*) with Krishna.

137.4 *his lovely image* The heroine is so upset that even after she shuts out the physical sight of Krishna (v. 3), she still has him before her eyes (v. 4). It is no accident where he appears—on her bed—and not mere happenstance that the poet designates this mirage with a term that plays an important role in the vocabulary of religion. It is "his lovely image" (*sumūrati*) that she sees, as if she were beholding an icon of Krishna in a temple. Involuntarily, she does the appropriate thing. She bends or bows (*jhuki*, v. 5) before the image, but it is a crouch of anger, as another meaning of the word *jhuki* makes clear, and her rage continues as she refuses to give in to any feelings of desire that may have caused the apparition. She rushes out into the courtyard and collapses as if in a seizure, in the course of which she sees the "real" Krishna before her. That is the image that leaves her speechless, for by now her sense of objectivity is gone.

137.7 *Desire* In the two concluding verses we see that the heroine ultimately yields: to her inner reality on the one hand—to Desire (*madana*, v. 7), the "beguiling" god of love, Kāma—and to Krishna's outer presence on the other (v. 8). In most poems concerning *mān* (e.g., §171), a go-between or confidante is required to break through the heroine's determined anger. Here, however, it is she herself who conjures up the intermediary being that acts as the agent of change. It is her own representation of Krishna—his "lovely image" (v. 4), her private icon—that ironically does the trick.

148.2 *pleasurable mixture* The cause of the *gopī*'s anger is obvious: Krishna has been with someone else. Her pleasure derives from the fact that Krishna has returned, and from his visual magnificence. The latter is heightened by an element of disarray, as harmony is sometimes made sweeter by the introduction of a certain amount of dissonance. There is an element of pleasure too, in the assuredness with which the *gopī* identifies the clues that point to Krishna's infidelity.

148.4 *both your yellow garments* These are apparently the upper and lower parts of Krishna's *pītāmbar*, the yellow garment he ties in the informal way a cowherd would by cinching it around his waist after the third fold. The one is carried loose or wrapped about his shoulders, the lower is worn as a *dhotī* tied at the waist. Their red discoloration comes, presumably, from the vermilion forehead mark of the woman with whom he has been, or from the rose-tinted powder (*aṅgarāg*) with which she has dusted herself after bathing. We are hearing the speech of a *khaṇḍitā nāyikā*, a *gopī* who welcomes Krishna back with distinctly mixed feelings after he has spent the night away.

148.4 *betel at your eyes* The expression *nain tamor* is probably to be taken as meaning "betel at your eyes," referring to stains from the other woman's mouth that would have been left around Krishna's eyes in the course of love-making. This confusion of mouth and eyes provides a suitable inversion for the "mascara on your lips" (*adharani añjana*) that directly precedes it. A simpler exegesis would explain *nain tamor* more loosely as "betel in your eyes," that is, the bloodshot color they display because Krishna has gone without sleep.

148.7 *confluence of child and youth* The glory of the "confluence of child and youth" (*baisandhi*, i.e., *vayosandhi*, v. 7) is at once too great and too subtle to bear description, for it stands at the point where one stage of life shades into the next. Sūr envisions this eclipsing of the possibility of poetry as a total eclipse—so total, in fact, that it takes place even before the dawn arrives (v. 8). For the "sun" that is Sūr (see §29.8), this means the end of speech, and the poem is quickly concluded. For the *gopī*, however, the meaning is different. When she uses the image of a solar eclipse, she is probably referring to Krishna's unwillingness to defend himself before her or interact with her in any way. He refuses to look her in the eye and show her his brilliant face. Or perhaps she has in mind the simple fact that his night-long dalliance has left his face without its customary glow.

163.5 *the master has no body* On Kāma as bodiless, *anaṅg*, see §62.6.

163.8 *minions mimic kings* In verse 5, referring to Krishna's curls, eyebrows, and eyes, the woman who speaks observes that the functionaries in this kingdom take their cues from their superiors. She refers to the upper tier as ministers (*mantrī*, v. 5) and says they have no fear—any more than their master has a body. In verse 8 she goes on to characterize the demeanor of a larger, somewhat lower set of actors—Krishna's remaining bodily features. Again she sees a multitude of functionaries doing the will of their chief, and she quotes a proverb to show how natural this is: "minions mimic kings" (*jasa rājā tasa prajā basīti*).

The traits that tie masters to minions vary in the two cases. The first time around, the *gopī* had described the upper register of Krishna's facial features as hovering about the royal face (vv. 3–5). Cleverly, she said their brazen absence of fear (v. 5) took its cue precisely from his absent body. Just as Kāma works with bent bows and sharp arrows, their deviousness showed itself in "crooked" (*kuṭila*, v. 3) curls and "convoluted" (*bakra*, v. 4) glances. But by the time she approaches the more "bodily" register extending from mouth to feet (vv. 6–8), she has a different trait in mind: the maddening laziness so typical of bureaucratic style. At first it may seem "gentle" (*manda*, v. 7) in its deliberate manners, but this is a "plague" (*īti*, v. 6) if you want to get anything done. Slow-moving bureaucrats like these are a far cry from the nervous sycophants who flit about the throne room centered on Krishna's eyes. This second tier of organs, extending from the lips downward, are his subjects (*prajā*, v. 8), his "minions," and we experience them not in lively interaction with the king but as dull administrators of his policies. The sounds of the original hint at the difference between these two tiers. Assonance and alliteration (*sacare śravana samīpa samīti / bakra bilokani bheda bhediyai*, vv. 3–4) accompany observations about mirrored deviousness at the upper levels, and when it comes to bureacratic sluggishness ("gentleness") farther down, there is outright repetition (*manda . . . manda . . . manda*, v. 7).

165.2 *this mantra* Rādhā's confidante—or Krishna's go-between—reports that like a yogi (or a sigh-filled lover), Krishna has adopted Rādhā's name as his personal mantra: *hā rādhā rādhā*. The name of Rādhā is indeed used this way in the practice of some Vaishnavas. Part of the power in its repetition comes from the fact that both syllables in her name are formed around the same open vowel. Another part comes from the fact that once this stream of sound gets moving and word boundaries fade away, adepts actually find themselves uttering the word "stream" (or "current," *dhārā*). There is something essential here, and the word *dhārā* sometimes connotes an infusion of energy, as we imply when we speak of electrical current.

165.4 *Like a great yogi* It is relatively commonplace in the *Sūrsāgar* for a comparison to be made between the rigors endured by a woman separated from Krishna and those that yogis (or *yoginīs*, their female counterparts) undertake in the cause of spiritual discipline (e.g., §261, 300). Here, however, the suffering renunciant is Krishna. There is room for a certain amount of skepticism about the truth of what she claims, since it is motivated by a definite aim: to stimulate sufficient sympathy in Rādhā that she will desist from her lonely sulking and go to Krishna's side. But whatever his true state, the description of him is a lovely one. It nicely sets out one of the four situations appropriate to *pūrvarāg*, the first stage in the growth of love—namely, a situation in which the hero has heard about the heroine but has not yet seen her (*guṇaśravaṇa*).

165.7 *libation . . . fire-oblation* The final action in the series of religious disciplines to which Sūr appeals (vv. 4–6) is one that has to do with sacrifice (v. 7): the rites of cremation (see Jonathan P. Parry, *Death in Banaras*, pp. 151–190). In an early stage in those rites, which extend over thirteen days, the ancestors and sages are satisfied, and the gods invoked, by means of water-offerings (*tarapana* < *tarpaṇa*); appropriately, these are analogized to Krishna's tears. Later, on the tenth and twelfth days, the fire-sacrifice (*piṇḍadān* or *piṇḍapradān*) commences, with its oblations (*havi*) of sesame seeds, barley seeds, and *ghī*, which are directed to the departed soul and other ancestors. This is the heart of the matter, and indeed the poet selects Krishna's burning heart (*hṛdai*, v. 7) as the proper analogue. Finally, on the thirteenth day, Brahmins are invited to partake of a meal on behalf of the person who has died and other members of departed generations. The poet seems to want to compare Krishna's "mutterings and lapses" (*bolata biśrāma*, v. 7) to this ceremony—the sounds perhaps being the feast itself, and the silences the rest that follows. The overall purpose of sacrifice is to ensure an act of reciprocal commitment on the part of the being to whom the sacrifice is made. In this case the person being propitiated is Rādhā—symbolically, the departed or "dead" Rādhā, so it is at this point that the go-between turns to her and asks her to respond, to come alive (v. 8).

170.2 *Lord of Love* Clearly Krishna (Hari, v. 1) is meant, but he is here designated *ratipati*, that is, Kāma. Kāma earns this designation because "love" or "passion" (*rati*) is the name of his wife. *Pati*, the other half of the compound, designates not only "lord" in a general sense, but also "husband."

170.4 *offering the liquid* The theme of the poem has particular force in Indian society, where traditions of hospitality are so important that they provide much of the basic language for worship itself. At several points early in the poem Sūr hints at this ritual context: he mentions offerings of water and the like (*araghādika*, v. 4) as well as incense and lamps (*dhūpa, dīpa*, v. 5). All this is fully appropriate for Krishna, the lover who is also a god.

170.6 *rare flavor* The female confidante or go-between whose persona the poet assumes urges Rādhā to supply five of the six flavors (*ṣaḍras*) that ought to be present in an ideal meal—sweet, pungent, bitter, sour, and salty (*madhura*, v. 6; *kaṭu, tikta, amala*, v. 7; *ṣāra*, v. 8)—and completes the picture by alluding to the *ghī* (*sarapi*, v. 8) that should be added as the final ingredient. There are also spices—in the form of "little bites" (*upadaṃsa*, v. 9)—and aromatics. Perhaps these supply the missing sixth taste, the astringent.

170.10 *your ritual, your vow* Through all this richness of amatory/gustatory connection, it is easy to forget the religious or ritual aspect of things, so it comes as something of a surprise when Sūr strikes that note again in the final line. This time he is much more explicit than at the beginning of the poem, for he speaks of merit (*punya*) and ritual vows (*brata* < Skt. *vrata*). Probably the sort of vow he has in mind is the kind that young women observe to obtain a good husband, and married women continue to use the same instrument to secure the welfare of the men in their lives, both husbands and sons. The performance of such a *vrat*, a particular feature of women's religion, demands a regimen of austerity, but the hardships described in this poem are remarkable indeed—not just because of their rigor but because of their use. These "salty . . . nail wounds" (*naṣaṣata ṣāra*, v. 8) and "hair tugs" (*kacagraha*, v. 8) and "little bites" (*upadaṃsa*, v. 9) are not to be endured passively by the woman involved; rather, she is to visit them upon the presumed object of her vow. Just as a fine meal is achieved through seemingly contradictory flavors, so the Lord of Love (*ratipati*, v. 2) is most deeply satisfied by contrariety.

171.1 *Rādhikā* An alternate form of the name Rādhā.

171.2 *so says Mādhav* The language of this poem is so forceful that it is hard to shake off the impression that we are hearing Krishna's own pleas, yet this inserted phrase makes it clear that someone else is actually reporting them. Perhaps it is the poet, in which case we are as close to Krishna's own language as we can get in this medium, but there are other possibilities as well. We may be hearing a woman sent by Krishna to intercede with Rādhā, whose art would precisely be to create a feeling of such verisimilitude that she could stir Rādhā from her torpor and achieve a reconciliation between her and Krishna. And there is a further possibility. If the supposed go-between were a dear friend of Rādhā's, she might be acting out of personal concern, eager to disperse Rādhā's sullen anger (*mānahi māna*, "so much bitterness," v. 7), and restore her mental and physical well-being. If so, she might find it convenient to speak for Krishna whether or not he had actually said the things she attributes to him. Thus in all likelihood we have the poet quoting a *gopī* who in turn quotes Krishna—or at least this is the likely situation up through verse 6. In the final couplet it is hard to tell whether the go-between intends her words to be perceived as Krishna's or whether she is speaking for herself. The use of the vocative *saṣi* ("friend," v. 7) could signal that change, although it is also conceivable that Krishna might use such a word.

172.2 *Love . . . fine traits* This evocation of spring, with its vivid, short lines, celebrates the time of year intimately associated with Kāma, whose approach is manifest in the signs of the season. They are spoken of here as if they were the very traits (*guna*) of Kāma himself. The person who formulates these words and addresses them to Krishna explains that Kāma is presenting these attributes as tribute, and proceeds to clarify the ways in which various features of the scene are actually aspects of Kāma's army that come into view as he approaches. First there are the flowers (vv. 3–6), his signature: in a well-placed pun, these "fresh-petaled" (*nava dala*, v. 3) flowers are simultaneously a "new battalion," and the metaphor opens out from there. Next come the birds of Brindavan (vv. 7–8), which are likened to elephants, cavalry, and infantry—three of the requisite divisions of a fighting force; the fourth, the chariot division, is inanimate, so it is compared to the high cliffs that form a natural habitat for birds. One also has the surrounding scene (vv. 8–12). On herald drums and kettledrums (*nisān, bheri*, v. 10) and their comparison to waterfalls and bees, respectively, see §173.5. Perhaps the most unusual simile in the group is the last (vv. 13–14), where an abstraction, beauty itself (*chabi*, v. 13), is brought into play. Here we have a kind of summary for everything that has been described since the third verse.

172.15 *the girl's plea* As the poet offers his own signature—uncharacteristically early—we are forced to consider the persona through whom he has been speaking.

The poet seems to address this directly, by naming the speaker with the word *bāla* (v. 15), but the gender of that word is actually ambiguous, particularly as a rhyme-word at the end of the verse. This term must refer to someone young, but it could be either a boy, one of Krishna's cowherd friends, or a girl, a *gopī*. If the manuscripts are any indication, some early performers understood it to be a youth, since they associated the noun *bāl* with a verbal form that is normally masculine (*badata*, A1, B3, B4). On this reading, we would form a picture of Krishna's cowherd friends observing the beauties of spring and moving on to ask Krishna to welcome it, apparently in a general way. The alternative, however, has a much stronger textual claim, since the preponderance of manuscripts construe the verb in the feminine (*badati*); hence "the girl" in our translation.

172.16 *Kāma cowering* The speaker's concluding remarks cause us to reconsider the couplet with which the poem began. We know that Kāma is bringing gifts (v. 2), but we are now pressed to ask why. In verses 16–18, we learn that it is because on an earlier occasion in which Kāma advanced into the presence of a god, he was badly burned—quite literally so. On that occasion he came bringing a beautiful woman, Pārvatī, and his intent was to seduce Shiva, who was lost in ascetic meditation, into a more active involvement with the world. In this mission he was serving as an envoy for the rest of the gods, who were threatened by a great demon that could only be defeated by an offspring of Shiva—provided, of course, that Shiva could be enticed into producing one. Kāma and Pārvatī ultimately succeeded in their mission, but in the process Kāma was defeated. Offended at the way in which he had been abruptly pulled from his meditation, Shiva turned Kāma to ash with the heat of his third eye, rendering him bodiless. It is the bodiless Kāma who is now to be seen in his attributes (*guna*, v. 2), since his own form is no longer visible. These attributes are the blandishments of spring.

The speaker goes on to suggest that Kāma's invisibility also has a specific and present cause. Kāma is afraid to show himself (v. 16), for fear that he will suffer the same fate he met when he encountered Shiva. So Krishna should reassure timid Kāma, a general who behaves in anything but a martial way, that he has no intention of doing battle with him but will rather accept the tribute he brings. He should offer a soothing pat of his hand.

In preparing the way for this royal gesture, Sūr makes a rare foray into Persian/Urdu with the word *gudara* ("tribute," v. 2). He names Kāma's ritual of humility in the language of the Indo-Muslim courts. In a different way he also evokes the language of court by his use of the word *śrī* (v. 1). We have understood its primary meaning as objective and have translated it as "splendor," but if one divided the first line differently it could be also interpreted as a very unusual honorific, as if intoned by the chief officer of protocol: "Behold Brindavan, Lord Lotus-Eye!" The closing gesture that would signal Krishna's acceptance of Kāma's act of self-abasement preserves this royal mood.

172.18 *a gesture of your hand* If the speaker is a *gopī*, she may be recommending a very direct way in which Krishna can restore Kāma to wholeness through a movement of his hand. He can reach out and touch her, accepting Kāma's timorous tribute in the bodily form that she presents it, and thus satisfying her desire (*kāma*). On this interpretation, the poem admits a new kind of closure, for the *gopī* herself becomes an expression of "Brindavan's splendor" (*brindāvana śrī*, v. 1). In the original Brajbhāṣā, there is no need for the masculine object that English requires in the final line. Since the object is unexpressed, Krishna may reach out simultaneously to him (Kāma) and to her. With respect to Krishna, she *is* Kāma—or so she hopes.

173.2 *the game that's played at Phālgun time* As understood in the Krishna traditions of Braj, Holi is the boisterous game in which the sexes confront one another in a tournament of fun and love. It transpires on the last evening of the waxing fortnight of the lunar month of Phālgun (*phāga*, v. 2), and continues into the next day, the first in the month of Caitra. Holi usually falls sometime in the month of March, so it is natural that Spring (*basanta*, v. 2), who is the chief courtier of Kāma (*madana*, "beguiling Love," v. 2), should play an active role. Men and women play Holi by showering flower petals and colored liquid on one other.

173.3–4 *palās panicles* At the onset of Holi a great bonfire is lit, in which millet sprouts are set ablaze as a firstfruit offering for the spring harvest. The poet describes a natural analogue to this moment by drawing attention to the *palās* plant, which comes to bloom at that time of year. The plant is sufficiently common that the woods are filled with the brilliant golden color of its panicles—a sight so memorable that the *palās* has earned the English name flame-of-the-forest. The poet actually provides that gloss ("rise like flames in a fire," *uṭhati agini kī nāī*, v. 3).

173.5 *ḍaph and herald drums* Holi is not just a matter of sights, but of sounds, and the poet does not neglect this aspect of his metaphor (vv. 5–8). He gives particular attention to percussion instruments, mentioning cymbals (*jhāñjhi*) and various kinds of drums. He likens the sound of waterfalls to the *nisān*, a kettle-shaped drum that is struck with a mallet and makes such a deep sound that it is often used to call attention to someone who is about to make a public announcement. Hence the translation "herald drum." The *ḍaph*, which follows, is a frame drum, much like a tambourine without the cymbals, but twice as big. Smaller than the *nisān*, it is used in Braj exclusively during the Holi season. Since he mentions the *ḍaph* in an intermediary way, it is not entirely clear whether Sūr intends to associate its sound with that of the waterfalls or of the bees; for metrical reasons we have chosen the former option. The third type of drum he lists in verse 5 is the *bheri*. This we translate "kettledrum" since it resembles the *nisān* in shape, yet it does not have so deep a resonance.

173.16 *the kingdom, oh Krishna, is yours* Just as Spring is king of the seasons (v. 14), so Krishna is king of "every pleasure" (v. 16). Not only is he the person to whom this description of nature's game of Holi is addressed, he is ultimately the object of the description. For as the final couplet says, everything that transpires in this "basil woods" (*brindā bipini*, v. 15; cf. *brindāban*) belongs to him. The "company" that surrounds him there (*samāja*, v. 15)—the special musical assembly that is constituted every year in the Holi season—has as its purpose the celebration of that fact. Such musicians could well be performing this very poem.

3. KRISHNA DEPARTS FOR MATHURA, NEVER TO RETURN

183.1 *Mathura has decked herself out* As Krishna approaches Mathura from the Braj countryside, accompanied by Balarām and escorted by Kaṃs's envoy Akrūr, the poet describes the welcome the city extends to him. It is that of a bride who awaits her bridegroom. The comparison is facilitated by the fact that the word Mathura—the first in the poem—is feminine in gender, and in succeeding verses the poet achieves an increasingly dense intermingling of the thing compared and the term of comparison by varying their positions in relation to each other. Rhymed in couplets, these verses display many more than the usual divergencies of line order in the various manuscripts where the poem is recorded. Thus the poem's "body," extending from verses 3 to 10, has many shapes. The critical version (following B1, B2, U1) is guided by a downward *śikh-nakh* (topknot to toenail) movement in verses 3–9, with a quick flourish back to the top in verse 10. Such an approach (or the reverse: *nakh-śikh*) is standard in the depiction of both male and female beauty, and the conceit of representing a city as a woman is an ancient one. It figures regularly in Sanskrit *kāvya* literature.

183.12 *conquer Kaṃs!* Only in the final verse does the poet swerve from the task of sustaining the mood of amorous attraction (*mādhurya*). Here, suddenly, we have the first mention of the ugly side of things—the evil Kaṃs—and we hear an exhortation to battle. This is heroism (*vīrya*) in quite a different sense from the erotic excellence suggested by the title *braj nāyak* "hero of Braj," which occurs in the preceding verse. In that earlier context, a hero (*nāyak*) was one who excels in the arts of love, and with his long and languid metaphor the poet has lulled us into believing that only such heroism is required for Krishna to be the "hero of Braj." Now, however, he startles us awake with the realization that the capital city of Braj finds itself in a desperate situation that demands heroism of a different kind. Krishna must defeat Kaṃs to earn the beautiful city/woman who is here described as his queen. To become her king, to ascend the throne that once belonged to Ugrasen and is now usurped by Kaṃs, he must fight.

186.2 *dressed like a fine actor* Everything reported in this composition leads forward, with an assured crescendo, to Krishna's victory over Kaṃs (v. 9). As in so many other poems of Sūrdās, the spectators' point of view makes all this difference, and the poet interprets the action he depicts as a type of performance. Already in the second line he describes Krishna as being "dressed like a fine actor" (*naṭavara bheṣa kāchi*), and the matter of dress echoes in our ears as we watch the hero perform his first deed once inside the city walls. He kills a washerman or clothes-dyer (*rajaka*, v. 3) who has greeted him with insolence, and quite pointedly distributes the washerman's load of clothes to his own company of rustic companions. If the cinching of Krishna's traditional yellow *pītāmbar* close around his legs serves to imitate the dress of a master performer (*naṭavara*, v. 2), a dancer, now the cowherds too have something appropriate to wear on their newfound urban stage.

186.4 *a sophisticated act* The dramatic motif continues here. When Krishna passes the seemingly impossible test of snapping the huge bow Kaṃs has set out for him, the poet says he does so as the play of an accomplished actor (*līlā naṭa nāgara*). It is in the dramatic sense "a sophisticated act." The word *līlā* connotes not only performance but ease—it is "play" in both senses—and the emphasis on ease is further strengthened when Sūr refers to the confrontation with the mad elephant Kuvalayāpīḍ, whom Kaṃs has set upon him. It is but play (*gaja ṣela ṣilāyau*): Krishna "made a mere toy of the elephant." And when the hero enters the wrestling ring in the following verse, the poet dubs the space surrounding him a stage (*raṅga bhūmi*, v. 5).

Typically, it is not the actual struggle to which he draws attention, but Krishna's gesture of challenge as he slaps his hands on his thighs in anticipation of the fight. Again drama is to the fore, and as in a play the result of the action is assured beforehand.

186.5 *Muṣṭik and Cānur* These are the two wrestlers Kaṃs has pitted against Krishna and Balarām. The confrontation has a David-and-Goliath quality as two mature, professional, and in most accounts unscrupulous wrestlers are matched with two unpracticed boys. Sūr draws attention to this imbalance by featuring the reaction of the women of Mathura, who berate Kaṃs for the inequality (*ayukta* > *ajaguta*, v. 6). Indeed, from Sūr's retelling it is not even clear that Balarām is on the scene to assist his brother—or perhaps it is only Krishna whose fate concerns these women.

186.9 *Kaṃs he killed* The killing of Kaṃs forms the central event of the drama, yet even in the midst of victory the poet maintains his emphasis on staging and audience reaction by directing his attention to those affected by the action. He goes on to refer to the crowning of Krishna's great-uncle Ugrasen, whom Kaṃs had deposed from the throne, by means of Ugrasen's reaction to the boy: Krishna "gladdened his heart" (*mana bhāyau*). And in the final scene, Krishna's release of his parents Devakī and Vasudev from the prison where Kaṃs had held them results in their singing his praises. Through and through, this is a poem not just about actions but about relationships and reactions. These are the touchstone of bhakti. Such relationships extend to the poet himself. By positioning his own name just before the final phrase in which he speaks of singing Krishna's fame, Sūr suggests that the last verse is also capable of the following interpretation:

> And when he [Krishna] released his parents from their bonds,
> Sūr sang songs filled with his great fame.

187.1–2 *Master Gopāl . . . Mohan* Mohan and Gopāl are familiar terms of address for Krishna, but the latter, with which the poet begins, is accompanied by an honorific (*jū*, translated as "master," v. 1). This immediately suggests a certain distance and sounds a bit awkward. Who can be speaking? As the verses proceed, it gradually becomes clear that this poem is spoken at the moment when, after Krishna and Balarām have defeated Kaṃs, Nanda must depart once again for Gokul, the place whose generic meaning is translated in verse 12 as "cowherd town." Nanda is the speaker. The contrast between the informal, rural ways of Gokul and the graded etiquette that structures affairs at an urban court like Mathura accounts for the unknowing "mischief" or "mistreatment" (*dhīṭhāī*) for which he apologizes in verse 3. Nanda had made himself part of the group that accompanied the boys on their mission to do battle with Kaṃs, but that victory brings Nanda more loss than gain: Krishna will stay in Mathura. Part of the poignancy of the composition is that the poet refrains from actually using Nanda's name until the last verse.

187.4 *Garg's words* The reference to Garg the astrologer recalls the ceremony held to honor Krishna's birth. On that occasion Garg was invited to analyze the child's horoscope, but when he did so it emerged that this was no ordinary child but a special, even divine being (BhP 8.19; cf. §3.2–4). Nanda's witnessing of Krishna's victory over Kaṃs and his minions confirms for him the truth of what Garg had said, and accords with the discovery that Krishna is really Vasudev's son (*basudyau suta*, v. 4), not his own.

187.12 *Daddy, Daddy* Unlike Yaśodā, to whom he must report (vv. 5–8), Nanda is able to comprehend the royal identity that Krishna displays in Mathura—an identity he has actually had since birth. Yet that does not alter his emotions. Nanda is forced into the awkward position of having to ask his own son (or rather his foster son—that is part of the problem) to project himself into the past. He asks him to pretend, if but for a moment, that things really haven't changed.

191.3 *You are the wife of Vasudev* Since there is no tradition of Yaśodā's going to meet Devakī in Mathura, we must assume that this poem records a message that she sends through an envoy. In what she says, we meet an exquisitely simple personality. The language is straightforward, and its content is distinguished only by a preoccupation with cows (v. 6) and cowherds (v. 8) and the prominent use of diminutives (*kanhaiyā*, "little Kānh," v. 8) and terms of affection (*merau lāla laḍaitau*, v. 4: "my darling boy").

191.3 *a boor from Braj* The audience derives its pleasure from watching rustic Yaśodā address sophisticated Devakī. When she characterizes herself as "a boor from Braj" (*gavāri brajabāsī*, v. 3), she makes use of a word that suits her station exactly, since it is a colloquial derivative of the general word for cowherd that she uses to designate Krishna in the end (*gvāla*, v. 8). She buttresses the latter with yet another expression of that same rusticity, this time the one that ties Krishna most directly to Yaśodā's mothering impulses: his insatiable appetite for butter. The message is clear: he belongs with her. That is where the real bond of recognition ("memory," *pahicāni*, v. 1) is to be found—the bond she could only tentatively seek with Devakī (v. 1).

192.2 *no one's fault* This poem records the lament of one *gopī* to another about the sufferings she has had to endure after Krishna has turned his attention from her to someone else. She explains how friendly, familiar, happy features of her environment—especially those with romantic associations—have through no fault of their own become inimical presences. It is the sight of Krishna, now lost, that has caused this syndrome, and her eyes are what provoke the sharpest concern. She can endure perversions of and intrusions upon the other senses, but when the eyes' ability to keep watch for Krishna is threatened by the dense foliage around her (v. 7), she must appeal for aid. She calls to her friend or the poet himself for assistance (v. 8), and with that departure from the stoic reportage announced in the refrain, the poem is at an end.

192.2 *turned his loving eyes away* The editors of the Nāgarīpracāriṇī Sabhā edition understood this poem as pertaining to the time when Krishna had left Braj behind. That is one legitimate way of interpreting the phrase "Hari turned his loving eyes away" (*hari hita locana phere*, v. 2), but not the only one. It is also possible that the woman who speaks is referring not to a general departure but to Krishna's having turned his eyes from her personally—in the direction of another woman. If that was the poet's intention, the poem should by rights be placed earlier in the collection.

193.1 *Wayfarer, see* With this composition one or more *gopīs* send a message of distress to an absent Krishna. It is natural to assume that he has departed for Mathura and that the messenger is Ūdho, though the latter is not actually named. The *gopīs* intimate the effects of their own *viraha* ("fever of longing," v. 2) by describing the way in which a similar longing seems to have afflicted the Jamunā, but only in the last line do they reveal their actual purpose in providing this portrait of the river's condition. They hope to stimulate Krishna's sympathy for their own affliction.

193.1 *dark Jamunā's blackened* It is not unusual to compare a river with a woman—certainly the Jamunā is always thought of as female—but this is a very successful example of the genre. (Contrast Daniel H. H. Ingalls' reaction to an extended, though strictly paratactic, metaphor of exactly this sort that appears in the *Harivaṃśa:* "The *Harivaṃśa* as a *Mahākāvya*," pp. 392–393). The stage is set in the title line when the river is identified by means of her second most frequently used name, Kālindī, a patronymic she earns by virtue of her descent from a Himalayan peak called Kalind. (Further on the Jamunā's lineage, see §431.) Here, however, the *gopīs* discern a different logic behind the name: it seems to them to contain the word "black" (*kālī* > *kārī*)—hence the translation "dark Jamunā" (v. 1)—a point that they drive home by saying explicitly that the river has turned "very black" (*ati kārī*, v. 1). At least by comparison with her sister the Ganges, such darkish hues are, in fact, the natural color of the Jamunā, but according to aesthetic canons prevailing in Braj culture they are not to be expected in a beautiful woman.

Hence there is a reason for the *gopīs* to present their interpretation of why the Jamunā appears as she does—not merely discolored but also displaying a whole array of symptoms that one would expect to see in a *virahiṇī*. For instance, her once full and healthy body—a torrent (*jala pūra*, v. 4)—has now grown so thin that only rivulets (*panārī*, v. 4) remain. Further, her hair is unkempt, like grasses and reeds (v. 5), and there is the suggestion that her anguish has caused some of it to turn dry and white, as one sees in the white-tasseled *kas* reeds on her banks. Her eddies and vortices (*bhaṅvar*) are likened to bees (*bhramar*), which turn them black in the process (v. 6). And the last in the list of symptoms that these *gopīs* provide concerns the Jamunā's deluded babblings. These they liken to the mournful sounds of the sheldrake (*cakaī*, v. 7), which spends the day with its mate but calls for it all night long, when the two are separated. The Jamunā's condition is even worse: she calls both night and day.

196.5 *sandalwood powder* Among the medications here mentioned as normally effective in bringing down a fever is sandalwood (*malaya*, v. 5). The *gopīs* make a liquid of it by mixing it with water, and they give it color and scent by adding in *kumkum*—that is, vermilion powder—and musk.

196.8 *Hari's lunar face* The moon is held to be cooling, since its light is much softer than the sun's, but it, in the form of Krishna's moonlike face, has been removed. When these *virahiṇīs* say that their heart-lotuses no longer bloom because the moon has been taken away, the variety of which they speak (*kumuda*, v. 8, a white lotus) is indeed the night-blooming sort.

197.1 *the memory of that passion* This poem presents us with a pleasing mix of the fleeting and the fixed, the happy and the sad, as a *gopī* (quite possibly Rādhā) calls to mind her memories of a night spent with Krishna. According to the interpretation advanced here, it was a night in which love was ultimately consummated, urging itself upon the actors—and perhaps particularly upon Krishna—despite the games of hide-and-seek that are recounted in verses 2–4. Otherwise the memory of "that passion" (*vaha rati*), announced in the title line, would not be so indelible.

The entire encounter is refracted through the lens of memory, and the night remains dark from the perspective of the day. Yet in another way, the events of the night are not so dark at all. As the repetition of the refrain after the final line forces us to recall, "the memory of that passion does not fade." Slowly, gently, the poet maneuvers us into the position of wondering whether the whole encounter transpired in a dream—a dream so vivid and deeply meaningful that it persists even by day. That would explain exactly how Night acted the part of a cheat (v. 6), robbing the heroine of her dream and taking Krishna along too as it retreated before the advancing light of day. For once it would be the night, rather than Krishna himself, who has cast her in the familiar role of a *khaṇḍitā nāyikā* (cf. §148) at dawn, and that would explain the paradox of how at one level—in dream—her desire could also have been fulfilled (v. 1).

201.2 *horn, earring* This composition, in which a *virahiṇī* ("lonely woman," v. 5) deserted by Krishna vows to take up the life of a yogi in hopes of finding him, carries strong echoes of a number of poems attributed to Mirabai. (See Hawley, *Three Bhakti Voices*, pp. 117–138.) It is, however, more consistent in its imagery, for the poet depicts a specific kind of ascetic—the Nāth Yogī. The accoutrements of such a yogi are listed systematically: the antelope horn he blows to announce himself (*sīṅgī*, v. 2), the glass or quartz earring he wears in one ear (*mudrā*, v. 2), the handleless bowl he uses to beg his food (*ṣappara*, v. 2), and the rough cloak he wears (*kanthā*, v. 3), which is made by sewing together spare pieces of cloth. Other practices mentioned here are more generally observed—the wearing of unkempt hair (*jaṭā*, v. 3), the habit of dousing one's body with ash (*bibhūti*, v. 3) and dust (*ṣeha*, v. 5), and the attempt to generate inner heat (*jārauṅ*, v. 5)—but these are features of the life of a Nāth Yogī too.

201.4 *I'd rouse old Gorakh* Most specific of all references to the Nāth order is the mention of its putative founder, the legendary Gorakhnāth (*gorașa*). Because he is considered by Nāth Yogīs never to have died but to have receded into a life of eternal contemplation, he is potentially available to give succor and guidance to those who can manage to awaken him. The *gopī* who speaks in this composition imagines doing so by casting herself in the role of someone to whom Gorakhnāth himself owes allegiance: his own guru, the great god (*mahesa*, v. 4) Shiva. Nowadays one occasionally sees ascetics dress up as Shiva by placing a cardboard crescent moon in their hair, carrying a trident in one hand and a little drum in the other, and so forth. This sort of show (*svāṅga*, v. 4) is what the *virahiṇī* proposes here.

201.6 *cobra that's lost the jewel* In the final line it seems the poet relaxes his grasp on the particular image he has adopted in the rest of the poem. He turns instead to the familiar metaphor of the snake that has lost the jewel said to rest at the center of its hood and guide its course: such is the state of Braj without Krishna. Actually, however, the poet has not entirely abandoned his yogic metaphor. The connection persists in two ways. First, Shiva has close associations with snakes, especially cobras: they serve as his jewelry. Second and less obviously, the poet makes use of a term that is central to the spiritual philosophy of the Nāths: the word *sūnau* ("empty"). As in Buddhist theory, it serves as the designation of ultimate reality—a state that, according to Nāth doctrine, can actually be attained at the apex of the yogi's climb to perfection. This is an exalted sense of the meaning of emptiness and here, of course, Sūr uses it tongue in cheek. The emptiness that yogis strive so hard to achieve is precisely the state that Krishna's *virahiṇīs* would love to escape.

206.1 *parting that cuts two ways* In this poem, so similar in spirit to many composed by the well known Maithili poet Vidyāpati, one of Rādhā's friends informs Krishna of the condition Rādhā endures when separated from him. Rādhā exemplifies the pain of separation at two levels: the simpler one, in which she reacts to Krishna's absence by making him verbally, mentally present (v. 3), and the deeper one, in which she becomes so absorbed in the presence she longs for that she is converted to her lover's role and feels disoriented at being separated from herself (v. 4).

This complex state, in which heroine and hero are inexorably intertwined, reminds one not only of Vidyāpati but of Jayadeva, author of the renowned twelfth-century Sanskrit *Gītagovinda*. Indeed, the name that the poet chooses to pair with Rādhā's own is precisely the one Jayadeva chooses in beginning the *Gītagovinda*: Mādhav. Jayadeva weaves the lovers' names into the dual construction *rādhāmādhavau*, and Sūr creates numerous echoes between them here. Despite this close association, however, the primary reality both here and in the *Gītagovinda* is one of separation, and Rādhā's remembrance of Krishna must bear great weight in holding the couple together. (See Barbara Stoler Miller, "The Divine Duality of Rādhā and Krishna.") Estranged from herself and estranged from him: these two separations (v. 1) are the two ends of the burning log in which Rādhā, like a desperate wood-bug (v. 5), finds herself trapped.

212.1–6 *my friend* This simple composition requires little comment—except, perhaps, to remark on that very fact. The repetition of the syllable *rī* at the end of every line, which indicates that a woman is being addressed, contributes to the folkish tone. Even the meter is rough, and the poet uncharacteristically (to judge by the rest of the early *Sūrsāgar*) and perhaps absent-mindedly repeats the word *biraha* (< *viraha*: "longing," vv. 3, 5).

214.5 *sheldrake* As in §193.7, the poet appeals to the sheldrake (*cakaī*) because it spends its nights separated from its mate, with whom it reunites when morning comes. But here, contrary to both nature and convention, we have the specter of a sheldrake couple united at night rather than by day. Small wonder, then, that when the *virahiṇī* seeks out her mate at dawn, expecting him to return like a morning sheldrake to its partner, he is nowhere to be seen. Thus the order of creation has been reversed, as the poor woman suggests by concluding the poem with a depiction of Brahmā, the Creator (*vidhātā*), as "menacing" (*niṭhura*). The sheldrake Krishna she saw by night was only a reflection of her own desire—a dream Krishna. The winds of wakefulness alter that perfect reflexivity of mind, and he is gone. Thoughts of him remain (v. 1), but it's not the same.

217.1 *With love* This is one of several compositions in which the poet gives examples from the natural world to illustrate the costliness of love. Here they are arrayed with an economy that is hard to rival: the moth, the dove, the deer (vv. 2–4; see notes on §§418.7–8, 13–15, 17–18). The rhetoric has a shape that is nothing if not obvious. All the way through verse 4, each line begins with the word *prīti*, "love."

217.5 *coos love, coos love* In verse 5 the pattern changes. On the one hand, we seem to have a relaxation, since the line no longer begins with *prīti*. On the other hand, however, there is a tightening, for in Indian love poetry the call of the cuckoo (*papīhā*)—*piu piu*—is heard as a variant of *priy priy*: "my love! my love!" In a sense, then, love is mentioned here not once but twice—a loose analogy to the "stretto" pattern that appears so often in the penultimate verses of Sūrdās poems.

217.6 *A lonely woman sets herself on fire.* Only in the last verse is love—at least, the word love—truly absent. This underscores the sad condition of the "lonely woman" (*birahini* < *virahiṇī*) whom the poet finally names there, suggesting by proximity that she cries out as tirelessly as the cuckoo. The human realm does indeed present stark examples of how "with love there's never a thought that one might die" (v. 1), as one senses in the most crucial word in the poem—its last, *pacārai*. There are two principal ways to understand this verb. If it means "to announce" or "to broadcast," then we form the picture of the *virahiṇī* as someone whose extravagent behavior—her sighs, her dishevelment, her uncontrollable fainting spells—automatically attracts attention. By going beyond all propriety, she has entered upon a death that is social in nature. One might translate:

> For what, says Sūrdās, might she fear?
>   A lonely woman broadcasts herself.

It is the second possible sense, however, that has been chosen for the main translation, with *pacārai* meaning "to burn" or, in context, "set herself on fire." This casts the *virahiṇī* in the role of an incipient *satī*, a woman who dreads separation from her mate far more than death. This seems the more dramatic interpretation of the two, and places the cuckoo to whom it metaphorically refers in a direct succession with the creatures described in the verses preceding its mention. They all rush forward to death.

219.1 *my letters* This well-known poem expresses the complaint of a *gopī*—Rādhā, Yaśodā, or some other—whom Krishna has left behind in Braj by going to Mathura. The focus is her letters, presumably dictated to a traveler (cf. §193). In verses 3–4 she hypothesizes about what might have happened to prevent her message from being delivered. Then in verses 5–6 she considers what might have occurred if they had been delivered but nonetheless left unanswered. The poet reports the *gopī*'s suggestions artfully, moving from the plausible (rain-soaked paper) to the impossible (an epidemic of cataracts) to show that actually she surmises the true cause of Krishna's silence: indifference.

219.6 *scribes, says Sūr, have gone blind* The last line may conceal a clever twist. On the face of it the poet has his *gopī* refer to servants (*sevaka*)—scribes, one would think—whose writing has made them go blind (*liṣai te āndhai*). She goes on to suggest a cause for the blindness: cataracts, a disease she designates in her rustic way as "stubborn doors for the eyes" (*naina kapāṭa are*). Yet at another level, in speaking of scribes such as these, the poet may be referring to himself, for he inserts his own name as a signature just after pronouncing the word "servant" (*sevaka sūra*). The poet's full name is Sūrdās, which means "servant of the sun" or of the sun-god Sūrya, and *sevak sūr* (that is, *sūr sevak*) would mean exactly that. Furthermore, Sūr is a blind poet, at least by reputation, so once again the shoe would seem to fit. If we take this verse as at some level referring not only to the scribes of Mathura but to the author of the poem, we have Sūr in effect blaming himself for failing to facilitate communication between this *gopī* and her lost love. Acting as her messenger, he has repeatedly sung her lament, probably in temples where Krishna is installed upon the altar. Yet still the Lord gives no response.

220.1 *thickening clouds* This is a poem of the rainy season—one of a dozen or so that appear in the early *Sūrsāgar*—and is therefore appropriate to sing once the monsoon arrives. In north India, this usually occurs in late June or early July. The theme of separation is prominent in poems of this type since the monsoon is apt to isolate lovers from one another, and at precisely the time when all the world seems to spring to life and love.

The present composition, which is evidently spoken by one *gopī* to another, is no exception. Although no mention is made of Krishna's being absent until the very end (v. 8), there is a gathering poignancy as this *gopī* describes the great, rolling clouds. For not only does she liken them to elephants in rut—indeed, elephants of Kāma (v. 2)—but she does so in a way that gives the hearer hints of her preoccupation with Krishna, even if she is unaware of it herself. The very mention of rainclouds (*ghana*, v. 1) is apt to call him to mind, since his complexion is frequently likened to them—so frequently, in fact, that one of his titles is "Dark as a Raincloud" (*ghan śyām*). Soon the second word in that title also appears: as the *gopī* surveys the clouds, she sees "fine dark bodies" (*syāma subhaga tana*, v. 3). In the original, the number is indeterminate, so the association with Krishna's own "fine dark body" is much closer than the translation would suggest.

220.5–6 *bounds of ponds . . . shores* This is weather that the *gopī* not only observes but feels. As the following verse makes clear, these rains suggest (or indeed, *are*) her own tears, or perhaps those of the *gopīs* collectively, and the ponds whose boundaries they defy are her eyes. The poet designates these boundaries with the word *avadhi* (v. 5), which also conveys the meaning of a boundary in time, and in Sūr's usage normally refers to the time at which Krishna is expected to return. This overtone persists in verse 6, where the word *belā* carries the same ambiguity: it can mean both "shore" (as in the translation) and "time." When Krishna does not return, when the eyes have waited too long in vain, the tears flood forth.

220.7 *Lord of Airāvat* The woman who speaks recalls the moment at Mount Govardhan when after great deluges the storm-god Indra, whose vehicle is the elephant Airāvat, joined his hands in a gesture indicating his submission to Krishna, the Lord of Braj.

223.1–6 *thunder . . . travelers* The monsoon is the season when lovers return to those from whom they have been parted. The rains make travel so difficult that one wants to begin journeying at the first sign they are imminent; otherwise the separation could be a long one. The *gopī* who expresses herself in this poem therefore laments the fact that Krishna has not returned to her—from Mathura, in all likelihood—and wonders why the signs of impending downpours have not made themselves manifest where he is.

She lists these portents systematically, beginning, obviously enough, with thunder. That calls to mind Indra, god of rains, and she speculates that Krishna has been so pleased by Indra's submission at Mount Govardhan that he has forbidden him to express his stormy anger in Krishna's presence any more. The mention of Indra in turn suggests the ladybug (*būḍha*, v. 3), since that insect's full name is *indrabadhū* ("Indra's daughter-in-law"). The ladybug is so called because it appears when the monsoon—Indra's rainy weather—begins; it is a sign of the season. When the *gopī* says the ladybug "can't find the earth" (literally "can't enter the earth," *dharani na būḍha prabesani*, v. 3), perhaps she is speculating that the bug has been detained in Indra's heaven. As a good daughter-in-law, she will not emerge from the family home until he does.

Among birds, herons (*bagani*, v. 3) are particularly associated with the rains (cf. §220.5), as are peacocks, wagtails, and cuckoos. The peacock performs its mating dance during the monsoon; the wagtail (*cātriga*, v. 4) is said never to drink except in the presence of a constellation that appears late in the monsoon (cf. *Sūr's Ocean* §264); and during the rains the cuckoo (*pika*, v. 4) is particularly vocal in its call. This call—*piu, piu*—sounds as if the bird were summoning its lover (*priy priy*, cf. §217.5). From a bird's song it is but a short step to the songs that women sing while swinging. In north India swinging is an activity specifically reserved for the monsoon season and is strongly associated with women, who typically sing songs of the season together as they swing. Such songs are often set in *rāg malhār*, the very raga with which most manuscripts associate the composition at hand (so B1, B3, J2, J4, K1, U1, but not U2, which employs *rāg naṭ*).

After mentioning all these marks of the monsoon, the *gopī* calls to mind one last feature, the difficulty of travel (v. 6), and that is the saddest of all. If no travelers appear on the road to Mathura because the road is closed, the rains must indeed have come there, and Krishna's failure to appear can only mean that he is occupied with some other love.

224.7–8 *dispatch a letter* The final two lines present a possible resolution to the monsoon plight of the *gopī* who speaks. A messenger is to be sent to the monarch of the realm to apprise him of the sad condition of one of his subjects. A subject's well-being is, after all, the test of a good king. Yet in this instance there is a crippling complication: the ruler—"the Yādav king" Krishna—is precisely the cause of the problem.

230.1 *autumn* Now the rains are over; the roads are passable again. If Śyām, "the Dark One" whose color matches the monsoon clouds, was prevented from coming to her all during the rainy season, now he has the chance. But still he has not come.

230.3 *kāṃs grass* When the *virahiṇī* points to various details of the autumn season, they produce very different sentiments from the ones they ought to elicit. Normally when the *kāṃs* grass, which grows amply near the Jamunā, produces its white flower, this is a welcome sign that the monsoon is over and the satisfactions of autumn are at hand. The water in ponds and rivers has cleared (v. 4), lotuses bloom there once again (v. 4), and the harvest moon shines with its "great drops of pollen" (*makaranda kanda*, v. 5) in the form of moonbeams.

230.5 *they frighten my heart* As the *gopī* recites these pleasures of autumn (vv. 3–5), we are lulled into forgetting her situation—perhaps she is, too. So when she begins to make the obvious comparison between the pollen-gathering bees and her heart as it drinks in moonbeams, we follow along. But then she stops short, right in the middle of the line (v. 5). Instead of finishing her simile, she pronounces the word "fear" (*ḍara*, translated through the verb "frighten"), and it comes as a shock. The remainder of the poem explains why she feels as she does.

241.4 *virtues . . . serpents do not know* Krishna's role in Mathura is to exercise sovereignty, but she protests that his true excellences (*guṇa*, "virtues") cannot be sensed in that mode. Cobras (*nāgas*) are the species that are classically seen to shield the heads of great sovereigns, and in this way they also belong intrinsically with Vishnu, the divine king who rests on or sits beneath the many hoods of his vehicle Śeṣ. Yet using the very word *śeṣ* (*sesani*, v. 4), she insists that "even thousand-hooded serpents" cannot know Krishna's truest virtues. These virtues, by implication, are the ones he has displayed to her in love.

241.6 *dancing street performer* The *gopī*'s constancy is the very opposite of Krishna's evanescence—the way he comes and goes, and with such damnable, thoroughly secular style. His instant brilliance ("flash," *caṭaka*, v. 6) is like lightning (*dāmini*, v. 5), and his easy changes of mood or preference remind of "a dancing street performer" (*naṭa nacata*, v. 6), a figure to whom Krishna is nowadays so frequently likened that the term *naṭ* figures in some of his most familiar epithets (*naṭavar, naṭ nāgar*). These translate loosely as "best of dancers" and "urbane dancer": see Hawley, *Krishna, the Butter Thief*, p. 156. Here, however, with the word "many" (*bahu*, v. 6) as a modifier, we form an impression of an agile street performer who shifts roles with the quick change of a turban—a one-man show (cf. §412). This is the Krishna for whom our *gopī* longs, not the personage who rules in Mathura.

4. THE BEE-MESSENGER

244.1 *Ūdho, go to Braj* This poem represents the speech of Krishna after he has liberated Mathura from the hands of Kaṃs. According to the Sanskrit Purāṇas, Krishna declines to accept the role of king after this victory, preferring to return the kingdom to its rightful leader, the elderly Ugrasen, who had been deposed by his son Kaṃs. In many poems in the *Sūrsāgar* this nicety is overlooked as the people of Braj, especially the womenfolk, use regal terms ("king of the Yādavs," "lord of the Yadus," etc.) to refer to the Krishna whose intimacy they no longer enjoy. That royal persona would also fit with the mood expressed here, though it is not strictly implied. Here Krishna dispatches Ūdho, his philosophically minded friend, to speak with the *gopīs* he has left behind in the Braj countryside. As such, narratively speaking, this poem belongs just before the substantial set that celebrate Ūdho's encounter with the women of Braj.

244.2 *Vedic revelation* The "Vedic revelation" that Ūdho is urged to preach is *śruti*, "that which is heard." This word designates the upper echelon of traditional teaching—as against the lower, *smṛti*, "what is remembered"—and usually refers specifically to the Vedas and Upanishads. Here, however, it seems to bear a broader meaning and refer to something like "elevated wisdom," the sort of thing philosophers and yogis such as Ūdho ought to possess. He is to make heard (*sunāi*) what has been heard (*śruti*). The concerned, common-sense tone that Krishna takes—particularly his use of such stock metaphors as the fire and the fish—foreshadows the futility of Ūdho's expertise. Its down-to-earth urgency matches poorly with the rarefied cure that Krishna sends Ūdho to dispense.

246.1 *uncanny resemblance* This poem captures the moment when the *gopīs* see Ūdho arriving in the distance, mounted on his chariot to bring them a message from his friend and master (cf. §244). The *gopīs* find a number of resemblances between him and Krishna. They marvel at these, hoping against hope that the apparition they see in the distance is somehow Krishna himself. Certain of these resemblances contribute to the *gopīs'* perception of both Ūdho and Krishna as bees, and this becomes the defining feature of a large and celebrated group of poems (*Sūr's Ocean* §269ff.) in which the *gopīs* actually address Ūdho as such. These are called *bhramargīt*, "songs of the bee" or "songs to the bee." They are at the core of a larger set of poems—to which this one belongs—that describe the interaction between Ūdho and the *gopīs*.

The title *bhramargīt* derives from a vignette reported by the *Bhāgavata Purāṇa* (10.47.11–21), in which the *gopīs* see a passing bee, that paradigmatic traveler among animals who gathers the sweet pollen associated with love. In their distress the women address the bee as if it were Ūdho. Ūdho hears their pleas and replies, as he continues to do in the fourteenth-century Marathi *Uddhavagītā*, where this moment is prominently celebrated, and in subsequent Brajbhāṣā accounts such as the *Bhramargīt* of Nandadās, who was probably Sūr's younger contemporary. (An English translation is given in Ronald Stuart McGregor, *Nanddas*, pp. 85–105.) In the *Sūrsāgar* itself, however, Ūdho is given little chance to speak. Here the *bhramargīt* belong almost entirely to the *gopīs*. Certain of these poems (e.g., §248) echo the program of yoga and rationality that Ūdho would press on them, but we hear very little of it from the man himself.

248.2 *parading it around* The *gopīs* object to Ūdho's manner in bringing them Krishna's message. Rather than treating it as a private communication—indeed, a communication between lovers—he veritably shouts it from the rooftops: he seems to brandish the letter on his head.

248.3 *the mark of hardship* The *gopīs* also criticize Krishna, saying that he "slaps the mark of hardship on every house" (*ghara ghara tapa kī thāpa*). They may simply be referring to the way in which boorish visitors pound on the door, or they may have in mind the red handprints that are placed on Indian doors at times of celebration as signs of auspiciousness. But if so, they mean it ironically. There is nothing auspicious about the handprint Krishna has figuratively slapped on their doors with the message he has chosen to send.

248.4 *unknowable, untellable, unmeasurable* Here the women refer to several terms (*avigata akatha amāpa*) that figure prominently in the "no traits" or "non-attribute" (*nirguṇ*) school of Indian philosophy as ways to designate the undesignatable Ultimate. So far, so good: these are the categories Ūdho himself would have used in trying to appeal to the *gopīs'* reason. But the *gopīs* stand them on their head, interpreting their intentional lack of specificity as reason to doubt that there is anything real or believable in what they describe. They suggest that this fancy negative language is merely evasive. In verse 5, they divulge what they believe to be the true cause for Krishna's "strange new way" (v. 3) of behaving. They propose that it was not really he who dictated this message but their rival Kubjā, the hunchback. Kubjā's influence in Krishna's court has become so powerful that the *gopīs* refer to her as his "chief minister" (*adhikārini*, v. 5). They picture her as standing before him, either telling him what to say, as our translation implies, or giving orders in his stead. If one follows out their logic, this would imply she even has access to the royal seal (*chāpa*, v. 1).

The word *kubijā* or *kubjā* ("hunchback") is often used in the literature of Krishna as if it were a proper noun, referring to the woman who welcomed Krishna to Mathura with a display of affection that is often treated as a subject of ribald humor. She was a masseuse on her way to deliver ointments to King Kaṃs when she beheld Krishna and Balarām. As reported in the *Harivaṃśa*, she was immediately infatuated with Krishna's beauty and offered him the massage instead, smearing her unguents on him and Balarām—a welcome gesture, since these two were about to enter a wrestling match. Krishna rewarded her by touching her in turn, gently removing her deformity, and that further magnified her desire for him. This caused Krishna and his brother to laugh heartily, and Krishna departed with a smile (HV 71.34–35). The *Viṣṇu Purāṇa*, picking up the thread, has Krishna extend the good-natured joke by promising to return to her (VP 5.20.12), but he never does. The *Bhāgavata* goes a step further, actually causing Krishna to come back later and satisfy her sexual appetite, as a reward for her good deed. In doing so, however, the humorless *Bhāgavata* is quick to tell us that Krishna is merely stooping to the (erstwhile) hunchback's level of physicality: it is a shame that she did not come to him for salvation instead (BhP 10.48.1–11; see Noel Sheth, *The Divinity of Krishna*, pp. 59–61).

253.2 *mark of fame* Ironically, the *gopī* depicts Ūdho as being beyond reproach. She says he bears the very crown—or literally, forehead mark—of good repute (*sujasa kau ṭīkau*).

253.4 *no-trait path* The speaker names the theme of Ūdho's philosophy correctly, as *nirguṇ* (> *niraguna*). She almost strays into denigration by characterizing this philosophy as "tasteless" (*phīkau*), but if one were being literal-minded, one might still take that as a fair description of the intent of Ūdho's yogic message. He proposes to wipe away the tastes and appetites that normally accompany sensory experience.

253.6 *singed with his own curse* In the first words of the second half of the composition the *gopī* abandons her tongue-in-cheek neutrality and presents her own understanding of these matters. The word she uses to do so is one with a usage hallowed in the annals of *nirguṇ* philosophy: *jñāna*, "knowledge." She couples this general concept, however, with the adjective "my," so it becomes quite individual: "to my way of thinking" (*merai jāni*). She goes on to speak of Ūdho as both giving a curse and suffering from it at the same time, and her evidence is that his body bears such a dark color. In India such things as curses and the evil eye are generally spoken of as black, so this makes sense, and the specific word she uses to describe the color is *syām*, which hints bluntly at the identity of the person who has given the original curse. Krishna not only curses the *gopīs*, but in cursing them, curses Ūdho too.

253.8 *he's like a snake* There is another reason why a body may turn black—snakebite—and in that case too the cause of the blackening is black itself: the *gopī* is thinking of a cobra. In one sense this cobra is Krishna, but in another sense it is Ūdho, for both of them are prepared to send the message of yoga and *nirguṇ* thought to Braj and then retreat: they "bite and scurry off." Under the circumstances, one should beware of thinking that the liquid they have to spread is innocuous (*phīkau:* "tasteless," v. 4), as this *gopī* at one point seemed to suggest. In the very next line, indeed, she had gone on to a rhyme that would suggest it was something else entirely: a matter of love—literally, "of the beloved" (*piya kau,* v. 5). Love is certainly not innocuous, and farther still from being the "juice of eternal life" (*amī* < *amṛt,* v. 8) that it masquerades as being. This stuff is poison!

261.2 *clad with the sky* This poem is a fine example of the comparison Sūr often makes in his *bhramargīt* poems between yoga and its rival, *viyoga*. These two terms mean literally "union" and "separation," and Sūrdās celebrates the bodily rigors of love in separation as exceeding the demands of conventional, Ūdho-style yoga (see Hawley, *Sūr Dās,* chapter 4). When it comes to ascetic discipline, Ūdho has nothing to teach the *gopīs,* who manifest the abilities of yogis without being instructed how to do so. Here it is specifically the *gopīs'* eyes that are cast as yogis, and yogis of the most stringent sort: *digambars,* literally "those who are clad with the sky." The *digambar* branch of the Jain ascetic community disallows the use of any form of clothing (cf. *ughāre,* "exposed," v. 4).

261.5 *the way ascetics die* Another direct reference to yogic practice is found in the phrase *sahaja samādhi,* which means "spontaneous concentration" or "simple concentration" but is also a technical term that refers to the custom of burying yogis in a seated, meditative posture when they die. The practice is especially associated with Nāth Yogīs (cf. §201). Cremation—the normal option, one that both depends upon and reinforces family bonds—is thought inappropriate for yogis since they undergo the rite of death at the moment they leave behind every societal bond to undertake a life of wandering and self-denial. The unbroken concentration of the *gopīs'* eyes makes the double meaning possible: they gaze so fixedly that one cannot tell whether they are dead or alive.

261.8 *haṭha-yoga eyes* As his "last word" in describing the *gopīs'* eyes as yogis, the poet calls them *haṭhī*. The term means fixed or implacable, and doubtless the poet wants us to hear it in that sense: "stubborn," as our translation says. But the word *haṭhī* suggests someone who practices *haṭha yoga,* the "stubborn" or "violent" sort especially associated with Nāth Yogīs. In *haṭha yoga,* one tries to break through to truth with a program of physical discipline that emphasizes difficult yogic postures. Women whose eyes have mastered the harsh, direct approach of *haṭha yoga* can scarcely be expected to respond to Ūdho's efforts to interest them in yoga of the more delicate, philosophical sort, which is so much more oblique and takes so much longer to produce results.

266.2 *these tactics* This poem is a comment from one *gopī* to another on Ūdho's presence in Braj, and it has the element of wit that has made Sūr's *bhramargīt* compositions famous. Although the focus is primarily on yoga (vv. 3–4), the techniques and tactics (*upajoga* < *upayoga*) he has learned from living with the people of Mathura may have both sexual and medical dimensions. In regard to the former, no practiced listener will miss the contrast between intimate union ("mating," *saṃbhoga* v. 5) and the disease (*roga*, v. 6) that is the true subject of this composition: *viyoga (biyog*, v. 4), that is, separation. As for the medical metaphor, every language must have its version of the saying the *gopīs* adopt as their punch line: "Physician, heal thyself!" It is not entirely clear whether the *gopī* who gives this speech intends it as a description of Ūdho or of the one who has sent him on his supposedly curative mission. Perhaps one need not choose. As in many other instances, the *gopīs* are happy to tar the master and his messenger with the same brush.

277.1 *Lord of the Milkmaids* This poem focuses on Krishna's use of the title *gopīnāth*, "Lord of the Milkmaids," and the issue is truth in advertising. The angry *gopīs* argue that if Krishna were in fact what his name claims him to be, he would return to Gokul ("our cowherding town," v. 2) and care for them. Instead he snubs their protestations of need by taking up with Kubjā—or so they allege. The *gopīs* dare Krishna to adopt the unappealing title "Lord of the Hunchback" if he is so smitten by her (v. 4). Then they go on to make some unkind allegations about the resemblance between him and an elephant—or literally, as befits his current role in Mathura, an "elephant king" (*gajarāja*, v. 5).

278.1 *it won't sell in Braj* This is one of the classic ripostes that the *gopīs* offer to the message of yoga that Ūdho preaches. They treat him as some sort of pedlar and predict only the worst for his business (*byaupāra*, "tradesmanship," v. 3), at least if their own reaction is any measure of future success. They are not to be fooled: this is false merchandise (*ṭhagaurī*, "dirty trick," v. 1) and the clever deceits that surround it will make no progress in the straightforward atmosphere of Braj. Maybe the wholesaler—Krishna—can be duped (v. 4), but not such seasoned buyers as themselves. They are not about to barter grapes, which in India are not only a sweet but a rare product, for the inedibly bitter and utterly common fruit of the *nīm* tree (v. 5). And it makes simple business sense that Krishna's "traits" (*guna*) are worth more than the "no-traits" (*niraguna*, i.e., *nirguṇ*) that Ūdho is peddling—or, as we have said in our freer translation, that taste counts for more than its absence.

283.4 *many forms of concentration* Ūdho may have his brand of yoga, but the *gopīs* have theirs, as well. They practice it "both night and day," disciplining themselves so that their minds become at least as sharp and unyielding as his (v. 1). The various techniques of concentration they employ in their attempt to focus on Krishna parallel the ones he would propose, and have already rendered their minds "stern" (*niṭhuratā*, v. 4). The *gopīs*' yoga derives its central power from memory (*surati*, v. 4). They explicitly contrast it to the sorts of "Pure Land" meditative techniques that call for the visualization of various heavenly realms (v. 5): these pale in power before the memory of Hari. This is so, they hint, because by focusing on Krishna they are mobilizing and refining their own karma—actual "patterns from the past" (*bāsanā* < *vāsanā*, v. 7). Although the term *vāsanā* sometimes refers simply to desires, it does so because wishes reflect mental predilections. As the general theory of karma states, these predispositions are inherited from the past, often from former lives. The lesson to be learned is that the memory of Krishna is something powerful: to ignore it is merely to invite it to return. The *gopīs*' yoga, then, involves not leaving the body in search of other realms of happiness—even the sort that Ūdho says his new form of mental discipline would make available—but the opposite. They must stay with their bodies so that karma can find its fulfillment in a future meeting with Krishna (v. 8).

287.1 *a secret liaison* In this poem the *gopīs* provide a character description of Ūdho and his master, evidently in response to a charge against their own character that they feel has come from Ūdho. The issue is framed by the phrase *gupitahi yārī*, "a secret liaison," which the *gopīs* repeat as if Ūdho had used it first. It is memorable in the context of the *Sūrsāgar* because it incorporates that rarety, a word of Persian origin (*yārī*). This term, with its aroma of courts and courtesans, has the effect of depicting Ūdho as a sort of professional gossip. The *gopīs* are not amused to see their tie with Krishna analyzed in this manner, and they resent the slimy suggestion that they have participated in something that could appropriately be cleansed by yoga (cf. v. 5).

287.2 *a turban of deceit* In response, the *gopīs* go on the attack. They turn the tables by characterizing Ūdho's deceitful (*ṭhagavārī*, v. 2) nature with the metaphor of a turban. A consummately public symbol, the turban is normally a sign of respectability, but when they describe the one they see Ūdho wearing, they paint a mixed picture indeed. His turban is evidently of the type one often sees in Rajasthan, in which the cloth is dyed in bands of several colors. The *gopīs* offer interpretations for each color, as if each performed the emblematic function we associate with flags. The yellow, of course, is for Krishna: this is the color of his garments and the one that pleases him most ("his favorite color," v. 3). After that comes Kubjā's color, red, which in this context symbolizes the life of passion. The third color is seemingly the one the *gopīs* would ascribe to themselves, since they identify it with Braj. This is white, the color of purity and good repute. Finally, there is Ūdho's own distinctive color, black, which pertains to him not just because of the darkness of his skin but because black symbolizes crookedness, dishonesty, and exploitation. Red, white, and black are the three basic colors in the Indian scheme of *guṇas*—representing *rajas, sattva,* and *tamas*—and the valuation the *gopīs* assign to each color in this context matches the general scheme.

288.4 *also four arms* Krishna's "four arms" (*caturbhuja*) are a mark of his divinity, and are not normally displayed when he manifests himself as a human being. In that capacity he has but two. Here, however, the *gopī* accepts both possibilities and adds them together to produce the number of legs a bee possesses.

289.1 *Don't take amiss* This light-hearted poem is well known in Braj, and it is no wonder, given the striking image that the poet develops here. In Indian society to call something black is no compliment, so it is appropriate that this *bhramargīt* poem begin with an apology, since Ūdho is himself black in color. Sūrely he will understand that he is the most immediate example of the products of Mathura's oven and will be dishonored—a grave offense to Indian canons of hospitality—so the *gopī* demurely excuses herself ("don't take amiss what I say") before forging ahead. This is especially critical since she speaks tongue in cheek, and her words do in fact conceal a pun (on *bilagu*, meaning "averse, offended" or "separate, different"). This hidden meaning in the first verse causes the poem to open, for knowing ears, in a way very different from what we have rendered in our primary translation:

Don't think Ūdho and our Dear One are different.
This Mathura—what a soot-blackened oven!
  Whatever comes from there is black.

289.4 *the shining jewel* Krishna is jewellike (*maniyāre*), she says—but what kind of jewel? This jewel is, if not quite black, the deepest blue (*nīla*, v. 5); it got that way by being pulled from a blueing vat (*nīla māṭa tai*, v. 5) and plunged into the famously dark waters of the Jamunā. This is faint praise at best. Krishna seems to have achieved his "rare . . . traits" (*guna nyāre*, v. 6) by epitomizing all that Mathura represents. In this context the expression *bali jāuṅ* ("I offer myself to you," v. 6) carries roughly the meaning "I give up!" (cf. §72).

289.5 *the blueing vat* The *gopī* who speaks uses this phrase *(nīla māṭa)* not as a general way to compromise the idea of Krishna's being some fabulous jewel, but specifically to suggest a story so venerable that it appeared in versions of the *Pañcatantra* dating back at least to 1000 C.E., perhaps considerably earlier. (On issues of dating, see Hawley, *Sūr's Ocean*, vol. 1, p. 503.) In that tale the protagonist is a jackal who wanders from the wilderness into a city and there, besieged by dogs, falls into a blueing vat. On emerging, he escapes the urban environment and returns to the forest, where he appears so fearsomely remarkable to the other wilderness creatures that he manages to install himself as their king. He treats most species with moderate consideration, but cannot abide his own: he treats the other jackals with contempt and banishes them from his presence. One day, though, he hears them howling and cannot help howling himself, thus revealing his true identity to his animal courtiers. A tiger (or lion) eats him on the spot. The story ends with a moral repeated many times in the *Pañcatantra:* never abandon your friends.

In the *gopīs'* use of this tale, it is clear who has abandoned his kin. Like the *Pañcatantra*'s jackal, Krishna has strayed inside the city walls from the forest where he belongs, and by a transformation that is mysterious to the *gopīs*, he has been welcomed as if he were some exotic jewel and exalted to royal status. Perhaps they hope their howling about his "rare traits" will make him howl back, and that Krishna will reap the appropriate reward.

289.6 *how rare your traits* In its oldest versions, this poem is full of guarded insult and double entendre, as in this slur on Krishna's "rare . . . traits" (*guna nyāre*, v. 6). Outright slander, however, emerges in a variant conclusion that appears first in manuscript G1. This variant is retained in the way the poem is usually recited in Braj today. In it, the first half of the final line becomes *tātai jamunā bhai sāṅvarī* rather than *kamala nayana bali jāuṅ tumhārī*, which changes the logic fundamentally. The earlier idea was that Krishna became black from a dunking in the Jamunā, but now we are asked to believe the reverse. One encounter with him was enough to discolor the poor river forever:

That's why the Jamunā has its darkish tone—
  from the unrivaled traits of Sūr's Dark Lord!

This is an appealing thought, but it leads in the opposite direction from what was originally intended when the *gopī* made her reference to the blueing vat.

290.1 *Those dark ones* This poem joins its immediate predecessor as a bitter meditation on the meaning of Krishna's dark color. His title Śyām (*vai syāma)*, "that Dark One") is the point of departure, and the refrain line can be heard as grammatically singular—a personal endictment of him: "That Dark One, my friend, what would he know of love?" Yet as the poem develops, we quickly become aware that the *gopī's* charge against Krishna is made in generic terms. She accuses him by leveling her charge against the class to which he belongs, and the phrase *vai syāma* and the verb it governs (*jānahi*) may also be understood in the plural: "Those dark ones, my friend, what would they know of love?" Bumblebees (*bhavara*, v. 5) do appear as examples of the genus "dark," and in certain late versions the poem is actually addressed to Ūdho as a bee (*madhukara*, v. 1: see NPS 4368.1).

290.5 *bumblebees . . . crows, and koels* In the original, the verse that lists these black creatures is so full of harsh "k"s that it feels like bouncing along the top of a picket fence (*bhavara kuraṅga kāka kokila kau kabi ati kapaṭu baṣānahi*, v. 5). Similarly, the thought: bumblebees are notoriously fickle and self-serving; crows are shameless scavengers and thought of as cunning; and the reputation of the sweet-voiced koel is tarnished by the fact that it is said to abandon its eggs in the nests of crows, hoping the lesser bird will care for its young (cf. *Sūr's Ocean* §267.3). These three are thus worthy to be described as "a very rotten lot" (*ati kapaṭu)*—a devious, unsavory bunch.

290.5 *black bucks* A problem arises, however, with the species called *kuraṅg*. Normally this word, which means "earth-colored," refers to a deer, and one of its most specific designations is the black female antelope. We translate "black buck," however, because elsewhere it seems clear that the poet is thinking of the male of the species. Perhaps he groups this creature with others in his list simply on the strength of the name itself—*kuraṅg* can mean "of bad behavior"—or perhaps the deer's quick and darting movements are meant somehow to connote deception. Alternatively, he may have a different animal in mind: *kuraṅg* may also denote "bay horses." This would be appropriate in that these are thought to be as unpredictable as the "dark horse" that figures in European proverbial speech, yet it is true that *kuraṅg* is much more rarely used to name a horse than a deer or antelope.

300.1 *just for ourselves* Here, as in certain other *bhramargīt* poems, the *gopīs* seem to address one another in Ūdho's presence, rather than direct their remarks to him. Yet he remains the stimulus for what they say, and in the end, if our interpretation is right, this indirection changes. They do turn to him after all (vv. 7–8).

300.2 *ten-day trial* The *gopīs* begin by announcing a surprising about-face. They abandon their stiff resistance to the yogic life Ūdho would foist upon them, but their acquiescence has an improbable, sardonic air. They say they are willing to sign up for "a ten-day trial" (*dina dasa dhauṅ*, v. 2) and in this spirit they list a series of yogic accoutrements they expect to be adopting (vv. 3–4). Some of these are eclectic: the staff and antelope's skin are widely used among ascetics. Equally common are the practices of smearing the body with ash and wearing the hair in unkempt, matted fashion. The mention of a whistle made from an animal's horn (*siṅgī*, v. 4) and of a rag quilt (*kanthā*, v. 3) are much more particular, however. These suggest the *gopīs* have Nāth Yogīs in mind as their model.

300.5 *arrows straight in the face* The *gopīs'* list of yogic practices piles up very quickly—so quickly that one may miss an intriguing fact: in the space of two verses (vv. 3–4) the *gopīs* have reeled off nine signs of the yogic life. This counts the smearing of ash on one's limbs and face as two separate practices, as the language of the original suggests *(aṅga bibhūti rahau muṣa mājai,* v. 3). If the *gopīs* intend each of these aspects of yoga to mark one day in their trial period, then by the fifth verse they picture themselves as set to undertake the tenth. They are "enlightened beings" (*sayānī*) ready to "suffer arrows straight in the face" without flinching or fleeing in any way. These, presumably, are the arrows of love's pain—the sting of separation from Krishna—and they signify an entrapment that is complete. If being impervious to any arrow of sensory stimulation denotes the ultimate stage of yogic attainment, the status of these arrows in the realm of love is the reverse. They are unbearable, and with their mention, as the poem enters its second half, the tone begins to change. The *gopīs'* light-hearted irony begins to slip into something more serious.

300.7 *yoga's fifth stage* At this point the *gopīs* turn to Ūdho, unable to carry the game any farther. They tell him what they think yoga amounts to in their own experience, and do so with impressive precision. They halve the number ten and refer to the fifth stage (*pañcamī*) in the yogic ascent as classically described in the *Yoga Sūtras* of Patañjali. This is the stage called *pratyāhāra,* the restraining of the sense organs. It is characterized by the attainment of a state of consciousness in which the senses and the organs of cognition that pertain to them are separated from their external, sensory objects; they follow the mind instead (*Yoga Sūtras* 2.54–55). To the *gopīs'* way of thinking, it is an alternate way of speaking about what they know as *viraha*—separation from the object toward which their whole sensory apparatus strains, namely, Krishna. As they set this "fifth stage" alongside separation, it feels to them like thunder in relation to the "murderous rains" (*bariṣā badhati,* v. 7; U1, B3, cf. B2, B3, J4, 5) or "monsoon" (*bariṣā avadhi,* v. 5; J1) of *viraha.* Ūdho's thunder announces a disaster they have already experienced. Further on possible meanings of the "fifth stage," see Hawley, *Sūr's Ocean,* vol. 1, pp. 521–522.

300.8 *took away our clothes* The *gopīs* conclude their argument with an example, as in the standard Indian form of the syllogism, and the example is not just hypothetical. To describe the killing rains of separation, they reach back to a moment when they were truly inundated, the time they undertook cold-water austerities in the Jamunā for the purpose of gaining a fine husband. It worked all too well. The very person they were thinking of—Krishna—materialized on the bank while they were still in the water, but all he did was confiscate the clothes they had left behind, causing them to walk a naked gauntlet before him as they emerged. This was indeed a kind of renunciation, to use the language of yoga. They left behind their bodily integrity and their reputation as members of a good families ("renouncing shame," *taji kula lājai*).

This time, Ūdho implies, it will all be different: their austerities will earn them the man himself. And indeed, the clothes-stealing episode is represented in the *Bhāgavata Purāṇa* (10.22.25–27) as being just such a preliminary test for achieving fully intimate union with Krishna. But it seems to these *gopīs* that it actually produced the awful separation they now endure. Why then should they set any store by renunciation in the new mode that Ūdho proposes? The ten-day trial has failed—or rather, in its desparate *viraha* way it succeeded long before Ūdho arrived on the scene.

313.1 *Bṛṣabhānu's daughter* This poem, presumably spoken by one of Rādhā's friends, offers a description of the heroine as a *virahiṇī*. In a summary phrase in verse 6, in fact, the word is used explicitly: *birahini*, "one who longs." In the title line Rādhā is introduced as "Bṛṣabhānu's daughter," but by the time the second line begins we are aware that she has come under the power of someone outside her own house—Krishna.

313.5 *burned again* The image is charcoal—burned once to make it ready for use as a fuel, and again when that use begins. The blackness of charcoal confirms the color suggested in the opening line: "utterly soiled."

313.6 *Nanda's darling girl* Instead of referring to Rādhā by means of a proper family name such as "Bṛṣabhānu's daughter," the title used at the outset, the poet designates her by means of her relation to—of all people—Nanda. She is called *nand dulārī* (v. 6), "Nanda's darling girl." This is a strange title indeed, one that could only be justified if Rādhā had become Nanda's daughter-in-law. By implying marriage, in fact, it makes us wonder whether the depiction of Rādhā in the previous line as a veritable corpse (*mritaka*, v. 5) may have been a gesture toward *satī*. And if, as the dominant conception has it, Rādhā was not really married to Krishna, then it draws even greater attention to the person who should by rights have made her an "honest woman," since *nand dulāre*, "Nanda's darling boy," is a familiar designation for Krishna. Is this the meaning of her being "utterly soiled" (v. 1)?

315.3 *shivered* The word is *pulaki*. A more precise rendering would make reference to the phenomenon of horripilation, which is actually what Rādhā experiences: she suffers from intense heat, as if in seizure. Among the various remedies sought, "something cool" (*usīra*, v. 5) might be a wet fan or some sandalwood paste. Lotuses (*kamala*, v. 5) might seem desirable because of the water trapped in their stems. "Poultices" (*kumakumā*, v. 5), finally, might refer to a number of substances, even some that come in liquid form and would be brought in a small vial. The snakebite diagnosis (cf. §253.8) connects to the motif of the *gāruḍī*, the snakebite-curer. The *Sūrsāgar* familiarly depicts Krishna in that role—as the doctor who is able to extract the poison of *viraha* because he himself was the one to inject it into a woman's bloodstream in the first place. His presence cures the disease that is his absence (see Hawley, *Three Bhakti Voices*, chapter 7).

316.1 *Hari has come* In this composition we hear the words of Ūdho as he reports to Krishna (Ramāpati, v. 7) what he has seen on his mission to Braj. The moment he calls forth is the one in which he met Rādhā. The title line seems innocuous enough until we recognize that it is delusionary. Hari has in fact not come, only his look-alike messenger. This—or perhaps the very illusion of his presence—is what triggers her seizure. When the poet says she "wraps herself in darkness" (v. 2), we see her eyes closing involuntarily. Other details of a seizure follow (vv. 3–5): the great trembling of body, the accelerated heartbeat, her lack of response to any attempt to grasp or restrain her, the hair loosening, and perhaps even the broken bangles as a symbol of bodily rigidity.

316.6 *two doves* The climax of Ūdho's tale comes when Rādhā's breasts are compared to doves (*parevā*). Although her separation from Krishna has worn her thin and her appearance is desperate and disheveled, one can still see in these normally hidden "birds" the plumpness and generosity of faithful love that animates her within. Evidently the vows read at her own "love marriage" (*prema kī parani*—a contrast to the *dhārmik* sort) are still being recited, although the marriage bangles have just been shattered.

316.7 *Ramāpati* A title of Vishnu/Krishna that refers to his role as the husband of Lakṣmī, for whom Ramā ("the pleasure-giver") is another name. Speaking in the voice of Ūdho, Sūr uses this vocative at precisely the same point in another poem as well (§319), and not just because it is metrically convenient. Rather, he wants to drive home to Krishna a sense of the responsibility that comes with being the husband or protector (*pati*) of the one who gives pleasure (*ramā*), one's mate. Vishnu is a paragon of such behavior, and in the minds of many, so is his avatar Rām, whose name is evoked but not denoted by the title Ramāpati.

316.7 *bewildered as a snake* As to the conceit about the jewel at the center of the cobra's hood (cf. §201.6), it means not only that the snake loses its sense of balance and direction without that gem—the Krishna gem in this case—but that all its life functions are impaired. The cobra continues to live, but without any strength: it lives, so to speak, without life. This is Rādhā's situation as Ūdho reports it, and before long the poet makes us see that this is Ūdho's condition as well. The reference to the snake is *ahi mani chīnī*, at the end of verse 7, and Ūdho's description of himself is the rhyming phrase *ajāna mati hīnī*, which concludes the verse that follows. Thus when Ūdho says, "It's as if I'd lost my mind" (v. 8), we understand that to proceed without the jewel of love is to have lost one's mind indeed. For a philosopher it is a serious thing to say "I know nothing" (*ajāna*, v. 8).

319.1 *you, Lord of Braj* This poem has sometimes been interpreted as being parallel to the previous one: a report by Ūdho to Krishna about Rādhā's sad state. This may be so, but the woman being described is not specifically identified as Rādhā. A more serious difficulty is raised by the presence in the best manuscript tradition of the feminine vocative *saṣi* ("my friend," v. 3), which at the very least complicates the idea that these words are being addressed to Krishna by Ūdho. One could perhaps conceive of Ūdho as the messenger for a sort of "oral letter" delivered to Krishna by one of Rādhā's friends, in which the *gopīs*' inveterate habit of speaking to one another persists despite the fact that they are addressing Krishna (vv. 1, 7–8). A similar pattern, though in reverse, can be seen in the oldest poem attributed to Mīrābāī (see Hawley, *Three Bhakti Voices*, pp. 104–105).

But there is an alternate approach. One could understand this as the speech of one *gopī* to another in the course of a conversation in which several of the women of Braj gather around the heroine. In that case the appeals to Krishna would be pleas directed to him in his absence, helpless gasps sent to the winds with the hope that somehow he might hear (in technical terms, *anyokti*, discourse apparently directed to one person but actually intended for another, cf. *Sūr's Ocean* §252). Such a scene would be particularly appropriate to the sense of isolation said to descend on women absent from husbands and lovers in the rainy season, which provides so much of the metaphorical background for this poem (vv. 1–6).

319.3 *glistening new boats* The likening of the heroine's eyeballs (*golaka;* in translation, "eyes") to "new boats" (*nava naukā*) may suggest that they have been so thoroughly washed with tears that they look bright and shiny. The ropes or chains that moor them would seem to be the lashes of the lower eyelids.

319.4 *tilak-mark tree* The reference is simultaneously to the tree of that name (*tilaku taru*), a small species notable for its bright red flowers, and the decorative mark at the center of the woman's forehead, which is also called *tilak* and is often red, like the flowers of the tree.

321.2 *hear me, Śyām* Plainly this is the speech of a go-between who bears news of Rādhā to Krishna, but one can conceive of this messenger in two rather different ways. Either it may be one of Rādhā's female acquaintances, traveling from one Braj locale to another, hoping to persuade Krishna to come to Rādhā's side, or it may be Ūdho meeting Krishna in Mathura after his encounter with the *gopīs*. The absence of any reference to Mathura, to Ūdho's mission, or to Krishna's royal station would seem to favor the former option; but the mention of Rādhā's friends (*saṣī*, v. 2), as if the speaker were at some distance from this circle, perhaps argues for the latter. Judging by other poems with which this one was grouped in early manuscripts organized according to a narrative format, most sixteenth-century performers (or audiences or scribes) understood it not as Ūdho's speech but that of a messenger *gopī*. This is clearest in the case of manuscripts such as U1 and A1, which plainly distinguish the *bhramargīt* from other poems of *viraha*, among which the present composition is numbered. Yet like poem 325, with which certain manuscripts (B1, B3) pair it, this poem is not easy to pigeonhole. This is to its credit: none of its beauty or value depends on being able to specify its exact narrative position.

321.3 *She tears wildflowers* Things that brought Rādhā joy in happier times—the color and scent of flowers; the comments of friends; the call of a bird; the refreshingly gentle light of the moon; the relief of cool breezes, sandalwood paste, or musk upon the body—all these now cause exactly the opposite reaction. She bristles at each, like the suffering patient who vents her overpowering anger by snapping at anyone who would venture to help her. Her pathological fear of anything that might reduce the heat (vv. 6–7) is especially poignant, since she suffers from the fire of separation.

321.5 *meshed windows* The poet uses the phrase *jālani kai magha* (literally, "through nets") to designate one of the routes by which a would-be attacker might gain access to Rādhā. In this case the enemy is the moon—she shrinks from its gentle, liquid beams—and there are two possible ways to understand what might be meant by "nets." The first is to take the word as referring to the latticework ("meshed windows" in our translation) used by Indian builders to filter out the full force of the brilliant sun. Rādhā's condition is so extreme that she fears moonlight, with all its amorous associations, and even if it comes only in broken form. Her response is to search for any opening in her clothes and mend it shut.

This activity suggests a second interpretation for the "nets" that concern her. Perhaps the poet intends us to think of these as belonging to the garments themselves—either tears that might have been caused by Rādhā's painful writhing, or tiny holes embedded in the weave itself, allowing the cloth to breathe. If the latter, we would be presented with a dramatic demonstration of the heroine's psychological state: would Rādhā try to sew up every little airhole in her sari?

324.2 *the monsoon . . . has arrived* This poem could be understood as spoken to Krishna either by Ūdho or by another messenger—one of the women of Braj. Whichever is the case, the messenger is adept in easing us into the words actually used by Rādhā's friends when they try to shield her from the painful knowledge that the rainy season has come, the season in which lovers should by rights reunite. In a similar way the messenger eases us out again (v. 7). The three intervening verses are entirely given over to direct discourse (vv. 4–6), and they share another bond, as well. They all begin with negatives (*nahi*, vv. 4, 6; *nāhina*, v. 5). As a result, we in the audience can effortlessly distinguish them from the rest and feel we have arrived at the core of the messenger's report.

324.7 *a cuckoo will open its throat* The call of the cuckoo (*papīhā*) is particularly devastating to Rādhā because the sharp "piu! piu!" it shouts to its mate are exactly the vocables she or any *virahiṇī* might use to call out for an absent lover. *Piu* is recognizably the same as *priya*, meaning "dear one" or "beloved" (cf. §217, 223), especially if that word is pronounced in a familiar or colloquial way. When the cuckoo cries out, then, all the efforts of Rādhā's friends are in danger of coming to naught. All these women can do is try to shoo the bird away.

5. LORDLY ENCOUNTERS—AND OTHERS

325.1 *It seemed* This composition presents an example of the genre of literature in which a battle scene is compared to a river, flood, or storm—or vice versa. The theme itself is not a novel one—not even novel for the incident here described (cf. BhP 10.50.23–28)—but the poet handles it artfully. He constructs the scene in such fashion that his audience is only gradually able to gain the footholds that enable them to see just what is going on. Many title verses in the *Sūrsāgar* describe clearly the subject of the composition to follow, but in this one the title line does the reverse: it plunges the audience into a confusion of battle and storm by beginning uncharacteristically with the word *mānau*, which means "like" or "as if" and is here translated "it seemed." By putting this word first, the poet prevents his listeners from concluding too soon whether a storm is so intense that it is being compared to a battle, or vice versa. This ambiguity persists all the way through verse 5 and is only resolved with the mention of "Vasudev's two sons"—that is, Krishna and Balarām—in verse 6. At this point the audience knows that the battle is real, and the storm is its metaphor. Even at this, a fair amount of dust remains to settle: Which battle is it? Where was it fought? Not until the locale (Mathura) is mentioned in the penultimate verse and Krishna's enemy (Jarāsandh) revealed in the last verse is the picture complete. Like the citizens of Mathura (v. 13), we do not quite know what has happened until we see "Sūr's Lord" (v. 14) emerge from the confusion of battle in the final verse.

325.11 *heavenly mansions* The kings mentioned here are presumably associates of Jarāsandh, but may also include some subordinate Yādav royalty. The poet attributes their courage to a promise widely assumed in martial literature: anyone who loses his life on the battlefield is heir to a "fine dwelling" (*subasa*, v. 11) in the realm of the gods.

325.14 *vanquished Jarāsandh* Jarāsandh, king of Magadh in the eastern Gangetic plain, is remembered in the *Mahābhārata* and the Purāṇas as one of Krishna's two great enemies, the other being Kaṃs. Indeed, Jarāsandh is the greater of the two. After Krishna had succeeded in killing Kaṃs, Jarāsandh—Kaṃs's father-in-law—went on the attack. Although he lacked the strength to defeat Krishna outright, the eighteen debilitating battles he waged were sufficient to force Krishna and his tribespeople to flee westward from Mathura to Dvaraka. Or so the situation is presented in the *Harivaṃśa*. Subsequent treatments, such as those found in the *Viṣṇu* and *Bhāgavata Purāṇas*, play down the seriousness of this combat and find various ways to avoid conceding that Krishna's Vṛṣṇi forces were ever routed by the Magadhans. The *Bhāgavata* goes so far as to explain that Krishna's several confrontations with Jarāsandh were motivated by a deliberate plan on his part: if he allowed Jarāsandh to regroup repeatedly, he would be able to relieve the earth of even more exponents of evil when the final confrontation came (BhP 10.50.8–9; cf. Sheth, *The Divinity of Krishna*, pp. 62–63).

A similar set of contrasts characterizes the various reports of the first battle in the sequence, presumably the one to which reference is made in the poem at hand. The oldest version, that contained in the *Harivaṃśa*, describes a conflict that focuses clearly on Jarāsandh and Balarām; Krishna is present, but only peripherally. The *Viṣṇu Purāṇa* radically shortens the episode and distributes the warfare vaguely between Balarām and Krishna. By the time the *Bhāgavata Purāṇa* picks up the thread, Balarām's role is even further reduced. Although the *Bhāgavata* still reports as his the actual hand-to-hand encounter with Jarāsandh, it has Krishna masterminding the whole affair and allowing Jarāsandh to be released. One can see Sūr's version as a further progression in the same direction. While both Yādav brothers do appear, Krishna ultimately receives the poet's attention and his accolades. Sūr clearly says that it was Krishna who defeated Jarāsandh (v. 14), although he did not kill him. That deed was left to Bhīm, forming the background of two other poems included in this collection (§335, 336).

326.1 *my friend* The first few words of this poem reveal that one woman is addressing another—the particle *rī* ("my friend") is characteristic in such circumstances—but the poet offers few clues as to the occasion on which the conversation might be taking place. The hearer's attention is deflected from this question as the details of Krishna's appearance are described in the body of this *darśan* poem—first the chariot in which he appears (vv. 1–4), then the Lord himself (vv. 5–8). The unsolved question lingers in the back of the mind, however, and is only answered definitively as the composition draws to a close. At that point the poet names the spectators as "the citizens of Dvaraka" (v. 10), and we know that we are seeing Krishna return to his royal city after the great battle in which he finally defeats Jarāsandh (§325).

326.7–8 *conch . . . gander* The sound of the conch is compared to the cry of the *kalahaṃsa*, the high-flying gander (*haṃs*) so dear to Indian mythology. Yet the visual element is also important, for the gander is white, like the conch, which we see against the background of Krishna's red lips. Their shape resembles lotus petals, and they are probably what the poet means by adducing the simile of "russet waterlilies" (*aruṇa kamala*). This would imply that the whole bird is being compared to the graceful shape of the conch, but it is also possible the poet wants us to see the conch as the bird's head. As Krishna uses his forearms to lift the shell to his lips, the long neck of the *haṃs* would be revealed, with the red lotuses as background scenery.

326.9 *his mother and father* Among those who welcome him are Vasudev and Devakī, his aging parents, and certain manuscripts (B1, B2, J2, J4) add other members of Krishna's family: his brother Balarām and son Pradyumna (*suta bandhu janani pitu*, "son, brother, mother, and father"). The woman who speaks the poem depicts herself as an onlooker in the throng as the tender scene of their reunion transpires.

327.1 *to see Dvaraka* It is understandable that a poet whose life work required him over and over to depict the bucolic joys of Braj might gladly devote a composition or two to urban scenes. We see this enthusiasm clearly in several poems in the *Sūrsāgar* that depict Mathura (§183, 186), Ayodhya (*Sūr's Ocean* §376), or, as here, Dvaraka. The narrative excuse for such a poem—the presence or advent of Krishna or Rām—can be quite thin if the poet's purpose is to focus on the rich environment of the city itself (cf. §183). Sanskrit poets shared this habit, since descriptions of cities constituted one of the marks of a great poem (*mahākāvya*), and the visual analogue can be seen in a wealth of miniature paintings. In both mediums one finds the convention of having heavenly figures gather to witness events on earth (v. 11), and in painting this has a particular force, since the celestials fill out space that would otherwise remain empty. This sense of density, so familiar in the visual arts of India, serves as a suitable component of a cityscape such as the one conjured up in the poem at hand, so it is perhaps no accident that the poet begins with numerous sages and ends with all the gods.

327.2 *Nārad and Sanak* Both figure among the sons of Brahmā, and in the original, both their names are followed by the suffix *ādi*, meaning "and so forth." Each of them introduces a whole class of beings—in Nārad's case, ten sons comprising the first generation of Brahmā's progeny, and in Sanak's case, four sons comprising the second. Nārad and Śanak are celibate; hence the reference to their "dispassionate state" (*virati*).

327.8 *Love* Kāma, here called Madan.

327.9 *mridangam* That is, *mṛdaṅg*. See §3.57, 36.3.

332.1 *Wine* As early as the Kuśāṇa period, the sculptors of Mathura were producing images that show Balarām with a flask, bowl, or cup of wine in his hand, and his womanizing, epicurean qualities have been celebrated ever since. Here Sūr adds his voice to the chorus with a poem that is packed with the delights of sound—alliteration and assonance are frequent—and fairly brims with the kind of drunken life it describes.

332.7 *His strength supports the earth* The poet does not actually tell us who this hero is until the next to last verse, which includes a version of one of his titles, Bhūdhar (*bhū dharaṇa*, "supports the earth"). It refers to the fact that Balarām is an incarnation of the primordial snake Śeṣ, who is said to bear the earth on his hood(s). Yet many other hints are dropped along the way: Balarām's weakness for strong drink (*bāruṇī*, v. 1), his flamboyant habits (vv. 1–3), his characteristic blue garments (v. 3), his bowl of wine (v. 4), the fair color of his skin (v. 7), and his legendary strength (v. 7). The last of these, actually, provides yet another clue, since the word chosen to denote Balarām's might is the short form of the god's own name: *bala* (v. 7). Indeed, the poet discloses this name in a subtle way much earlier in the poem, for *bala* is also its second word ("strength," v. 1).

333.1 *Kālindī, do what I say* This poem gives us a second look at Balarām. Here too we meet the matter of liquor, this time not in the first word of the poem (*bāruṇī*, "wine," §332.1) but in its last (*matavārau*, "drunk," §333.8). Of course, knowledgeable listeners recognize that wine is at issue much earlier on, but part of their pleasure comes from the fact that Sūr withholds the verbal verdict about Balarām's drunkenness until the last verse—and even then delivers it only indirectly, by having Balarām deny it. This is a lovely touch, calling to mind the words every culture must have heard from the lips of its lushes: "I'm not drunk, you know."

As for the episode that reveals Balarām's drunken character, it is perhaps the most famous of all his exploits: the moment when he used his plough to change the course of the Jamunā. The author of the *Bhāgavata Purāṇa* makes an effort to mute the bawdiness of the story, but it is perfectly apparent in earlier versions, particularly that of the *Harivaṃśa*, and Sūr hardly lets the flavor fade. In the *Harivaṃśa* we hear how a drunken Balarām addressed the river as a beautiful woman (*rūpiṇī*) and declared his desire to bathe in her (HV 83.28). Rebuffed, he dug in with his plough, an implement whose shape the *Harivaṃśa* likens to the cobra hood that shields his head. That hood indicates not only Balarām's high status but also his membership in the great clan of serpents or Nāgas (see §16). Thus he lowers his own head as he digs with the plow. In consequence the river is drawn into his drunken state, as it were, and specifically as a woman, even a woman under his sexual control: a wife (*vanitām*, HV 83.32). This renders her unchaste with respect to her proper future husband, the ocean, with whom she desires to unite.

333.5 *spread out your whirlpools* Compared with the *Harivaṃśa*'s telling, Sūr's seems modest, but he does suggest Balarām's drunken sexuality in the peremptory language he uses from the outset. The element of sexual innuendo becomes more explicit when Balarām uses a term that could also refer to a bed: the word *pravāha* denotes both the flow of a river's current ("your water course") and the riverbed itself. Sūr reinforces this in his choice of a verb: even in the *Harivaṃśa*, Balarām is not so crude as to demand the river to "spread out" (*pasārau*).

And spread out from what? Certainly from her self-importance, her sense of her own virtues (*jiya kau guṇa*, v. 3); and from her obstinacy (*satara*, v. 3), her native opposition to him. To construe the word *satara* this way is to associate it with the Sanskrit term *śatru* ("enemy"), but the poet may also intend a pun on the Perso-Arabic *saṭr*, which refers to a line or row and connotes straightness—in this context, even tightness. If this is what Sūr's Balarām has in mind, it adds to his lewd tone. He is telling her to loosen up, and in a sexual sort of way.

335.1 *mounted on Garuḍ* This poem, one of the more dramatic in the *Sūrsāgar*, describes the moment when a messenger arrives from Magadh and makes his appearance at the court of Dvaraka. He acts as emissary of the many kings whom Jarāsandh (cf. §325) has imprisoned in his capital city Girivraj (also called Droṇagiri or Giridroṇī). The words he speaks have been dictated by the imprisoned monarchs themselves, as is made clear by the use of first-person forms in verses 3 (*mama*) and 6 (*hama*).

As one would expect in such a formal petition, considerable time is spent in praising the person to whom the message is sent. In the first two verses, many of Krishna's familiar titles are brought forward—first and foremost *garuḍagāmī*, "you who are mounted on Garuḍ, the bird." The use of this epithet is significant because the kings are hoping for a hasty response, and it is a long way from Dvaraka, on the Arabian Sea, to Magadh, which is situated in the heart of the Gangetic basin. In the last words of the poem Krishna justifies their hope. The poem does not mention it, but the chariot Krishna summons at that point (v. 10) bears the flag of Garuḍ. Hence by the time the poem is complete, Krishna is, figuratively, "mounted on Garuḍ," just as the refrain says he should be.

335.3 *Jarāsandh, blind with drunkenness* The route Krishna will take to Magadh is not direct. He will first go to Indraprastha, where Yudhisthir, eldest of the Pāṇḍav brothers, has begun preparations for an elaborate, two-year-long *rājasūya* sacrifice. Yudhisthir has already erected the sacrificial post (v. 8) upon which a horse will ultimately be sacrificed, and proposes to dedicate the sacrifice to Krishna. Its purpose is to consecrate his reign, and as part of its enactment, representatives will have been sent to each of the cardinal points, assuring that the entire territory claimed by the Pāṇḍav throne has in fact been pacified. The results of these sorties are positive, with one exception: the party dispatched to the east reports that Jarāsandh refuses to submit.

This situation confirms what Krishna hears in the message delivered in the poem we are now considering. Jarāsandh is powerful. As a result of his military prowess, he has been able to imprison many kings at Girivraj—almost a hundred, according to the *Mahābhārata*; fully 20,800, according to the *Bhāgavata* (BhP 10.73.1). These kings warn Krishna of Jarāsandh's obduracy (v. 3) and point to his lack of chivalry by venting their rage at being imprisoned after he had defeated them in battle (v. 4). Such was not the royal code (Mbh 2.20.6–9, but cf. §336). They worry that Jarāsandh's knowledge of the flourishing Pāṇḍav kingdom, as symbolized in the *rājasūya* sacrifice, will cause him to take the form of sacrifice itself (*tadrūpa hvai*, "react in just that mode," v. 8), committing atrocious acts that will produce devastation across the earth. They also fear for themselves, concerned that they will be the most prominent and perhaps the most immediate among Jarāsandh's sacrificial victims. The *Mahābhārata* (2.20.9) hints that he had already imagined such a fate for them in any case. Hence they appeal to Krishna, Jarāsandh's long-time enemy.

335.4 *bhṛṅgi bee* The *bhṛṅgi* is a large, black, bee-like insect that builds its hive of clay and immediately forces smaller insects inside. It buzzes around the outside of the hive while its victims produce a similar sound from within.

335.7 *Bhaum and Keśī* In the list of Krishna's accomplishments that the kings recall to persuade him to come to their aid are several deeds they hope will act as harbingers of their own salvation. The mention of his defeat of Keśī is one, for Krishna did this by forcing his elbow into the horse's mouth and cracking his jaw in two. The poet has the kings make use of the verb *bhidana* ("you split apart") to describe this action, and the kings' choice of words seems to presage the moment when Krishna will break into the prison to liberate them. Metaphorically, this prison is a "mountain cave" (*giri guhā*, v. 4) since the word "mountain" (*giri*) figures in the name of his capital. An even more obvious parallel is created by their mention of the evil king Bhaum, who had imprisoned some sixteen thousand princesses. Krishna subsequently freed them (BhP 10.59).

335.7 *Madhu, Kaiṭabh* Madhu and his twin brother Kaiṭabh were at one point responsible for attacking Brahmā and stealing the Vedas. Born from the wax of Vishnu's own ears as he lay recumbent on the Milk Ocean, these demons secured from Devī a boon that they would be invulnerable; it was this that gave them the wherewithal to start on a rampage in which they asserted their power. Vishnu managed to circumvent the boon by appealing to Madhu and Kaitabh for a counter-boon, which committed them to a conflict with him that they ultimately lost.

335.7 *Mur . . . Bhaum* The demons Bhaum (also called Narak) and Mur appeared as Krishna's opponents during his rule at Dvaraka. Both were protected by seemingly impregnable mountains, which Krishna shattered with his mace. The resonance to Jarāsandh (v. 4) is plain. Krishna ultimately killed both demons by means of his disc, and after thus beheading Bhaum, he released some 16,000 women he had imprisoned (BhP 10.59.1–38). This provides a second resonance to the situation of the kings who appeal to Krishna from Girivraj.

335.7 *Kaṃs's clan* Finally, the kings call to mind Krishna's killing of King Kaṃs, which was indirectly responsible for their present plight. Jarāsandh had married his two daughters to Kaṃs, so when Kaṃs was killed he felt duty-bound to send his armies against Krishna. In a long series of battles, Krishna only barely managed to survive Jarāsandh's onslaught; indeed, he had to retreat from Mathura to Dvaraka to do so. When Jarsandh allied himself with Kālayavan, it seemed that Krishna would finally be overwhelmed, but through a clever stratagem he managed to set the sleeping monarch Mucukund against Kālayavan. It was Jarāsandh's fury at seeing his plans frustrated once again that moved him to imprison whatever other rulers he could find. The kings say it was "for no cause at all" (*binu kāja*, v. 3), and in their case that is true, but Krishna bears an onus of responsibility.

336.1 *He conquered Jarāsandh* Here we have what is effectively a sequel to the previous poem (§335), but we must remember that they were in all likelihood designed as entirely independent compositions, as their separation from one another in most manuscripts suggests. Krishna has now traveled to Girivraj in the company of Arjun and Bhīm, all three of them disguised as Brahmin mendicants. Jarāsandh dutifully receives them as guests. Once admitted to the palace, Krishna reveals his true identity and that of his Pāṇḍav companions, challenging the king to engage in individual combat with whomever of the three he might choose. Jarāsandh opts for Bhīm, who slays him, according to the *Bhāgavata Purāṇa*, by ripping him in two from bottom to top. Actually this is Krishna's vicarious doing, for he signals to Bhīm how Jarāsandh might be defeated by picking up a two-branched twig and tearing it in half (BhP 10.72.42–43, cf. Mbh 2.21.20–2.22.5).

At this point Krishna proceeds to the Girivraj jail and releases the many kings whom Jarāsandh had imprisoned there in the course of his successful battles. In the epic this imprisonment is decried as an act contrary to the *dharma* of a warrior king and deserving of redress (Mbh 2.13.64, 2.14.10–20, 2.20.10–12). In the *Bhāgavata*, by contrast, little interest is taken in the ethics of the situation: the scale of the event and the kings' gratitude absorb the writer's attention instead. The *Bhāgavata* devotes half a chapter (10.73) to recounting the thankful paeans they raised to Krishna on being freed.

336.7 *Holi's crackling fire* The comparison of king's liberation to that of the pious boy Prahlād from the clutches of his evil aunt Holikā or Holī (v. 7, cf. §399) seems entirely original with Sūr. Every year Holī is symbolically consumed in an early morning bonfire that brings on the festival of noisy abandon known by her name; yet by afternoon of the same day a greater peace prevails than perhaps at any other time in the Hindu year (cf. §173). At the most obvious level, then, Sūr's comparison is aural: uproar turns to silence. But at another level he establishes a connection between two acts of deliverance that have, in Krishna (or Vishnu), a common cause.

337.2 *Dvaraka's so close* Here is the story of Sudāmā, and by the time a singer gets to the middle of the second verse, every member of the audience has it clearly in mind. The mention of Dvaraka and a Brahmin in the same breath does the trick, and by the end of that verse there is absolutely no question: Sudāmā's wife is urging her Brahmin husband to go to Dvaraka to plead his poverty before Krishna, Lord of the Yadus. Sūr's listeners know the rest: how Sudāmā became so poor in adulthood—and his wife and children so threatened by starvation—that he availed himself of his last resource. Aware that Krishna had become king of Dvaraka, and urged on by his wife, he went off to seek the monarch's help. All he was able to take as a gift was a few grains of rice (v. 7), which he wrapped in the end of the simple cloth he wore about his shoulders. Sudāmā had not seen Krishna since the days when they were at school together in Ujjain, living at the home of Sāndīpani, their common guru, so he had no way of knowing whether he would be recognized or received by his great friend. Any fears were for naught, however. Krishna received him royally, yet at the same time bringing himself to exactly the same level as his old school chum by immediately consuming the little rice gift he had brought (see §338).

337.6 *a tulsī leaf in exchange* The few grains of rice that Sudāmā tucks away in his clothes are famously the sign of his poverty—even these his wife has had to beg from a neighbor—and that in turn represents the larger cultural stereotype of the poor Brahmin. Sudāmā's wife anticipates the reception that awaits this meagre offering with an allusion to a celebrated verse in the *Bhagavad Gītā* (9.26):

> The leaf or flower or fruit or water
> that he offers with devotion,
> I take from the man of self-restraint
> in response to his devotion. (Miller, *Bhagavad-Gītā*, p. 86)

Sūr is not the first to quote the *Bhagavad Gītā* in connection with the story of Sudāmā: the *Bhāgavata Purāṇa* itself chooses this verse as its point of departure, quoting it in full (BhP 10.81.4). Sudāmā's wife aligns the leaf that opens this *śloka* with the tiny leaf that is understood as being the one dearest to Vishnu, namely, the leaf of the *tulsī* plant. Sūr weaves in the rest of the verse, too, as explained in Hawley, *Sūr's Ocean*, vol. 1, p. 592.

337.7 *set off with the sun* The poet encodes his own presence in this *darśan* scene. The term *sūrija* is a common designation for the sun, and that is its essential meaning here, but it is also a form of Sūr's own name and functions simultaneously as his signature. The unusual position of the signature in the penultimate line, rather than the last, draws attention to this pun.

338.2 *Śrīdāmā* Once again we encounter a poem that reveals Sūr's detailed awareness of facets of the Sudāmā story that emerge in the *Bhāgavata Purāṇa*, some of which appear in the poem's own narrative and some of which are telling in their absence. Sūrdās accords Sudāmā the alternate name Śrīdāmā (v. 2), which appears in the colophon to the *Bhāgavata Purāṇa* 10.80 but not in the text itself. Krishna too is given a distinctive name. He is designated Balabīr, that is, "Balarām's brother" (v. 1).

338.6 *clothes* The manuscripts are not in agreement about what the last word of this line should be—*cīra* ("clothes"), as I have translated, or *bīra* ("friend"). One could make plausible arguments for either alternative, but at Rupert Snell's gentle urging (e-mail communication, July 27, 2008) I have chosen the former against the Bryant edition. The opposite choice, the *lectio difficilior,* would translate as "Why still hide it now, my friend?"

338.8 *he remembered and Kamalā* There is an important ambuiguity about just who is doing the remembering here, one that is hard to carry over into translation. The original gives us only the noun "remembrance" (*surati*), positioning it between the poet's name and Krishna's act of chewing (*sūra surati cāvara cabāta hī*). If we are to understand that Krishna is doing the remembering, we probably find him in a reverie about how he and Sudāmā went looking for fuel at the request of Sāndīpani's wife and were marooned in the jungle overnight by a thunderstorm. Perhaps he also remembered that they had only a little bit of food with them, a detail unknown to the *Bhāgavata* that came to loom large in other versions of the story.

But what about Kamalā—that is, Rukmiṇī? Apparently this is her remembrance too, as the remainder of the line suggests. Her fear seems to arise because she remembers the rest of what Krishna said when he discovered Sudāmā's rice (v. 6), at least as the *Bhāgavata* reports the incident. In recognition of the power of devotion and of a Brahmin's humility, Krishna affirms there that "The beaten rice will satisfy not just me but the entire universe" (*tarpayantyaṅga mām viśvamete pṛthukataṇḍulāḥ*, BhP 10.81.9). With his first taste of rice, he satisfies himself. Rukmiṇī fears that if he were to take a second, he would fulfill his own pronouncement, satisfying the cosmos and inviting it to dissolve. Since Krishna actually is the entire cosmos, he has this power. That is why she grasps his hand: to restrain him and save the world—and at the same time, at least as important, to save him for herself.

Then too, there is the poet's remembrance. In the original, as we have seen, Sūr's name directly precedes its mention (*sūra surati*). Whoever else can claim to own the process of remembering that Sūr calls forth in this striking last verse, surely Sūrdās owns it as well:

> Sūr's remembrance:
> the moment he chewed the rice,
> Kamalā gripped his hand with fear.

For a more detailed analysis of this poem and its dramatic conclusion see Hawley, *Sūr's Ocean*, vol. 1, pp. 593–596 and *Three Bhakti Voices*, pp. 226–231.

339.1 *it left him at a loss* When Sudāmā encountered Krishna after such a long absence, he was so absorbed in restoring his childhood friendship that he quite forgot to achieve the purpose of his visit. The whole point was to get assistance from Krishna and thus save himself and his family from death and ruination, yet Sudāmā was so overcome at the joy of seeing his old friend that he did not even think of such matters. Only on the way home, as he anticipated facing his wife again, did the unpleasant memory of his present straits return. And then, in this state of agitation, he arrived at the place he thought was home, only to find that his simple hut had been changed beyond recognition. Thanks to Krishna, it had been transformed into a palace.

339.8 *set foot inside your home* The words Sudāmā's wife uses to welcome her husband are in the spirit of this grand transformation. Somewhat grandiloquently, she bids him not just enter his new domicile but "place his foot inside" it (*pāu dhāriye*). Finally, the word the poet chooses to designate this "it" is by no means the ordinary word for house. It is the loftier term *dhām*, a word that can refer to "homes" as grand as the cities that house the gods at the four great pilgrimage centers that mark the compass points on the Indian subcontinent. Sūr gives this special term for "home" the place of greatest honor in his poem: he lets it be the last word.

340.4 *Kailāś* The peak at the top of the Himalayas upon which Shiva is said to live, engrossed in meditation. In addition to the impression of divine grandeur that this name calls forth, there is the suggestion that Sudāmā's new house has great height: the *Bhāgavata Purāṇa* tells us the new structure was seven stories high (BhP 10.81.21). The same verse reports that it shone like sun, fire, and moon (*sūryānalendu*), and this may have been the stimulus for what Sūr says in verses 5–6. In the *Bhāgavata*, Sudāmā is overawed to see that shining surface and the various gardens and lotus ponds that surround it, but Sūr turns this vision into further cause for desperation on Sudāmā's part. In his disorientation Sudāmā quotes the common saying "Fate attacks the weak" (*drubala ghātaka bidhi*, v. 5) and goes on to depict himself as a poor lotus that tried to find more water (and perhaps light) than its little jungle pond initially afforded, only to be burned by the much stronger sun that illuminated its new, more open environment. Sūr may have in mind the way snow-covered Mt. Kailāś glistens almost gold in the midday sun, and indeed the word he chooses to designate the sun (*hem*, v. 6) is a close relative of the word for snow (*him*). One is reminded of a contrasting passage in the *Sūrsāgar* where a lotus (*nalinī*, as here) is the victim of frost (*himakar*, *Sūr's Ocean* §308.4). It is possible that the poet has this dimension in mind here too, since the *Bhāgavata* specifies that the mansion's walls were made of clear crystal (*svacchasphaṭika*, BhP 10.81.31).

340.7 *the manse* When Sudāmā initially comes upon the site and looks for his old house, he designates it with the simple term *ghar* (*gharu*, v. 1). But when his wife comes out the door, descends the steps, and bids him enter, she uses a different permutation of the same word—the fancy Sanskrit *tatsam* form *grih* (*griha*, "manse," v. 7) rather than the humbler *tadbhav* Brajbhāṣā alternative (*ghar*). This transformation of language parallels what has happened in Sudāmā's "real world," and recalls the careful use of *dhām* in poem 339 or again the *ghar/grih* disparity in *Sūr's Ocean* §342.

340.8 *wishing tree* The poet likens Sudāmā's new home to the fabled wishing tree (*kalpataru* > *kalapataru*). In ancient literature the *kalpataru* is sometimes depicted as one of five miraculous trees that grow in (Indra's) heaven, but here it is apparently conceived in the more general sense it had come to have by Sūr's time.

347.2 *if . . . I travel there with you* Here, in an episode that apparently has no basis in the classical mythology of Krishna, a *gopī* addresses someone who is traveling to Dvaraka. It seems he has offered not merely to take a message to Krishna for her, but to take along the *gopī* herself as a companion.

347.6 *a connoisseur of love* This composition gives poetic expression to the theology so clearly enunciated by Rūp Gosvāmī in his *Bhaktirasāmṛtasindhu:* there is no meeting point between *aiśvarya ras*, the emotion of lordliness, and *mādhurya ras*, the mood of love. Sūr does not actually use these terms, but he approaches them in interesting ways. In verse 6, he has his *gopī* speak of the Braj-dwelling Krishna as a *rasik*, which we translate "connoisseur of love" because of the way the *Sūrsāgar* typically uses this term to designate one who appreciates the arts of love. This is the erotic *mādhurya* element. Then in the following verse we meet the *aiśvarya* counterpart, the lordliness or majesty *(prabhutā)* featured in the expression *prabhutā rata* (i.e., *prabhutā rati*, J1), its marginal variant *prabhutā laga* (i.e., *prabhutā lagi*, J1), or the critical edition's *prabhutā rasa* (cf. *jo ta rasa*, J2). The phrase *rasika binu* in verse 6 has two possible connotations. Either the *gopī* means that she could hardly explain the meanings associated with the principal features of her native land to someone who was not "a connoisseur of love" or she means she cannot explain what they have become without that connoisseur. Either way—or both—it is clear that for a *gopī* such as this, and particularly for her eyes, love and lordliness do not mix.

355.1 *Nothing now remains* This poem gives a version of the well-known episode in which Draupadī, the common wife of all five Pāṇḍav brothers, was in imminent danger of being denuded and disgraced before the Kauravs. For all its fame, this tale is not included in the critical edition of the *Mahābhārata*, but is listed as an interpolation to the *sabhā parvan*, at 2.68.40 (Franklin Edgerton, ed., *The Mahābhārata*, vol. 2, p. 304). The situation was that the Kauravs, led by Duryodhan, had maneuvered their Pāṇḍav cousins into a game of dice, in which the Pāṇḍavs gambled away everything they had (cf. v. 3). The last and most precious item to be staked in the game was Draupadī herself, and when she was lost, Duryodhan sent his brother Duhśāsan to fetch her. Duhśāsan pulled her by the hair into the midst of the assembly as Duryodhan indecently exposed himself; then he began pulling on her sari.

In this composition Sūr recalls what happened then. Draupadī appealed to Krishna for help, although he was not present, and miraculously he supplied her with infinite lengths of cloth. Sūr anticipates this outcome by having Draupadī imply that in an interior way he had sheltered her all along: she "wore the mantle of [his] mercy" or, more literally, she had the sheltering wrap of his feet (*hutau kahū mana oṭa carana kī*, v. 4). The external manifestation is that the harder Duhśāsan pulled to unravel her sari, the more cloth there was to replace what had been lost. Ultimately he gave up and her honor was saved.

355.6 *sea of compassion* Sūr tells the tale with a nice twist by making creative use of one of the titles most frequently heard when needy devotees address petitions to Krishna. The title is *karuṇāsindhu*, "sea of compassion," and although Draupadī is not depicted as invoking it herself, she reaps its ocean of benefits: "its water, a current of cloth."

356.1 *Mādhav . . . took the wheel* This poem refers to events that transpired on the third day of the great Bhārata war (Mbh 6.55.83ff.) and assumes a knowledge of the way that story is reported in the *Bhāgavata Purāṇa* (especially 1.9.37–39). Bhīṣma, the aged but ever-agile commander of the Kaurav army, was the staunchest devotee (*jana*, v. 2) of Krishna, who had joined the forces of the opposite side as Arjun's charioteer but had vowed never to take an active role in the fighting. It was Bhīṣma's fondest wish to see Krishna arrayed against him in battle, however, and he attempted to provoke Krishna to fight him by raining countless arrows upon Krishna and Arjun, both of whom sustained multiple wounds. When Krishna sensed in Arjun a residual unwillingness to retaliate against Bhīṣma, who was his own elder and preceptor, he feared for Arjun's safety and sprang into the fray himself, thus fulfilling Bhīṣma's wish. In doing so, he broke his earlier oath, "the word of the Veda" (v. 2), but all in the cause of making a countervailing vow come true—the vow of his devotee. Bhīṣma had vowed that he would cause Krishna to take up a weapon in the Bhārata war, and when Krishna reached for the wheel, that vow was complete.

The *Mahābhārata* is content to present this about-face in its own terms, but the *Bhāgavata* is more guarded. Rather than have Krishna simply attack with his own weapon, the *sudarśan* discus (cf. Mbh 6.55.83–86), it depicts him as having been unarmed. He therefore has to reach for the wheel of the chariot he was driving (BhP 1.9.37) and use that as if were his accustomed discus. Sūrdās does not definitively commit himself to the latter position, in that he designates the weapon with the word *cakra* (v. 1), which can mean either "wheel" or "discus," but the fact that he "takes it in his hand" (*kara līnau*, v. 1) does seem to lean in the direction of the *Bhāgavata*. The "fine vision" (*sudarśan* > *sudarasan*, v. 7) that Bhīṣma then saw was at once the gorgeously bloody sight of Krishna that Sūrdās conjures up in verses 5–6 and the disc of that name, whether in function (if it was the chariot wheel) or in essence (if the discus itself).

356.7 *Brahmā saw* The pun on *sudarśan* guides the poem to its completion and introduces another startling juxtaposition. It is this. Clearly the person who sees this vision is Bhīṣma, who bows before Krishna and, according to the *Bhāgavata*, delivers an extended hymn of praise describing what he sees (BhP 1.9.32–36). Bhīṣma is the devotee, servant, or subject (*jana*, v. 2) to whom reference is made near the beginning of the poem. Yet when the vision has been described and the poet uses his signature to indicate that he is about to conclude, he suddenly changes perspective by naming the beholder of the vision not as Bhīṣma but as Brahmā (*birañci*, v. 7). The gods are often thought of as witnessing momentous events in the life of Krishna, so Brahmā's presence makes sense to that degree, but there is a more particular stimulus for the confused manner in which Brahmā reacts to seeing Krishna. He is disoriented by the affinity between the sight of Krishna raising the wheel or discus on his arm and the image of a lotus emerging from the dark waters of a lake on its stem. He finds himself in a powerful time-warp since he himself was emitted from the navel of Vishnu on an umbilical lotus at the beginning of time. Considering the vast destructive power of Krishna's discus, this vision of a return to creation is a stark event, perhaps foreshadowing the new age that will emerge from the global carnage of the great Bhārata war as a whole. In the *Mahābhārata* (6.55.89–90) the simile of the primeval lotus is used to describe the appearance of Krishna's arm and weapon at this moment, but it is apparently Sūr's own invention to bring Brahmā himself on the scene.

357.4 *Like a lion* The content of this poem closely resembles what we are given in poem 356—in fact, they share the first half of verse 3 verbatim—but the mood and perspective differ significantly. Here we see events directly through Bhīṣma's eyes; it is he who speaks. In consequence, the principal metaphor he offers for what he sees—that Krishna's wild hair looks like the dusty mane of a lion moving in for the kill—is more in keeping with his own dramatic situation. It is martial rather than cosmological.

357.5 *Gopāl . . . fulfilled my vow* This vow refers to Bhīṣma's pledge to see Krishna standing before him as a warrior before he dies. To fulfill this wish, Krishna must abrogate his own pledge, his Vedic oath not to step upon the field of battle and take sides in the Bhārata war (BhP 1.9.37). Like the author of the *Bhāgavata*, Sūr depicts Krishna as a person who places the honor and desire of those devoted to him above any other morality, even when the latter is thought of as being sanctioned by the Veda as in the case of a promise that ought to be kept. In both texts—the *Bhāgavata* and the *Sūrsāgar*—the lesson is that with Krishna the religion of bhakti is victorious over its predecessor, the religion of royal and martial *dharma*.

357.6 *so near* When Krishna comes to Bhīṣma's aid, drawing near to fulfill his vow, everyone in the audience knows what form this help will take: death!

359.3 *the Badarī forest* Only in verse 3 does the poet indicate that his subject in this composition is Ūdho. He accomplishes this by telling us that Krishna (*hari*, v. 1) is commanding the speaker to depart for the Badarī (jujube tree) forest. It was Ūdho who received that command, and the knowing audience then quickly understands the source of his consternation. Like that of the *gopīs*, it is caused by separation from Krishna, and it ironic that Ūdho tried to dissuade them from the emotions that accompany such a state.

359.5 *As I come to understand* In the *Bhāgavata Purāṇa*, as the story continues, Ūdho does accept Krishna's charge, and in the course of time he achieves the full reality of Krishna. But Sūr is not interested in any of that. He sticks with the moment that precedes the parting, giving no sense that Ūdho's pain will ever be mitigated. To the contrary, Ūdho's stewardship of knowledge makes his pain all the more intense (vv. 6–8).

359.8 *My deeds cook through* According to the theory of *karma vipāk* (> *karama vipāka*), the "ripening" or "cooking" of karma, actions earn their own recompense, and in kind. Ūdho confesses, in effect, that it is now his fate to suffer the pain he inflicted on the *gopīs* by trying to convert them to his persuasion. They burned at being separated from Krishna. Now, as the last word of the poem (*dahau*, v. 8) makes clear, it is his turn to burn instead.

360.4 *my will . . . my feet* This poem explores the same moment that occasioned the last, but this time an even greater emphasis is placed on Ūdho's tortured ambivalence. Ūdho contrasts the admittedly unhappy obedience of his will (or mind: *mana*) with the total rebellion of his feet. Then interestingly, he turns the ambivalence just the other way around. Borrowing the famous metaphor that concludes the first act of Kālīdās's *Śākuntala* (1.30), he likens his body to a flagstaff, and his mind (or consciousness or heart: *cita*, v. 6) to the flag. The staff—the body—is rigid, but it can be carried off by force, yet there is no way to keep the flag—the mind—from flapping in the wind. It vacillates, and not only that, it vacillates backwards. It points in the direction (literally, "toward the face," *sanamuṣa*, v. 6) of Krishna's feet, that magnet of devotion.

360.7 *this heart of mine* In the final couplet Ūdho seems to reverse course once more. Earlier it was the body that was brittle; now it is the heart (*hṛde*, v. 7). Ūdho cannot fathom how hard it must have become, considering that it does not break upon hearing Krishna's charge.

361.1 *a Brahmin dwarf* The incident described in this poem is the one in which Vishnu/Krishna confronts King Bali by taking the form of a dwarf (*vāman*), who is usually calculated to be Vishnu's fifth avatar. Self-denying rightousness has made Bali great in the earth—so great that his power threatens the hegemony of the gods; Vishnu steps in to restore the gods to their proper degree of influence. As part of a stratagem calculated to reduce Bali's power, he himself adopts a reduced form—that of a diminutive Brahmin, a dwarf—and comes before the king's palace reciting the Vedas. When the upright Bali wishes to reward him for his fine chanting, the dwarf humbly asks for the amount of earth that would fit in the span of three steps, refusing the scale of magnanimity of which kings are capable when pleased with their Brahmin retainers. His purpose, he says, is to erect—or literally "spread" (*chāvana*, v. 4) or thatch the roof of—a hut, the sort that would be appropriate for conducting a fire sacrifice. This seems not only a pious but a modest request, yet in the end it provides Vishnu more than enough scope to conquer Bali. In three remarkable steps he is able to spread himself over the entire world—including, of course, all the king's dominions.

In the Sanskrit Purāṇas, the story is told in two basic forms. According to one version, it takes Vāman his three steps to vault the universe. The first step is a tiny one, but the two succeeding steps are gigantic. According to the alternate version, however, Vāman is able to encompass the universe in only two steps, which precipitated a new problem: how could Bali remain true to his word, since he had offered Vāman three steps? The answer is the answer of devotion. Bali offered himself as the location where the divine dwarf could place his foot the third time. He prostrated himself, and Vāman stepped on his back. For a review of the sources provided by the Sanskrit Purāṇas, see

Deborah Soifer, *The Myths of Narasiṃha and Vāmana*, pp. 128–129. Surprisingly, the tradition that interests Sūr comes not from the *Bhāgavata Purāṇa*, which says that Vāman steps on Bali's head (2.7.18; 8.22.2), but from the *Brahma Purāṇa* (73.51), which prefers the back. A translation of this passage can be found in Clifford Hospital, *The Righteous Demon: A Study of Bali*, p. 127.

In the poem at hand, Sūr presents yet a third version of the story. Here the dwarf playfully asks for three and a half steps (*auṭha peḍa*, v. 4) rather than the customary three. It is the final half-step that causes the problem—or rather, for bhakti, the opportunity (cf. *Sūr's Ocean* §363). In Sūr's telling, this half-step is what remains after Vāman has stepped over the universe, and that is what Bali accommodates by offering his back. When Vāman accepts, we have a touching moment in which the great bows before the small as the emperor humbles himself before the penurious scholar. Yet Sūr's audiences know that the Brahmin is in reality greater than the king; they can supply from memory the events that dramatize this truth. These are events that have directly to do with the dwarf's (Vishnu's) foot, so the poet pointedly concludes with just this word—*pāvana* (v. 6).

361.3 *his feet* It is not accidental that, as the poem begins, it features the visitor's standing pose: he is on his feet. Soon we see the king giving the most solicitous attention to those feet (v. 3)—bathing them and, in an act of humility that is sometimes practiced in *bhakti* circles, drinking the water in which they were washed, as *prasād*. Then, as in the central story, those feet become the focus of the dwarf's request. Everything else—jewels and whole towns (or cows, if we adopt an alternate interpretation of *gāvana*, v. 5)—is kept at bay.

361.6 *his foot* Finally comes the moment when the dwarf's foot enacts the king's step-offering, and here the poet's choice of words is doubly apt. *Pāvan*, the last word in the poem and the climax to which it rises, means not only "foot" but "that which purifies," as in Krishna's celebrated epithet *patit pāvan*, "Purifier of the Fallen" (see §397). The audience recognizes that the touch of Vishnu's foot is precisely the means by which he grants salvation to those who come before him, even when they are not really "fallen" but righteous.

362.3 *the language of animals* Representing Vishnu's fifth descent (Skt. *avataraṇa*) into the welter of earthly affairs, the dwarf incident logically succeeds other descents in which Vishnu becomes wholly or partially an animal, for the dwarf is not quite a full man. The poet gives a small hint of this liminal status when he says that Vāman "understands the language of animals—two legs, four legs, or none." (v. 3). The term *apasu* may either refer to animals not appropriate for sacrifice, a meaning that would stress the priestly expertise of a Brahmin, or it may refer to animals that fit neither the two- nor the four-legged category—reptiles, insects, and so on. One variant construes them as birds (*pakṣī*, A1, B3).

362.5 *his own . . . sacrificial offerings* Bali has gathered a number of seers to perform a sacrifice. Most Purāṇas identify this as a horse sacrifice, but sometimes, as here and in the *Matsya Purāṇa*, no specification is given. The *Kūrma Purāṇa* (1.16.46), interestingly, calls it a sacrifice to Yajñeśvar, "the lord of sacrifice," that is, Vishnu, and the idea echoes elsewhere as well (*Brahma Purāṇa* 73.42, BhP 8.23.15). With this in mind, it is both appropriate and ironic that Vishnu himself—disguised—should arrive and be in attendance (cf. v. 13).

Bali is the principal sacrificer, and the sacrifice is already proceeding: the materials to be offered to the fire (*āhuti*, v. 5) have already been set out. The dwarf chooses precisely this moment to manifest himself, and Bali is sufficiently sensitive to his capacities that despite the advice of his family priest Śukra, preceptor to the *asuras*, he drops everything when the dwarf appears. The king offers him anything he wants if only he will participate. It was the custom that if anyone came begging at the door during a major sacrifice, the sacrificer had the duty to offer largesse, so Bali is eager to comply. And the visitor's status as a Brahmin scholar—a pundit, as the original says (v. 1)—seems to make his hospitality doubly appropriate.

362.18 *gained a whole new realm* The poet depicts the nobility of King Bali at every turn, right down to the last line when he sums up by saying that "he smiled and gave up all" (*hasi sarbasu dīnau*). Not until the following phrase does either the king or the poet's audience learn that Bali receives anything in return. As the story goes, Vishnu rewards him by making him the ruler of *sutal lok*, the third level of the netherworld (e.g., BhP 8.22.32). There Bali will rule until he becomes Indra in a subsequent emanation of the world.

6. *RĀMĀYAṆA*

366.1 *this jungle . . . Jānakī* Here Rām is speaking to Lakṣmaṇ, bewailing the loss of Sītā (through her patronymic Jānakī), whom Rāvaṇ has stolen away. Thinking of little else as he makes his way through the wilderness, he sees this theft everywhere, blaming it not on Rāvaṇ but on the jungle itself. In this guise the poet asks us to consider whether the horror of the fact of the theft is perhaps exceeded by the way in which it is accomplished. If Sītā were simply absent, that would be one thing, but the forest simultaneously provides a cruel illusion of her presence. It furnishes the flora and fauna that would normally appear not in their natural form but as terms of comparison for describing Sītā's beauties. Which is the real, and which the copy? That is the dementia induced in Rām by Sītā's absence, at least as seen through a poet's eyes.

366.3–6 *The lion has her waist* A number of standard similes appear in this composition. Lions and beautiful women are alike in having slim waists (v. 3), and the koel, the Indian cuckoo, shares with a lovely woman its mellifluous voice. An attractive woman must have the wide eyes of deer (v. 4) and pure white skin that resembles the bloom of the *campā* flower (v. 5). The seeds of the pomegranate resemble Sītā's teeth, both because they are arranged in neat rows and because their light, almost translucent tone contrasts to the deep red of the fruit's skin (v. 5). The deliberate, graceful walk of the *haṃs* or *marāl* bird ("swan," or more properly "ruddy goose," v. 6) is an appropriate feature of female beauty, and the brilliant red flower of the *bandhūk* plant (v. 6) corresponds to the color of her lips.

Although these similes are standard, Vidyut Aklujkar has made the intriguing argument that the particular ones arrayed here may not have been assembled for the first time by Sūrdās. Six of the ten he mentions are also clustered together in the Sanskrit play *Hanumannāṭaka* (act 5, verse 3), probably composed in stages between the tenth and fourteenth centuries (Aklujkar, "Battle as Banquet," pp. 358, 360). Although they appear there in a different order and with certain variations of detail, it is striking that both sets of verses—the Sanskrit and the Brajbhāṣā—refer to the same point in the Rām narrative. Aklujkar's suggestion is that Sūr knew the *Hanumannāṭaka.*

366.8 *his own* After Rām has catalogued these erstwhile similes, the poet returns us, in the final words of the poem, to one of the key words in the first line: *nija*, the adjective describing what is one's own. In the opening line Rām had used this word to address Lakṣmaṇ as "my own little brother." But the other person who had belonged to him—Sītā, the third member of their wandering triad—is gone. When the poet uses this word a second time, in concluding, he not only reminds us of the power of that loss, but states that in a sense Rām has disappeared as well. He has lost all sense of the majesty that is rightly his—"his own"—in consequence of his absorption in her. Sītā has been stolen by the forest, and Rām by Sītā.

367.1 *Now that you've seen me* The person who speaks in this poem is Sītā. After considerable effort, Hanumān, an emissary of Rām, has located her in the grove of *aśok* trees where Rāvaṇ holds her prisoner in Lanka. Rāvaṇ has given her a year to determine whether she would prefer to marry him or die; of this period, ten months have already elapsed. When Sītā begins by saying "Now that you've seen the state I'm in," she knows that Hanumān has seen a great deal indeed.

367.2 *guard the breaths* The poet conveys a sense of Sītā's great courage not only by highlighting her preference for silence over complaint (vv. 1, 5), but by having her present herself not as victim but as warrior. Rather than dwelling on her own imprisonment, she reverses the picture and depicts herself as a guard (*paharau*, v. 2; cf. *rāṣati*, "restrain," v. 4). Her unruly charge is her own life, which is eager to put off its current entanglements and escape into the peace of death. In typical Indian fashion, Sītā refers to her life as a series of "breaths" (*prānani*, v. 2)—the English translation reduces them to one "lifebreath"—and describes how they clamor for release through the main gate of egress, her mouth (vv. 3–4). Rather than allowing them to do so by emitting a series of deep sighs, she channels them into an invocation of the name of Rām. This works very well, for each time she intones his name, the sighing, open-mouthed vowel "ah" is followed by the labial "m." This makes the lips close, and the sigh—the breath—is time and again prevented from escaping.

367.5 *so humble a thing* The penultimate verse can be interpreted in more than one way. The option chosen for translation in the main text emphasizes Sītā's characteristic modesty: *itanī bāta* is rendered "so humble a thing." It is also possible, however, that the poet has a strategic aim in mind when he has Sītā return to the theme of wanting to say only a little (*itanī bāta*, "just this much"). Her laconic brevity may be caused by a desire not to attract the attention of Rāvaṇ's guards to her conversation any more than necessary—perhaps for Hanumān's sake more than her own. We might translate:

Hanumān, it causes me to feel some fear
even when I tell this much to you.

On either interpretation this verse gives us a last glimpse of Sītā's noble restraint before the dam bursts, in the last line, and we hear just how great her suffering is—but again, in precious few words.

369.2 *this jewel* This poem also reports on Hanumān's visit to Sītā in the *aśok* grove, and, reading it in this collection, it is easy to forget that it would very likely have been independent in its original performance setting. This gave Sūr the opportunity to disguise its narrative location until halfway through the second verse, when he begins to give it away by mentioning a certain jewel (*mani*). Then, if we are quick, we recognize the voice as Sītā's, and in the third verse that fact becomes plain. Thus our memory becomes clear at just the same time when Sītā herself speaks about memory—and that, for the sake of causing Rām to remember.

369.2 *my name . . . Raghunāth* The poet emphasizes Sītā's proverbial modesty by constructing what she says in such a way that although she talks of her own name, the name she actually pronounces is one of the public titles of her husband: Raghunāth. Yet what she is about to do—namely, send Rām the jewel with which she once tied her hair (*cūḍāmaṇi*)—is a gesture that requires a certain abrogation of modesty. Sītā must convey her feelings of loss and abandonment, which she measures against the recollection of better times, and that means recalling those times in the presence of Hanumān, who is by sex if not species another man. "Monkey, how can I say it?" (*kahā kahūṅ kapi*, v. 4), she asks. He is to be merely the messenger, of course—really she is addressing Rām—but as she compromises her marital privacy in this way, we too have the privilege of being able to listen in.

369.3 *on the banks of the Mandākinī* Sītā recalls one moment from their intimate history—something that happened when they were alone, something only she could know—as a way of signaling to Rām that the message Hanumān will be conveying is genuine. As in Vālmīki (5.36.12–31) and the *Adhyātma Rāmāyaṇa* (5.3.53–60; cf. RCM 3.1–2), she turns to the time when Lakṣmaṇ was not present as she and Rām bathed together in the River Mandākinī, which flows by Citrakut. Yet the moment she recalls is not exactly the one to which the two Sanskrit *Rāmāyaṇas* draw primary attention. They depict Sītā as calling to mind an attack on her by a crow—an attack between the breasts in the southern recension of Vālmīki, but to her toe in the more prudish *Adhyātma Rāmāyaṇa*—and Rām's vivid response: how he invested the energy of the miraculous *brahmaśiras* weapon into a blade of grass and hurled it at the crow, extracting its right eye in punishment. The import of the remembrance is clear: if Rām was so protective of Sītā then, why does he not come to her aid now?

Sūr's Sītā is different. She is so completely enveloped by ties of love, it seems, that she neglects to mention the episode of the crow, which would introduce a third being and in that way compromise the remembered lovers' idyll. Instead, she moves on to a moment of complete privacy, one that savors not of heroism but of *śṛṅgār*, the realm in which love is expressed in beauty and ornamentatation rather than in conflict and protection. The moment she recalls is the one in which Rām, seeing that Sītā's *tilak* mark had been erased as she bathed with him (both in the river and in his embrace), sets a new one on her brow, using the red ochre available in the forest. In that moment they would both have had to be still, in an exquisite face-to-face encounter (*muṣa muṣa jori*, v. 4). Sītā's memory of this incident does appear in Vālmīki (5.38.4–5), but it occurs alongside her mention of the blade of grass Rām turned into a weapon. Here, by contrast, we have only the loving intimacy, and no intruder. Of course, our knowledge of the unmentioned intruder in Sītā's current situation—Rāvaṇ—hovers over the entire scene, but that merely heightens the wonder of Sītā's intense concentration on nothing else but love.

369.3 *the memory of love* It is possible to take the term *surati* not just as "memory" but also, through a different derivation, as "loveplay"; hence the translation, "the memory of love." The future implied by that past is Sītā's desire to see Rām again, and just as the word "memory" (*surati*) is heavy with religious overtones, so Sītā invokes this future in the language of religion. She asks to be shown Rām's "image" (*mūrati* < *mūrti*, v. 6). At an obvious level this is the simple sight of him, but in a more specific way it is also the sort of image one might find in a temple or on an altar, with its power to save (v. 6). Sūr also likes to make use of this double meaning when his *gopīs* speak of remembering Krishna, and one tantalizing parallel even involves the memory of erotic play on a riverbank (*Sūr's Ocean* §292).

369.4 *if I say it, it'll be now* A poignant aspect of Sītā's speech is her hesitation (cf. §367). Perhaps the cause of this is modesty, but perhaps she also fears that activating the memory of Rām in words will cause her further remorse.

369.6 *this awful flaw* The poet refers to her present torment with strong alliteration—*dusaha doṣa duṣa* ("this awful flaw, this pain," v. 6). The "flaw" or "wrong" (*doṣa*) from which Sītā asks to be delivered is often felt, among those who revere her, to be not just the wrong committed against her—the abduction—but the sin she involuntarily commits by being apart from the man she loves and serves. Yet judging by her words in this poem, she has in mind neither that nor the lapse of Rām's protection of her. It seems, instead, that the great "flaw" to which she refers is the simple fact of their separation. The ideal, healing moment she pulls forth from their past in Citrakut epitomizes not Rām's ability to rescue her but the completeness of their love—"face joined to face" (*muṣa muṣa jori*, v. 4), as the original literally says. The absence of that union is the unendurable flaw in her present life, and only the sight of Rām can wipe it away.

370.2 *the Sāraṅg bow* The weapon by which Rām is known. Sāraṅg (< Śārṅga) means "horned."

370.3 *Yama, Kuber, and Indra* As apparent supporters, Rāvaṇ has deities who rule three points of the compass—south, north, and east, respectively—and the fourth, Varuṇ, is already in Rāvaṇ's camp because he controls the sea, which Rāvaṇ rules from his island, Lanka. The special knowledge attributed to these three divinities—namely, that Rām is actually a form of Vishnu (vv. 3–4)—gives a hint of what the outcome of the battle will be, but this knowledge is not transmitted to Rāvaṇ.

370.4 *light from the sun* The very hypostasis of night, Rāvaṇ is unprepared for his confrontation with the sun. That sun is Rām, who earns the association because the Raghu dynasty, of which he is the leader (*raghupati*), is among those that trace their ancestry to the sun (*sūryavaṃśa*). There is also the suggestion that his arrows are the sun's rays: they glisten (v. 2; cf. *Sūr's Ocean* §368.4–5).

370.5 *many drums sound* In the last two verses, the sense of Rāvaṇ's impending doom becomes even more palpable. In the title line, Sūr had focused on his battle roar, and now he returns to that theme, specifying that this is the cry of the leader of a fighting force, "the vanguard battle cry" (*agahuṇḍi*, v. 6). He likens it to the boistrous drumroll that is sounded as a woman who has decided to become *satī* processes to the pyre. The demon (*asura*, v. 6) who shouts this cry is Rāvaṇ, and he is said to be already in Death's power. The name Sūr chooses to designate Death (Yama) at this point is Antak, "the one who brings an end to things" (v. 6), and Rāvaṇ's end is indeed at hand as he walks into the brilliant sacrificial conflagration that will express the full power of the sun.

372.6 *Shiva smiles and weeps* Rām is Shiva's devotee, but Rāvaṇ is too, so on the one hand he laughs with pleasure to see Rām's impending victory and on the other he bemoans the fact that he cannot bring well-being to Rāvaṇ. The failed "promise" (*bacana*) of which mention is made seems no more specific than that.

372.8 *the twelve suns rise* When time maintains an orderly succession, these twelve are associated with the twelve months of the year—the sun governing each is accorded a special name—but at the time of cosmic dissolution (*pralaya*) time folds in on itself and they are gathered into a single brilliant blaze.

372.15–18 *the sighs of Sītā . . . ants* The heat released in the sighs of a woman separated from her beloved are proverbial (cf. §367), but here they are drawn out of their familiar amorous context into a very different, martial world. The heat first kindled by the poet in verse 8 culminates in a full forest fire (vv. 15–17), the description of which takes us through the penultimate verse. Then in the final line, with a characteristic shift, Sūr changes his metaphor to speak not of burning but crushing. This enables him to conclude an expansive composition that involves the pantheon, the heavens and depths, and all points of the compass with—what else?—ants (*kīra*, v. 18).

374.1 *Look, there he is!* This composition celebrates the moment when Rām returns to his natal city of Ayodhya after vanquishing Rāvaṇ at Lanka. The chariot he rides, called Puṣpak, is a huge, shining affair that speeds across the sky as the monkeys in Rām's army race across the forest treetops beneath. The monkeys are his vanguard, showing the way (v. 4), and they present an astonishing sight to the residents of Ayodhya, who have had no word of Rām's adventures in the jungles of the south (v. 9). Much of the interest of the poem, therefore, turns on the simple fact of Rām's needing to make introductions from one side to the other. Given Sūr's preoccupations throughout the *Sūrsāgar*, it comes as no surprise that distance and separation are the motifs from the *Rāmāyaṇa* that fascinate him most. Here, however, they form the background for a celebration of their opposite, a great reunion.

374.7–9 *Vasiṣṭa . . . Daśarath* Daśarath fathered Rām, Bharat, and the twins Lakṣmaṇ and Śatrughna by three separate wives. Bharat is the half-brother of Rām who served as his regent while he was absent from the throne of Ayodhya. Śatrughna also remained in Ayodhya during Rām's exile, and is therefore the other of the two "younger brothers" whom Rām introduces to his animal army in verse 6. Nor is Lakṣmaṇ absent from the scene. In verse 9 we have an implicit reference to him as one of the two "sons of Daśarath [who] went into the forest." Among the residents of

Ayodhya yet to be mentioned are the general population, whom Rām presents as "my beloved subjects" (v. 6), and last but not least, his preceptor Vasiṣṭha (vv. 7–8). Vasiṣṭha served as the intimate advisor of Daśarath, thus becoming the guru of the entire royal family, so by both age and rank he deserves the special attention that Rām accords him. It is he to whom Rām speaks the first, brief account of his adventures while absent from Ayodhya (vv. 8–11).

374.12 *his servants' praise* Sūr adds a nice touch to the final verse by calling back into service at that point the word *jan*, which we translated "subjects" when it occurred in verse 6, referring to the citizens of Ayodhya. On the face of it one might expect that these are once again meant when, in concluding, Sūr speaks of Rām's proclivity to deflect attention from himself and "sing his servants' praise" "as he enters his city." Yet the "praise" that rings in our ears just then is not praise for them, but for his monkey ally Sugrīv, his fighting partner Vibhīṣaṇ, and Rām's simian army. These are the ones who have turned back the "burn" of separation ("what burned them," *taba ju jarata*, v. 10) through the burning of Lanka. Thus the poet makes the point that Rām's realm, as represented by the subjects (*jan*) who belong to him, is far wider than might be included in any city's boundaries. Were it not for these outsiders, in fact, Rām's subjects in the narrower, more formal sense—the citizens of Ayodhya—would never have seen him again. Hanumān, Sugrīv, and the rest have been his subjects (or "servants," v. 12) by ascription, not birth or law.

Hence we arrive at a third level of meaning present in the term *jan:* "devotee." This sense is almost always felt when *jan* is used in a bhakti context, as here, and it is not surprising to have it surface when a poem typically spreads its net the widest—in its concluding verse. By having Rām introduce his Ayodhya *jan* to his jungle *jan*, Sūrdās suggests yet a third type: a wide community of "devoted subjects" or simply "people" who might hear this poem and sense something of the fealty that ties the first two groups to Rām.

377.1 *you who know from within* This hymn of praise to Rām celebrates his prowess in battle from a bhakti point of view. As the two elements in the title line suggest, his heroic actions spring from his sympathy for those he regards as within his orbit and charge. He too dwells in the "dreadful wilderness" (v. 3) that they inhabit, so he "understands [his] servants' [or subjects'] pain" (v. 2). The latter phrase is almost a gloss on the title "one who knows from within" (*antarajāmī*, v. 1), which in Upaniṣadic times meant "one who controls from within" but as the centuries passed came to refer to powers more of perception than of control (cf. §359.2, 397.7).

377.3–4 *Bāli . . . Sugrīv* The episodes chosen to illustrate Rām's passionate protection of those who cling to him are those having to do with conflicts between brothers. Verses 3 and 4 concern the rival monkey kings Bāli and his brother Sugrīv. After a series of incidents for which he bore no fault, Sugrīv was intently pursued by Bāli and ultimately allied himself with Rām, who found a way to slay Bāli and install Sugrīv as king.

377.5–6 *ten-headed forest fire of rage* Rāvaṇ and his brother Vibhīṣaṇ form a similar pair to Bāli and Sugrīv. Rāvaṇ's identity is announced by his title "ten-headed"; his anger against Vibhīṣaṇ, for siding with Rām, is described as a forest fire; the breezes that fan it are Rām's sighs on account of being separated from Sītā, whom Rāvaṇ holds hostage; and when Rām rescues Vibhīṣaṇ from Rāvaṇ's hot anger, it is with the "well-drawn" (*sukarasita*, v. 6) water of his tears of affection. Rām greets him with these tears when Vibhīṣaṇ arrives in his camp, to struggle against Rāvaṇ. Once again, then, it is the innocent brother expelled from his position of royal authority—this time Vibhīṣaṇ, this time in Lanka—who was defended by Rām. And again the end result was that he was installed as king.

377.8 *Rāmacandra* The title Raghubīr ("hero of the Raghus," v. 1) refers to Rām by locating him in the clan named after ancient king Raghu, a member of the solar dynasty. It closely resembles the title Raghupati ("Lord of the Raghus," §§370, 374). Rāmacandra ("the moon Rām," v. 8) is the most familiar variant on the name Rām and has a summational effect.

7. THE POET'S PETITION AND PRAISE

384.1 *ignoring Hari* In other poems in which Sūr confesses a misspent life, he tends to portray himself as a down-and-out, but here he depicts himself as having lived in style (vv. 3, 4, 6). Hence when he says he lived "without remembering Hari" (*hari sumirana binu*, v. 1), it sounds somewhat less like forgetfulness than willful neglect.

386.1 *that cow* The poet never actually names his elusive cow, yet there are a few clues. Hearing the poem as a whole, we find ourselves forming a collective impression of a "cow-of-the-senses," and indeed in its classical usage the Sanskrit word *go*, to which Brajbhāṣā *gāi* ("cow") is related, does indeed have "the senses" as its major second meaning, after "cow." Certain of Sūr's hearers would doubtless make this association right away. Others, less literate, might take a cue from a popular etymology that is sometimes offered for the name Mādhav, the title of Krishna which Sūr uses as the very first word in this poem. The name Mādhav is actually a patronymic. Madhu and Yadu are the two great ancestors of the Vṛṣṇi clan, but the derivative forms Mādhav and Yādav end up customarily denoting different entities: Krishna in the first instance, and his clan in the second. Not everyone knows this, however, and a folk etymology has emerged which constructs Mādhav from the words *māyā* and *dhav*, so that it means "master of illusion."

In fact, these two rather different approaches ultimately converge. From a subjective point of view, the cow represents the senses: their voraciousness eats up the world. From an objective point of view, however, the cow is *māyā*, the magical power of illusion that gives the senses such overwhelming force. It is hard to disentangle the two, and that is part of the reason the poet must appeal to Mādhav for help.

386.3–4 *Veda-tree . . . eighteen jars* The poem derives some of its attraction from the enumerations that appear throughout. It is possible that the phrase *nigam drum* (v. 3) is meant to be understood as plural, in which case one would have four Veda-trees rather than the one indicated here. The number eighteen, which appears in the next verse, refers to the Purāṇas, and to make the sense clear we have included that word in the translation.

386.5 *six kinds of taste* See §24.2.

386.8 *fourteen worlds* Seven above the earth, seven below.

386.10 *all three elements* The poet's final enumeration invokes the familiar picture of the universe as woven together from three qualities (*triguṇ*): the slothful, passionate, and truthful. These are often associated with colors—dark (here *nīla*, "dark blue," v. 9) for sloth, red for passion, and white for truth or purity. The poet links these with portions of the cow who has conquered the world (v. 9). In so doing, he suggests a pun on the word *triguṇ* (v. 10). On the one hand, it clearly denotes these three qualities specifically. They are manifest in the cow as three segments of its body—lower, middle, and upper—and they appear in the poem as two related triads: first hooves, belly, and horns (v. 9); then nails, heart, and head (v. 11). But the word *triguṇ* also has a second, more general sense. It means "threefold," suggesting the enormous size to which the cow has grown. This size makes it easy for her to deal with the massive, threefold world, and commensurately hard for anyone living inside that same phenomenal world to cope with her.

386.12 *deftly decorated* Another pun is concealed in the word *birañci* (or *biraci* in certain manuscripts), which, when coupled with *raci*, as here, means "decorated deftly." When it appears alone, however, *birañci* has a very familiar meaning that builds on this idea of deft creativity. *Birañci* is a title of the creator god Brahmā. This gives the phrase *raci birañci* a second sense, according to which the cow's head has "created the Creator." Her uppermost part has taken over—and perverted—the supernal role once exercised by Brahmā, and indeed it is her head that she uses to battle with the gods, who are denizens of the upper world. She upends them with a buck of her horns (v. 11).

386.13 *Nārad and the rest* In the penultimate verse the poet's schemes of enumeration break down. He grinds to a halt, reporting that even divine sages such as Nārad and ascetics like Śuk and Sanak (see §327.2) have worn themselves out chasing this cow-of-the-senses. The poet's own fatigue is suggested by the fact that he contents himself with the vague pluralizer *ādi* ("and the rest," "and so forth") in naming their cohort; the word is almost formulaic in this context. Indeed, Sūr must be exhausted after trailing this cow from verse to verse, and in the final verse he says so. He expresses his exasperation outright: how can his words ever capture her?

389.2 *fetal blood* Hindu rituals treat birth as a joyful event, particularly when a boy is born, but it is simultaneously polluting, since it involves organic remains and great quantities of blood. It is on this latter aspect that the poet fastens here. He looks with horror at the womb and the vagina so as to strip away all bodily pride from the sinner to whom he addresses himself—quite possibly himself, first and foremost.

389.2 *harsh karmic past* Most aspects of the poet's references to the physiology of conception and gestation are sufficiently obvious that they require no comment, but a word may be in order about the moral dimension—the relation of past actions (in this case "the harsh karmic past," *kaṭhina karama*) to present birth. On this point the range of theory is considerable, but the central conception would be that the newly gestating embryo is animated by a subtle body (*sūkṣma śarīra*) whose qualities are constituted from traces of past deeds and thoughts. This subtle body is the vessel for a life-essence that is variously named. It becomes manifest in the corporeal realm during intercourse. Then, as the classical medical text *Suśruta Saṃhitā* says, in sexual excitement "through the intermingling of heat and wind the seed flows forth; it enters the womb and combines with the menstrual blood" (*Suśruta Saṃhitā* 3.3, as translated by Heinrich Zimmer in *Hindu Medicine,* p. 187).

390.2 *toiling like a dog* Except in urban, middle-class enclaves influenced by European ways, the dogs of India are anything but carefully bred, well-coddled household pets. Some do serve as guards and are fed by their masters, but they are rarely encouraged to come inside. Many others are left to fend for themselves in the streets and fields, where they are lean, sometimes diseased, and often bruised from a life of fighting with one another over territory and scraps of food. Regarded as unclean because of their carnivorous habits, they often receive little better treatment from human beings than they do from fellow canines. To choose such freedom is to sentence oneself to a life of very hard labor.

391.1 *your devotion* As this poem begins, one thinks one knows what one is hearing. From the sound of the title line, this seems to be a composition of the classical *vinaya* sort, in which the poet humbly requests the only boon that is ultimately worth asking for: devotion (*bhakti* > *bhagati*) to the god before whom he bows. But that seemingly simple, prayerful mood is soon broken (v. 3), so the audience revises its expectations, understanding this now to be a poem of the "best of sinners" (that is, worst of sinners) type, which Sūr also develops elsewhere (e.g., §397). His apparent purpose is through confrontation to shame the Lord into submission: what will people think if they see a reprobate wailing unheeded at the door of someone whose reputation is built on being merciful to those most in need of mercy (*kṛpā-nidhi*, v. 13)?

391.7 *Once there was a time* Sūr recalls an incident recorded in the *Bhāgavata Purāṇa* (1.16–17), in which a personified version of the *kali* age flails and tortures the bull of *dharma* and the cow of Earth. These are the cattle (*pasu*) to which he laconically refers in verse 7. In translating, we offer the phrase "cattle of truth" to help supply the context; in the original, the poet calls forth this knowledge from his audience. They are expected to remember that in the *Bhāgavata Purāṇa* the cow weeps from weakness, and the bull is forced to hobble about on a single leg. The *kali* age, after hunting down these two creatures, would have gone on to kill them as well, but King Parīkṣit, a descendent of Krishna, comes to the rescue. Parīkṣit is ready to rid the earth immediately of the scourge of *kali,* but *kali* begs for his life. Parīkṣit honors this act of self-denigration by banishing *kali* rather than killing him. He purifies the realm in which *dharma* and the earth live by dispatching *kali* to a region inhabited by five species of unrighteousness.

The mention of Indra in verse 8 may be a further reference to this episode told in the *Bhāgavata Purāṇa*, for a scarcity of rain is mentioned there as one of the manifestations of the reign of *kali* (BhP 1.16.20), and Indra is the god of rain. Or Indra's role may be more general. He is traditionally reckoned the leader of the gods, who are said to suffer for want of sacrifices in the *kali* age (BhP 1.16.20). Sūr returns to this theme when he alludes to his own *kali*-like condition (v. 10), saying that his atrocious acts caused the gods to flee before him in shame when they found themselves impotent to stop him.

391.9 *burned myself alive* Sūr highlights his repeated resolve to take his own life, an act that Hindus reckon a very serious crime. He describes three sorts of suicides he has accomplished, and in verses 11–12 he boasts that he has committed them numerous times.

391.14 *Toss me out* To be touched by the Lord at all, even in anger and disgust, is its own form of blessing, and the Vaishnava tradition records that many a demon was rescued from perdition in just this way (cf. §55.5). Just as opposition is the appropriate form of bhakti, given who Sūr is, so the bhakti he craves in response is a rough devotion, a commitment to a real confrontation.

397.2 *Purifier of the Fallen* This poem is a member of the group that presents Sūr's most frequently heard challenge to Krishna's reputation. In it the poet questions the efficacy of Krishna's title as *patit pāvan*—"purifier of the fallen" or "savior of sinners"—and does so by asking how, if the name fits, he himself could have escaped salvation. After focusing on this one name throughout the first six verses, the poet shifts ground and uses the tripartite stretto so familiar in the penultimate line to introduce three of Krishna's other titles: *syāma sundara*, "the beautiful dark one"; *kamala naina*, "lotus-eyed"; and [*sakala*] *antarajāmī* (i.e., *antarjāmī*), "the one who knows [us all] inside." These could be expected to herald a marked change of mood, since as a group they are normally found not in the *vinaya* corpus, as here, but in poems that describe Krishna's loveliness and his loves. Often Krishna's lovers use these terms of address: even *antarjāmī* ("clairvoyant, perceptive of what is within") can be used by a *gopī* to designate a consummate lover's power to detect what is in the mind of someone who loves him (see *Sūr's Ocean* §107).

397.8 *cruel . . . crooked . . . craves* For all its promise, this shift of approach from accusation to appeal does not achieve its result by the time the poem concludes. Rescue is not yet at hand. Instead, the change of mood merely enables the audience to listen afresh to the poet's description of his own character, which he supplies in the words that conclude the poem. He offers a trio of terms that answer, implicitly, to the three titles he has just used to characterize the Lord. He says he is one "who is cruel, who is crooked, who craves" (*kūra kuṭila kāmī*, v. 8). In the original this self-description is even sharper to the ear than its alliterative translation would imply, since two other words in the last line—five of a total seven—also begin with "k." Furthermore, they contrast to the softer sibilant alliteration used to characterize people of the opposite type at the beginning of verse 5: *sukṛtī suci sevaka* [*janu*]. These words mean (in an altered order) "virtuous, obedient, pure," as translated above, but one would need a more roundabout rendering such as "virtuous, venerating, valued" to convey the way in which their sound runs parallel to, yet veers away from what the poet later says about himself. If the worthy of this world are "virtuous, venerating, valued" (v. 5), then the poet-sinner is "cruel, crooked, crude" (v. 8). Why have these qualities not attracted the Purifier of the Fallen?

399.1 *Rām* In the most convincing manuscript tradition (J1, B2) the "God" to whom reference is made is called Rām, but that term is here used in its overarching sense, not its sectarian one. As the body of the poem makes clear, "Rām" includes at least the other avatars of Vishnu, and not Rāmacandra alone. A similar catholicity would be implied by the variant Hari (U1), and a series of manuscripts avoid the quandary altogether by omitting any specific designation for the deity being described.

The poem gives a broad roster of figures who have benefitted from Vishnu's divine touch—both demons and devotees, as in similar lists elsewhere. Some of these encountered Rāmacandra; others, Krishna; still another, Narasiṃh.

399.2 *the four goals of life* The first person on the list is Sudāmā, the penurious boyhood friend of Krishna whose boon from Krishna as monarch of Dvaraka (§339, etc.) is generalized so that he attains "the four goals of life (*cāri padārath*), that is, the four ultimate aims for which a person can strive. These are *dharma*, *artha*, *kāma*, and *mokṣa*—righteousness, gain, pleasure, and release.

399.5 *Prahlād* The son of the demonic Hiraṇyakaśipu, who was attacked by his father for his devotion to Vishnu. In many tellings of the story, Hiraṇyakaśipu first enlisted the services of his sister Holikā, hoping to incinerate Prahlād in her lap, since she possessed a boon rendering her immune to burning (§336). But Vishnu intervened to reverse the fate of these two, and later, when Hiraṇyakaśipu attacked in person, Vishnu assumed his man-lion avatar (Narasiṃh) to save his youthful devotee from death. Narasiṃh emerged suddenly from a pillar in Hiraṇyikaśipu's palace when the latter struck it to ridicule Prahlād's assertion that Vishnu is everywhere—even in stones, trees and, yes, pillars. Thus Vishnu "justified the claim he made."

399.5 *Indra . . . a sage* The famous encounter between Krishna and Indra took place at Mount Govardhan (see §55). The reference to Indra's being made wise would apparently involve the revision in Indra's estimation of himself caused by his acknowledgment of Krishna as his superior. For someone who regarded himself as the captain of the gods (*surapati*), this was a profound act of learning.

399.6 *Sūrdās . . . without his very eyes* At the opening of the final verse, the poet places himself on the list of persons benefiting from Vishnu's generosity—and definitively so. For while it is possible, even usual, in the *Sūrsāgar* to omit any explicit grammatical connection between the poet's signatory name and the content of what he utters—the verb "says" is merely understood—here he uses the postposition *ko* to ensure that his name be understood as an integral part of the body of the poem. As soon as this *ko* is sounded, the hearer knows that Sūrdās intends himself to be a recipient of the Lord's benefaction, just like all the others.

Our translation suggests that the reference is to the poet's physical blindness—or at least a severe visual impairment—and if that is correct, it is the only such reference in this early stratum of the *Sūrsāgar*. The poet hardly understands this condition as a sign of grace, as some later hagiographies tried to make out by claiming that Sūr demanded blindness as a favor from Krishna, to protect his internal, supernal vision from being sullied by worldly sights. To the contrary, the poet seems here to be demanding the restoration of his vision as evidence of God's active involvement in his world. It is unclear whether Sūr is aligning himself with the demons he had listed or with the devotees, but his mixing of the two suggests that the question ought not to matter. Rām—that is, Vishnu—has built a reputation for being merciful to both, and it is his job to uphold that reputation now that the poet's own turn has come. By adding his name to the list, right here in the most intensely lit spot in the poem, Sūr hopes to shame the Lord into rescuing him like all the rest.

400.1 *danced too much* In the *Sūrsāgar* this classic *vinaya* poem is probably the best known of its genre. It is the self-portrait of the poet as dancer—a professional, but an exhausted one; someone sufficiently competent to entertain at the Lord's royal court yet sufficiently scandalous to call up in his patron the desire that he be paid off and sent away. At the conclusion of the poem Sūr explains why there should be this oscillation between adornment and embarrassment, praise and blame. He says that "the many artful steps" (*jo bahu kalā*, v. 7; J1) he knows are really not a form of knowledge (*vidyā*) but of ignorance (*avidyā*, v. 8). And just what is this dance? Sūr describes it as comprising all the cravings of the senses, and at one point he suggests that bad company may have played a role in fanning the flames. The words *asata saṅgati* ("movements to a dissonant pulse," v. 6) may simply refer to a dissonance between the musical role taken up by the voice and that played by the accompanying drum. These are, respectively, the "roar" (*nāda*, v. 5) and the "pulse" (*cāla*, v. 6). But the same phrase may also refer to "movements in the company of evil people"—people who provide not "the company of the good" (*satsaṅg*) but its opposite.

The "aging dancer" trope that Sūr elaborates here appears with different inflections in *Sūr's Ocean* ∫407 and in several poems that apparently enter the *Sūrsāgar* at a later date (see Hawley, *Sūr Dās*, pp. 166–167). Other poets worked with it, as well. For comparative purposes I have elsewhere translated an example attributed to Kabīr, and an even closer match can be found in an early Kabīr poem translated by Charlotte Vaudeville, with the title line "Now I can no longer dance" (Hawley, *Sūr Das*, pp. 139–140; Vaudeville, *A Weaver Named Kabīr*, pp. 286–287). All this raises the question of authenticity in a pointed way, since the present poem has frequently been seen as epitomizing a certain distinctive voice in Sūrdās.

400.8 *Nandalāl* If Sūr's poetry is his burden, it is also his offering. So it is touching that when he offers it up for a last time, he directs it to Krishna with a familiar and tender epithet, one that belongs not in a royal court but in a bower or even a nursery. The last word he speaks is Nandalāl, "Nanda's dear one," and it is hard to miss the strange, sad affection that goes with it.

402.1 *so many other sinners* In the course of this poem, Sūr gives Vishnu credit for having accomplished a great deal. The following are said to have been recipients of his salvation:

(1) Gajendra (v. 3), the elephant whose foot Vishnu saved from the jaws of a crocodile;
(2) an unnamed prostitute (v. 3), most likely Piṅgalā, whose life changed dramatically when, after waiting half the night for a customer, she considered how much more would be gained by waiting expectantly for Vishnu;
(3) King Nṛg (v. 3), explicitly named in several manuscripts but identified in others only by the manner in which he encountered Krishna: he had been cursed by Brahmins to undergo many rebirths until, born a chameleon, he would be fished out of a well in Dvaraka by Krishna and restored to his kingly status;

(4) the dissolute Brahmin Ajāmil (v. 4), who at death cried out for his son Nārāyaṇ but was answered instead by Krishna, who also bears the name Nārāyaṇ;

(5) a hunter (v. 5), perhaps Jar, whose arrow was responsible for Krishna's death as a mortal, but who received no punishment on that account;

(6) the vulture Jaṭāyu (v. 5), who fought with Rāvaṇ to prevent Sītā's abduction and was mortally wounded by him, but received from Rām and Lakṣmaṇ funeral obsequies that secured his passage to heaven;

(7) a monkey (v. 5), presumably the monkey king Bāli, who was similarly killed by Rām, and in the course of being killed, saved. It was Bāli's ill-treated brother Sugrīv who requested Rām to kill Bāli, an act that brought him to the throne;

(8) Ahalyā, the hermit Gautam's wife (v. 5), who was seduced by Indra and therefore cursed by her husband to be a stone in subsequent rebirths until Rām's foot should touch her and bring her back to life;

(9) a deer (v. 5), undoubtedly Mārīc, the demon uncle of Rāvaṇ who transformed himself into a golden deer to lure Rām away from Sītā so that she could be captured. Mārīc was killed by an arrow from Rām that simultaneously conveyed, by its very touch, his mercy;

(10) Kaṃs (v. 6), the evil king of Mathura who, like Bāli, was granted salvation by the very touch that killed him, though this time the touch was that of Krishna rather than Rām;

(11) Keśī (v. 6), the horse-demon who battled with the youthful Krishna;

(12) Kuvalayāpīḍ (v. 6), the mad elephant selected by Kaṃs to kill Krishna as he entered the tournament field at Mathura;

(13) Muṣṭik (v. 6), one of the wrestlers deputed by Kaṃs to battle Krishna and his brother;

(14) Pūtanā (v. 7), the demoness who flew into Braj as a heron, then metamorphosed into a woman, insinuated her way into Yaśodā's circle, and attempted to poison Krishna as she suckled him;

(15) the laundryman or clothes-dyer (*rajaka*, v. 8) in Kaṃs's service who insulted and was drawn into conflict with Krishna as the latter entered Mathura;

(16) Pralamba (v. 8), the demon who entered into a jumping game with Krishna and his young friends in hopes of carrying the lad off to his destruction;

(17) Nalakūbar and his brother Maṇigrīv—literally "the Nalakūbar pair" (*jugala nala kūbara*, v. 8)—who were cursed by Nārad to assume the form of trees called Yamal and Arjun until the infant Krishna pulled a heavy mortar between them, uprooted the trees, and revealed the persons they hid;

(18) Śiśupāl (v. 9), who spoke demeaningly of Krishna in the course of ceremonies marking the coronation of Yudhiṣṭhir, thus turning events that should have been auspicious to the opposite;

(19) Agh (v. 10), the snake-demon who attempted, on Kaṃs's instructions, to swallow Krishna and his boyhood friends as they played by swelling to such an enormous size that his mouth appeared to be a cave;

(20) Bak (v. 10), the heron who attacked the boy Krishna with his huge beak;

(21) Tṛṇāvart (v. 10), the storm-demon who attempted to kill the cowherd Krishna by sucking him into the vortex of his tornado;

(22) Dhenuk (v. 10), the ass-demon whose fierceness created havoc in the forest where Krishna and Balarām played as youths until they killed him. Presumably the "good" (*guna*) of the demons mentioned in this line refers, as in the case of Śiśupāl, to the single-minded concentration they directed to Krishna, albeit with intent to destroy; and

(23) Pāṇḍu's daughter-in-law (v. 11), that is, Draupadī, whose shame Krishna averted by supplying her with endless lengths of cloth (§355).

Not surprisingly in a poem of this length and structure, some manuscripts make omissions from or alterations to the list. In place of the dramatis personae that appear in the critical text of the first part of verse 8, for example, one may find the wrestler Cānūr or the forest-fire demon (J1) or alternatively Droṇ and Duhśāsan (B3, A1). Yet the force of the overall roster is little changed. Vishnu's many encounters—all of them salvific, even the violent ones, according to many interpreters—create plenty of room for variation without changing the general sense of the poem.

409.5 *Ajāmil* See §402.4.

409.7 *hunter, harlot, vulture* See §402.3–5.

409.8 *Council of Five* In the last line the poet plays his final card. He says he is dying of shame to have been excluded from a group of "five sinners" (*pāñca patitani*). At that point we begin to wonder if perhaps he has a sort of *pañcāyat* in mind. *Pañcāyats* are the "councils of five" constituted to provide the leadership needed in Indian villages when disputes between various groups require arbitration across caste boundaries. In the present context these leaders are the sinners whose notorious example singles them out from among their peers. Four of these—Ajāmil, the hunter, the vulture, and the prostitute—have already been listed, both in the poem and, so the poet reports, by Govind (vv. 5–7). When Sūr reveals his own signature, we have the fifth. The intrinsic structure of the *pad*, which demands the poet's signature before it can be complete, thus forces Sūr's own name onto Krishna's list. He says that the Lord forgot him when it was his turn to be enrolled (v. 8), but his very act of saying so would seem to correct the omission. But is this poem the official roster? It is Sūr's, we know, but is it the Lord's?

412.3 *noose of illusion* It is not entirely clear what sort of trap this is, but the poet is probably thinking of something fashioned of rope, perhaps quite specifically a noose. One tradition of interpretation, as represented in manuscript V1, makes this explicit; in verse 2 it speaks of a rope (*ḍorī*) and knot (*ganṭha*). The central issue remains the loss of sure footing—"stumbling" (v. 1)—but the idea of a rope trap, as in V1, allows for the possibility of the sort of snare that can be hung from a tree so as to pull an animal off the ground and suspend it from a branch upside down. The poet seems to follow out this image in the next verse by speaking of "hanging in air" (*laṭakai*, v. 4) once one has lost hold of those two guides to righteous living, "songs of the Lord" (or "the worship of Hari," *hari bhajana*, v. 4) and "gatherings of the good" (*sādha samāgama*, v. 4). If one stays aloof from these, then one is "left . . . hanging in air without either," as at the moment the stool is kicked away from beneath the feet of a man being hanged.

412.5 *acrobat* The poet portrays himself as a common performer (*naṭa*), an acrobat cum musician cum magician—just the sort of person who might find himself suspended in such an awkward position. In referring to the *naṭ*'s proud repertory of little acts (*bahu bidhi kalā*, v. 5), he humorously denigrates the tricks of his own artistic profession. If we think of him as constructing his own noose, these are the tools. We are reminded of the manifold abilities of the artful dancer in poem 400.

412.6 *husband . . . gone* The poet compares himself to a widow who in defiance of Hindu custom continues to display her wealth after her "dear one" (*piya*, v. 6), her husband, has passed away. From the poet's point of view, such an indiscriminate display of wealth serves only to incriminate the owner, pointing to the fact that this is not true wealth at all. In the same way there is something baseless and sad about an indefatigable performer whose desire for one more coin in the cup means he can never stop the act. It shows, perhaps, that an act is all it is.

413.7 *they'll be writing my horoscope again* The reference is clearly to rebirth and, with it, the determination of a new horoscope, but who does this "writing"? Sūr may be thinking of the fates—Brahmā is often considered to play this role, using an individual's forehead as his slate—or he may have in mind the astrologers who decipher the cosmic notation to which it corresponds (cf. §3.2–4).

416.4 *cooked like an eggplant* The mention of being "head-first thrust in filth" (v. 4) apparently refers to existence in the womb and particularly to the moment of birth, in which the child not only enters the world through the genital passage but arrives, once delivered, amid the disintegrating placenta of afterbirth, which many Hindus consider to be ritually polluting. The reference to being "cooked like an eggplant" in the same line is if anything more vivid. In Braj a favorite way to cook an eggplant (or potato) is first to suspend it in a fire until it is baked, allowing it to shrivel and sometimes even burst. Then the eggplant is peeled, and the inner contents are crushed and once again submitted to the fire, this time to be fried. The result is called *bharatā* or *bhuratā* (cf. *bharata*, v. 4). One aspect of the poet's comparison is the upside-down position of both vegetable and fetus, but the main point has to do with the elaborate, tortuous process of gestation that the fetus must endure.

416.8 *like the deer* Here is another reference to the belief that agile, restless deer are rendered temporarily immobile—and therefore easy targets—by a certain pleasing sound that hunters can produce (cf. §217, 418). Deer are said to be particularly entranced by anything sung in *rāg sāraṅg*, the "deer" raga.

418.1 *Sūr's twenty-five* This poem is one of the most unusual entries in the *Sūrsāgar*, so unusual that it has traditionally been accorded a title separate from the rest (*sūrpacīsī*) and has sometimes appeared in anthologies where the rest of the *Sūrsāgar* is absent, such as Anup Sanskrit Library, Bikaner, no. 70, *phuṭkar kavitā*,

V.S. 1752 (1695 C.E.). The name *sūrpacīsī* means "Sūr's twenty-five" and refers to the fact that the poem is a compilation of 25 *dohās*—rhymed couplets in which each verse contains 24 instants, 13 coming before the caesura and 11 after (vv. 3–52). In addition there is a refrain containing 16 instants (v. 1), complemented by a rhyming verse in *dohā* meter (v. 2). As one might expect in a poem of this length and type, there is considerable variation from manuscript to manuscript in regard to line order. Because the *dohā* is a self-contained unit, it was easy for the couplets to be heard and remembered in varying sequences. Yet even amid this diversity the basic structure of the poem is little altered.

It has two parts. The first is a litany to love that stresses the trials lovers are willing to endure for the sake of their love (vv. 3–24); in a number of examples that trial is death itself. Here the poet works adroitly to shape seemingly isolated *dohās* into a cohesive whole. Several repetitions of the word "love" in its various forms—*prīti, piya,* and *prema* (vv. 1, 5, 16, 17, 20, 21, 24)—serve to keep the overarching theme of the first half in the listener's ear, and the tropes enlisted to illustrate it are by now familiar to readers of this volume. The second part of the poem portrays a particular act of love (vv. 25–48): the one by means of which God creates, nourishes, and sustains individual beings in this world, and human beings above all—again, a familiar theme. Addressing his soul or mind (*manā*, v. 1), the poet asks himself how he could have spurned and ignored such a love.

418.17 *the turtle dove* The bird mentioned here is the *parevā*, whose every movement is said to be motivated by a search for its mate. This is what enables sportsmen to train such birds to stay aloft for days or more at a time. They will drop to earth from exhaustion before abandoning their love-search; the bird to stay aloft the longest wins for its owner the prize, and for itself, death (cf. §217). Here, however, death comes into play in a somewhat different way, as we may deduce from Abū'l Fazl's catalogue of types of pigeons kept for sport at the court of Akbar ('Allāmī, tr. Blochmann, *The Ā'īn-i-Akbarī*, pp. 312–314). Abū'l Fazl uses the special designation *khernī* (our *parevā*, evidently) to refer to a type of high-flying pigeon particularly noted for its devotion to its mate. Even if the bird flies at altitudes that make it invisible to humans, it is able to see its mate once the cloth covering her cage is removed, and will descend instantly to be with her. The taxonomist in Abū'l Fazl is interested in the ways different *khernīs* choose to make this precipitous descent—with two wings spread, or with one, or with none at all—but what our poet cares about is the risk involved. The wingless pose seems particularly apt as a demonstration of how the bird willingly courts death for the sake of love. And from Abū'l Fazl's description, one wonders whether the *parevā*'s death-defying descent may not have been especially responsible for the fact that, as he notes, Akbar referred to pigeon-gaming as *'iśqbāz*, "love-play."

418.42 *messengers of Death* Emissaries of Yama, whose task is to bring down the curtain on individual lives by ushering the souls concerned to the netherworld, where Yama reigns (e.g., §391.11–12).

418.47 *Smṛti* A class of religious literature comprised primarily of texts devoted to legal matters (*sūtras* and *śāstras*). The word *smṛti* means "that which is remembered" and refers to works understood to be products of human reflection. These contrast with *śruti*, "that which is heard" or revealed, namely, the Veda (e.g., §33.7–8).

419.1 *Turn away, mind* This poem is one of the most intriguing in our collection since it is the only one ever to be accepted into the scriptural corpus of the Sikhs. It title line appears in the Kartārpur Pothī of 1604 (v.s. 1661), showing conclusively that the poem was in circulation by the end of the sixteenth century but perhaps also showing, as Gurinder Singh Mann has suggested, that the Kartārpur editors did not know exactly what version of the poem they should record. They left a space blank as if expecting to complete their work at a later date, and went on to record Guru Arjan's warm response to Sūr's poem, in which he elaborates on the contrast between the ecstasy of a life spent hearing and seeing Hari or Śyām Sundar and the degradation of a life spent gratifying the senses. A later scribe, in the Khārā Māṅgat Pothī of 1642, filled out the body of the original Sūrdās poem with a version that is quite close to the one found in manuscripts on which our critical edition is based. (Mann, *The Making of Sikh Scripture*, pp. 116–117, 175. Guru Arjan's response is found on p. 1253 of the standard edition of the *Gurū Granth;* it is also available in transliteration and translation in Deol, "Surdas," p. 184, accompanied by a textual analysis that extends through p. 193.)

419.2 *giving cobras milk* In north India, offerings of milk to placate cobras are common at the festival of *nāg pañcamī*, which occurs during the monsoon, when snakes become particularly numerous and dangerous. They are also used in connection with the worship of the apotheosized hero Gugā (or Gogā).

419.3 *camphor* The breathing of camphor is a technique for soothing and improving the voice, which results in more beautiful singing. Sūr says it is hopeless in the case of crows. Alternatively, he may be referring to the use of camphor as a medicinal purifier useful for stomach disorders. Considering what crows eat, any good effects would soon be rendered nil.

419.5 *arrows cannot pierce a stone* Here the poet adopts the proverbial observation that "you can't pierce a stone with an arrow." Unlike Kabīr, who often uses the figure of an arrow to stand specifically for the sharp truth revealed inwardly by the True Guru (Hawley, *Sūr Dās*, p. 136), Sūr seems to be speaking in a plain, nontechnical way. In specifying that the unyielding target stone is "fallen" (*patit*), the poet uses the word that most familiarly designates moral degenerates, a word we have heard time and again in the title that praises Vishnu/Krishna for being "purifier of the fallen" (*patit pāvan*).

419.6 *once a blanket's dyed black* In its use here, this familiar idiom contrasts broadly with instances in which it is mobilized to provide a commentary on the enduring visibility of Krishna's (Hari's) excesses in the color of his skin (e.g., §289).

420.1 *O cakaī* The *cakaī* represents the bird of the soul, motivated to take flight by its separation from the One it loves. The *cakaī*, female of the species, is said to endure such a separation from its mate each night; the two are reunited only when morning comes. The poet calls to the *cakaī* through the night as if he were her mate, the *cakavā*, urging her to abandon the darkness that is the cause of loss and separation, and fly with him to where there is only day.

420.1–8 *those feet, that lake* Upon hearing of this "foot-lake" (*caraṇa sarovara*), experienced listeners will think immediately of *mān sarovar*, the "spiritual lake" cradled at the tip of the Himalayas. The poet encourages this process. He draws out associations between this lake and Brahmā, whose sagely son Sanak (§§327, 386) appears here along with Brahmā's vehicle, the *haṃs* bird (loosely translated "swans," v. 3). The *haṃs* is characteristically thought of as making a migrational journey to this high Himalayan home. *Mān sarovar* is even more fundamentally associated with Shiva, whose abode on Mount Kailāś it borders, and Shiva too appears in verse 3, accompanied by his cohort of ascetic metitators. Yet both Brahmā's contingent (*sanaka sahaṃsa*, "Sanak . . . with swans," v. 3) and Shiva's (*siva muni jana*, "Shiva and sages," v. 3) are transfigured. They become denizens of the lake itself, their status modified and reduced to that of fish and waterfowl. They spread a sort of Vedic emulsion that is suspended across the poem until the line in which the poet announces his signature (v. 7).

At that point something happens. We learn that the central players in this magical scene are not these two members of the *trimūrti* but the missing third, Vishnu, who has so far not been directly mentioned. Far from suffering demotion, however, Vishnu gets the main billing, along with his consort Śrī. The picture of the poet prostrating himself in reverence to this divine couple (*praṇamata sūrija dāsa*, "Sūrdās prays," v. 7) calls to mind the feet that actually constitute the lake inhabited by other members of the *trimūrti*. For to prostrate oneself is to bow at another's feet—in this case, the feet of Vishnu. Not accidentally, these feet also figure in images we have of Vishnu and Śrī as they relax in water play: on the primordial Milk Ocean, Śrī passes her time massaging them. But Vaishnavas also conceive Vishnu's feet—specifically the toenails (cf. v. 3)—as the super-Himalayan point from which the Ganges descends to earth (§432), so here we have a new conjunction. The poet envisions Vishnu's feet as the source and essence of a body of water filled with "pearls of freedom" (*mukati mukatāphala*, v. 5) and good deeds (*sukṛta*, v. 5); his glistening toenails are its source of never-failing light (vv. 3–4). Step by step we discover that the lake so closely associated with Shiva and Brahmā (*mān sarovar*) is really the lake of Vishnu's feet (*caraṇ sarovar*), and the refrain keeps our eyes on this point: "flee to those feet, that lake" (v. 1).

428.2 *searches the jungle for a jewel* The metaphorical connection between a lost jewel and the forest is somewhat imprecise, so it not surprising that two manuscripts, both of them relatively late, attempt revisions. G1 speaks of a bead lost from its necklace, which then is sought throughout the world (*jag*), not the forest (*ban*). V1 retains the forest or jungle of the core tradition, but supplies a new subject, namely, the deer who searches everywhere for the source of the musk he smells in his own navel.

428.5–6 *face . . . in a mirror* In the present context, the vignette of the face in the mirror is particularly deft: to clarify the reflection of something soiled is further to illuminate the sorry state of the thing reflected. The "inky filth" on the face of which it speaks (*muṣa malina . . . masi*) is just the sort of thing one might connect with a past so reprehensible that it seems to add up to nothing (*aleṣai*, "futile," v. 7).

428.8 *being blind* We cannot know whether a blind man was the first to perform the poem, but in certain other poems we have hints that Sūr's blindness was understood (either by "the real" Sūrdās or by others who used his name) to have been the result of a gradual process that became conclusive in old age (see Introduction). If that was the common understanding when this poem first circulated, then its content would have seemed even more effective than otherwise, for the last couplet suggests an inverse relation between physical and spiritual blindness: only as the body weakens does one's sense of truth grow strong. Gradual or not, the central force of the motif of blindness in the hagiography of Sūrdās is that very often the sighted are blind, while the blind can truly see.

429.1 *offering of lights* The comparison upon which this poem turns (other poets of Sūr's period also employ it) is with the *āratī* ceremony. It is performed with a cruse of oil or, as in this case, clarified butter (*ghī*) to illuminate an image of a deity. The person officiating—a priest in a temple, a householder at home—lifts the lamp with circular motions to bring light to the often dark recess in which the image is housed. Such images are typically installed on thrones (*siṃhāsan* or *āsan*), as is specified in verse 3.

429.3 *tortoise . . . Śeṣ* The trick here is that the deity being illuminated is also the officiant—Hari himself—and the ceremony is all creation. This accounts for the references to the myth of the churning of the Milk Ocean, in which Vishnu participates by allowing himself to be used, in his tortoise avatar, as the base upon which the great world-churn can be mounted: Mount Mandar upended and pulled back and forth by a cosmic snake. This snake is customarily identified as Vāsukī, but here a more intimate connection with Hari/Vishnu is suggested, for the snake is Śeṣ, who served as the couch upon which Vishnu reclined in the long period of rest that preceded creation and who is, as his name "Remainder" suggests, an overflow of Vishnu himself. By assigning Śeṣ to Vāsukī's role, the poet strengthens the sense of Hari's self-sufficiency.

429.4 *Island Earth* This phrase translates the word *dīp*, which carries a double meaning. In the first instance it is, as the variant *mahī* in several manuscripts makes plain, the earth, conceived as the island-continent Jambūdvīp (*dvīpa, dvīp* = *dīp*). The second meaning, however, refers to the lamp itself (*dīpa* = *dīp*), which the earth also is, according to the metaphor that guides the poem. Mount Mandar, the axis mundi, then becomes the wick that is placed in the cruse, and the seven seas that surround Jambūdvīp are the *ghī*. Thus one has a colossal vision of cosmogenesis as the Deity's illumination of himself. The Milk-Ocean myth is mapped onto an image of the physical world, with the earth below as the long-handled ritual cruse and the sky above it filled with the light of heavenly bodies—the glow of the *āratī* flames.

429.7 *Shiva . . . Prajāpati* Once the basic metaphoric connections have been established, the poet peoples the scene with living beings, especially divine ones. Notably, these include Prajāpati, the creator deity who first emerges in the late philosophical hymns of the *Rig Veda*. Sūrdās thus presents his Vaishnava creation scene as logically prior to that.

429.9 *those who love the Lord* Namely, *bhaktas* (*bhagatani*). Thus as the poem draws to a close, listeners have the challenge of fitting themselves into the picture along with everything else.

8. TO THE HOLY RIVERS

431.1 *Oh Kālindī* This composition, a praise-poem and plea for forgiveness, is unusual in the *Sūrsāgar*, both for its brevity and for its subject. Although it is possible to think of it as being spoken by a *gopī*, since the speaker claims to have been favored (*kripā*, v. 2) by Krishna, that is by no means requisite. In fact, the mood is so direct that it might characterize the thoughts of anyone who comes to the Jamunā in an act of worship. If a *gopī* speaks here, she is a devotee like any other; all can claim to have been favored by Krishna. In a similarly general way, it is impossible to know the exact cause of the petition for forgiveness that is made here. Perhaps there is none. After all, as the final verse implies, the quality of defilement is built into the very nature (*prakriti*) of the worshiper's condition, and bathing in the Jamunā is intended to wash it away.

The title Kālindī (*kālyandrī*, v. 1) derives from Kalind, a mountain in the Himalayas. This title is patronymic in a loose sense, in that the Jamunā is said to have descended onto the great plain of north India from Kalind, where she originates.

431.1 *whom Keśav loves* Next comes her association with Keśav, that is, Krishna. Because the river provides him with most of his favorite places, she is designated his beloved (*pyārī*, v. 1). Some say that she is his wife too, as is stated in *Bhāgavata Purāṇa* 10.58.17–23 and emphasized in the Vallabh Sampradāy. Indeed, "wife" is another sense of the word *pyārī*, though not the dominant one, and the *Bhāgavata* reports that when Krishna does wed in Dvaraka, one of his eight wives is named Kālindī.

431.3 *Yama's elder sister* After that the poet greets the Yamunā (Brj. Jamunā) in her capacity as the sister of Yama (Brj. Jam). Yama and Yamunā (or as she is alternately called in this context, Yamī) are understood in various texts to be twin offspring of the sun-god Vivasvant (or Sūrya) and his wife Saraṇyū. But Yamunā is the elder of the two, "Yama's elder sister" (*jama jeṭhī*), which seems a logical step on the way to her being exalted as "mother of the world" in the phrase that follows. The Jamunā's close linkage with Yama, as his twin, gives her leverage over matters of life and death. For that reason Brajbāsīs annually propitiate her along with him in the festival of *bhāī dūj*, which is celebrated as brothers bathe with their sisters in the Jamunā on the second day of the bright fortnight of Kārttik. The festival of *bhāī dūj* would provide an apt ritual occasion for voicing the sentiments expressed in this poem; but especially in Braj, where the Jamunā is worshiped so widely, they hardly need be confined there.

431.3 *mother of the world* Finally the river is addressed as a mother (*jaga kī mahatārī*, "mother of the world," v. 3). Along with Mount Govardhan, the Jamunā is regarded as one of the two primeval *tīrthas* of the Braj country, having existed since time immemorial, during each of the four world ages (*cahūṅ juga*). This timeless presence is a nurturing one; she is therefore the mother of all who live in Braj.

432.1 *From the lotus of those . . . feet* This poem is a paean to the Ganges, and at the same time to the feet of Vishnu/Krishna, from which it is said to flow (§10, 433). In the most venerable manuscripts the poet proceeds very gradually, leaving it to the audience to identify the subject of the poem as it unfolds. Only in relatively late manuscripts, beginning with V1 (1756 C.E.), do we find the opposite approach. They replace the word *piya* with *hari*, announcing that the feet mentioned in verse 1 are not "beloved feet" or "the feet of the beloved" (*piya pada*), but specifically "Hari's feet." Then anyone who knows the mythology can quickly deduce that the "nectar" in question (*makaranda*) is the Ganges.

432.4 *known by Shiva* In the older manuscripts Sūr takes pleasure in deferring the discovery of the Ganges's identity. Not until verse 4, when he speaks of its falling on Shiva's head, do we know he is singing the praises of the Ganges, since that is the river said to descend from its heavenly home to earth by cascading upon the head of Shiva as he sat meditating in the Himalayas. Even then the poet does not actually divulge the river's name. He waits until the final verse, at which time, with a familiar appellation, he calls her "River-of-the-Gods" (*surasari*, v. 6).

At that point Vishnu's identity also comes clear, for Sūr's audiences know that in Vaishnava tellings of the myth of the Ganges's descent, her point of heavenly departure is Vishnu's toe. The Ganges is said to have begun to flow when Brahmā honored the appearance of Vishnu's foot in his realm at the pinnacle of creation by pouring water upon it (e.g., BhP 5.17.1ff.). This incident forms a part of the story of how Vishnu became a dwarf (§361, 362). According to the *Bhāgavata*, it was when Vāman stretched to the conclusion of his first step that his foot appeared in Brahmā's kingdom, Satyalok.

432.4 *casting aside the moon* Here another level of mythological resonance is brought into play. The poet remarks that the attraction of Vishnu's Gangetic nectar is so strong that Shiva feels no further need for the cooling moon that is lodged in his unkempt locks, or for the snakes and mountains that serve, respectively, as his jewelry and abode. So far, one can think of these as merely features or emblems of Shiva, but as verse 5 continues the poet speaks of *asura sura sau banda*, "the duel in which the gods and anti-gods were bound." This transports us to quite a different landscape—the one in which the gods and their opponents churned the primeval Milk Ocean to gain access to the liquid of immortality (cf. *amrita*, v. 3: "ambrosia, the liquid of deathlessness;" *sudhā*, v. 6: "immortal [liquid]"). In this cooperative tug-of-war the gods and demons used a great snake as their rope and an upended mountain as their churning stick. The elixir itself is sometimes said to have emerged in a vessel provided by the moon. All these elements are present in Shiva's paraphernalia, so the poet is able to move deftly toward the cosmogonic churning scene and give the poem a dimension of added density that is appropriate to the penultimate verse.

432.6 *all three worlds* *Tihū lokani*, that is, the heavens, the atmosphere, and the earth. The Ganges is accorded a certain supremacy because she connects these various levels of the cosmos by flowing between them, while Shiva is confined somewhere in the middle. The poet underscores this transcendent aspect of the Vishnu's grace—his Ganges—by constructing an impressive alliteration that culminates in the last word of the poem. He describes Vishnu's foot-nectar as *sugama surasari sudhā [sūra] suchanda*: "[says Sūr] that River-of-the-Gods/is immanent, immortal, and so free." The final word, *suchanda*, means "independent," "self-willed," "spontaneous," or, as translated here, "free." By implying that Vishnu's grace is even freer than Shiva, the poet says a great deal about how Shiva and Vishnu are to be ranked. At the same time he says something more. What makes that grace most praiseworthy is precisely that it transcends measurement and rank. It flows like a river—everywhere, uncontrollably—and its ultimate greatness is that it is freely accessible to all, in all three worlds (*tihū lokani sugama*).

433.1 *Mādhav's Braid* This poem of praise is addressed to Venī Mādhav, "Mādhav's braid" (*mādhau bainī*), the deity who governs and is consubstantial with the great confluence of rivers at Prayāg. It is here that the Ganges meets the Jamunā, and one sister mixes with the other to constitute the great watercourse known thereafter as the Ganges. According to Hindu perception these two manifest rivers are joined by an invisible third, the Sarasvatī, and for that reason the place is conceived as a triple confluence (*trisaṅgama*, v. 6). Hence the metaphor of a braid (*bainī* < *veṇī*, v. 1) is apt. This confluence is commonly called *triveṇī*, a braid of three elements, and in Sūr's time the short designation *veṇī* was evidently common (e.g., *benī* in RCM 2.106.3).

In his image form at Prayāg, Venī Mādhav is a black, standing, four-armed Vishnu who appears alongside his consort Lakṣmī. In this poem, however, the poet's attention focuses not on what one might see in a temple but on the deity's physical presence as the sum of three rivers—the "braid" that is most familiarly called Gaṅgā (the Ganges) as it stretches downriver from Prayāg. (Further, see Hawley, *Three Bhakti Voices*, chapter 10.) This Ganges cleanses the *kali* age (*kali kāla*, v. 3), and she is the natural enemy of death (*kāla*, v. 3, in another meaning; cf. *jama*, Yama, v. 7) because she ferries her devotees to new forms of life (as in verse 8). Even the myth of her origin pits her against death, for she washes clean the ashes of the sons of Sāgar ("Ocean"), who would otherwise have been trapped forever in Yama's netherworld kingdom (cf. §391, 418). This action becomes the paradigm of hope for all who come to the Ganges, especially at Prayāg, seeking release.

433.3 *Trivikram* Sūr takes all the potencies of the Ganges and relates them to Vishnu—Trivikram (see below)—as would have been especially appropriate if the poem was originally created for performance at the temple of Venī Mādhav itself. Expositing the name of the temple, he takes the triple confluence at Prayāg and turns it into an aspect of Vishnu—a weapon he bears, a great sword (*taravāri*, v. 4). The purpose of this sword is to cut away the harsh, crooked (*kaṭhina . . . kuṭila*, v. 3) deformations of the *kali* age and reinstate a supple unity, as the metaphor of the braid suggests.

The title Trivikram (*tribikrama*, "Triple-Victory Lord," originally v. 4; in translation, v. 3) belongs to Vishnu primarily in consequence of the might (*vikram*) he exerts through taking three great steps (*kram*) as the dwarf Vāman. Although narratives of the incident vary (§361, 362), the title generally signifies Vishnu's hegemony over all three facets of the universe—earth, atmosphere, and heaven in the older conception; earth, heaven, and the netherworld in the more recent. Here we do have echoes of such a cosmology ("their hells," *niraye*, v. 8), but the main targets of Venī Mādhav's campaign are the three divisions of Yama's army of heretics.

433.7 *Greeks, Kāpālikas, Jains* As symbols of the confused dispersion that is rife in the *kali* age, the poet seizes on another triad—three groups he portrays as being soldiers of Yama, the death-force that rules the *kali* age. Not coincidentally, these three are in various ways opponents of Vishnu, and therefore heretics from a Vaishnava point of view. The evil triad comprises Greeks (*jamana* < Skt. *yavana*)—that is, barbaric outsiders from the west; Kāpālikas—skull-wearing devotees of Shiva who flout normal laws of morality; and Jains, who reject the authority of the Vedas. As a set, they have a somewhat archaic ring, as if the poet intended them to signal something of the manner in which the *kali* age got started on its crooked course. The term *yavana* goes back to the Alexandrian period; the Kāpālikas appeared in the early centuries C.E.; and Jainism formed around a core that probably dates to the ninth century B.C.E. Yet each of the three continued to be represented in Sūr's own time. Jains and Shaivas (if not specifically Kāpālikas) were certainly a part of his ambiance, and when he used the term *yavana* (i.e., *jamana*), his audiences would quickly have made an association to the major group of conquerors from the West who succeeded the Greeks and were designated by the same name. These were the Muslim rulers who constituted a permanent presence in the Delhi region and elsewhere from the twelfth century onward.

433.7 *the merest sight of it* Trivikram is envisioned as bearing (and the Triple Confluence as being) a sword, as he would be expected to do—among other weapons—in the venerable theological system called Pāñcarātra. There the Lord is conceived as manifesting himself in four *vyūhas* ("dispositions" or "formations," but also specifically "battle arrays"). The third of these, called Pradyumna, is associated with lordship and heroism (*aiśvarya* and *vīrya*); heroism is understood as the Lord's ability to remain unaffected by changes he brings about. Sūr may be taking advantage of the fact that Pāñcarātra theology specifically identifies this quality of heroism with Mādhav. Similarly, Pāñcarātrikas conceive Trivikram in his image form as one of three subsidiary "inner formations" (*antaravyūha*) of Pradyumna, and in that guise he bears four swords.

If Sūr has these Pāñcarātra perspectives in mind, he nonetheless reduces the four swords for his present purposes to a single entity, the confluent Ganges. He sees its hilt as Mount Meru (v. 5), which presumably stands for the Himalayan range. From there the Ganges descends to earth, slashing through the north Indian plains. Its axis is north-to-south, which makes sense when one considers that Yama, the deathly enemy against which it is aimed, is inevitably pictured as residing and ruling in the south. Overall, Pāñcarātra ways of thinking would be consonant with an understanding of this river/sword as Vishnu's *tejas*, his radiant power, so it is no surprise that the poet makes mention of how its liquid body flashes forth in waves (*sobhita aṅga taraṅ ga*, "the waves of its body glint," v. 6).

The best introductory statement on Pāñcarātra doctrine relevant to this theme is that of Hudson, "Vāsudeva Kṛṣṇa in Theology and Architecture," pp. 139–158, and I am further indebted to Dennis Hudson for conversation relating specifically to this poem (January 5, 1999). For various Pāñcarātra strands relevant here, see also Klostermeier, *A Survey of Hinduism*, pp. 246–248; Gonda, *Viṣṇuism and Śivaism*, pp. 48–61; and Gonda, *Medieval Religious Literature in Sanskrit*, pp. 59–61. In regard to the association between Mādhav and *vīrya* in the iconographic program of the Pāñcarātra temple of Vaikuṇṭha Perumāl at Kancipuram, see Hudson, *The Body of God*, pp. 143–145.

433.8 *its name—one name* Pāñcarātra theology may also lie behind Sūr's depiction of Trivikram as one who not only defeats heretics and outsiders (v. 7) but also saves them at the same time (v. 8). Pāñcarātra understands Trivikram as that aspect of Vāsudeva Krishna according to which he protects unclean or demonic persons if they take refuge in him through a Vaishnava preceptor (*ācārya*) who wields the power of mantric rites. No preceptor as such is present here, but the poet hints that that role has been assumed by Venī Mādhav himself. When "Yama's soldiers" cast their eyes upon the confluence which his name represents, they come under the protective power of that "one name" (*eka nāṅva*, v. 8) and leave behind the hellish realms (*niraye*, v. 8) where they had been stuck. Pāñcarātra theologians saw this process as giving hope especially to Śūdra rulers, whom they epitomized in the figure of Bali, with his associations to subterranean Pātāl or Sutal; Trivikram simultaneously subjugates and saves Bali. Sūr's use of this material gives an interesting twist to the classic Trivikram story according to which Vāman grants Bali his netherworld kingdom as a boon (cf. §362). Here it seems that the *asuric* figures involved travel not downward but up, "leaving the hells" (*taji niraye*, v. 8) that symbolize their status as minions of Yama. Yet a measure of ambiguity remains, for Bali's kingdom is usually described as just the sort of "fine peaceful realm" (*bhūmi sucainī*, v. 8) that Vishnu's three opponents would now be abandoning for a finer realm still.

In making the Ganges a scimitar, the poet transports this Pāñcarātra theology, whose refinements would presumably have been familiar to at least some of his listeners, to a register that makes his meaning more widely and vividly accessible. He calls the river's current (*dhāra*, v. 6) the edge or blade of the sword, and that is a second meaning of the same word. Both meanings of *dhār*—"current" and "blade"—are retained in our translation. He also puns on *nāṅv* (v. 8), a word that can mean either "name" or "boat." Here, as we have said, the "one name" ("one boat") Sūr has in mind is presumably Venī Mādhav—at once the confluence and Vishnu himself—and there is a particular logic in specifying that it stands alone. After all, foreigners (Greeks, i.e., Turks/Muslims), apostates (Kāpālikas, who may possibly stand for all Shaivites) and heretics (Jains) also orient themselves to "names," but their names are of lesser import, or simply false. For there is only one true name, the name of Vishnu. When Greeks, Kāpālikas, and Jains see Vishnu's "one name" embodied at the confluence as *venī* (or *triveṇī*), they abandon their former allegiances, merging their three names into the one true name like strands in a braid. In doing so, they enact yet another pun. They "flee" (*bhaje*, v. 8) from their erstwhile selves at the very moment that they "sing" (again, *bhaje*) of Venī Mādhav. Alas, only the first of these two meanings emerges in translation.

433.9 *heavenly damsels* In the penultimate verse, "heavenly damsels" (*dibi sundari*) appear. They celebrate "that water war" (*jā jala juddha*) between Venī Mādhav and the three forces of Kali or Death, which the poet sees shadowed in the roiling confluence of the three rivers. These celestial beauties point even more unambiguously to the One about whose name the poet has been speaking all along. For when they present their garlands to the Ganges, in a gesture that has for millennia fallen to creatures such as they, they do so in the name of Nārāyaṇ (*narainī*, v. 10). They garland the victor in battle.

433.10 *river of Nārāyaṇ* Nārāyaṇī (*narainī*) is one of the names of the Ganges, which it earns because it is said to originate in the heavens at the toe of Nārāyaṇ, that is, Vishnu (§432). This name, with which Sūr concludes his poem, is thus appropriate to the heavenly women with whom the poet associates it. Is it also, from their perspective, the "one name" forecast in verse 8?

433.10 *says Sūr* Finally we must ask who is speaking in this poem. In an obvious way, it is the poet himself—that must remain the best answer. But once the "heavenly damsels" are introduced, at the end, it becomes possible in hindsight to construe the speech of the first eight lines as their hymn of praise, their "great uproar" (*kulāhala*, v. 10). In performance, the return to the refrain after singing the final line would particularly suggest this. As the maidens prepare to garland the Lord as Ganges, the "hails" (*jai ho jai*, v. 1) we hear might well be theirs.

Bibliography of Works Cited

Abbott, Justin E., and N. R. Godbole. *Stories of Indian Saints: English Translation of Mahipati's Marathi Bhaktavijaya*. 2 vols. Delhi: Motilal Banarsidass, 1982 [originally Poona: Scottish Mission Industries, 1934].

Agravāl, Vāsudev Śaraṇ, and Daulatrām Juyāl, eds. *Nal Daman*. Agra: Agra Viśvavidyālaya, 1961.

Aklujkar, Vidyut. "Battle as Banquet: A Metaphor in Sūradāsa," *Journal of the American Oriental Society* 111:2 (1991), 353–361.

'Allāmī, Abū'l-Fazl. *The Ā'īn-i-Akbarī*. Translated by H. Blochmann; edited by S. L. Goomer. Delhi: Aadiesh Book Depot, 1965 [originally 1871].

Askari, Syed Hasan. "Historical Value of the Afsana-i-Badshahan or Tarikh-i-Afghani," *Journal of Indian History* 43:1 (April 1965), 183–200.

al-Badā'ūni [al-Badāoni], 'Abd al-Qādir. *Muntakhabu-t-tawārīkh*. 3 vols. Translated by W. H. Lowe. Delhi: Idārah-i-Ādābiyat-i-Dillī, 1973 [originally 1899].

Bāharī, Hardev, and Rājendra Kumār Varmā. *Sūr Śabd-Sāgar*. Allahabad: Smṛti Prakāśan, 1981.

Behl, Aditya. "The Magic Doe: Desire and Narrative in a Hindavi Sufi Romance, circa 1503." In Richard M. Eaton, ed., *India's Islamic Traditions, 711–1750*, 180–208. Delhi: Oxford University Press, 2003.

———. "How Newness Enters the World: Inaugurating a Genre." Part I of "Shadows of Paradise: An Indian Islamic Literary Tradition, 1376–1545." Lecture delivered at the École des Hautes Études en Sciences Sociales, Paris, June 8, 2005.

———. "Presence and Absence in *Bhakti:* An Afterword," in J. S. Hawley, ed., *The Bhakti Movement—Says Who?*, 319–324. *International Journal of Hindu Studies* 11:3 (2007).

Behl, Aditya, and Simon Weightman, with S. N. Pandey. *Manjhan: Madhumālatī, An Indian Sufi Romance.* Oxford: Oxford University Press, 2000.

[Bhāgavata Purāṇa] Śrīmadbhāgavata. Varanasi: Paṇḍit Pustakālay, 1965.

Bikhārīdās. *Kāvyanirṇaya.* Edited and annotated by Javāharlāl Caturvedī. Mathura: Kalyāṇdās and Brothers, 1959.

———. *Kāvyanirṇaya,* with notes by Ved Prakāś. Delhi: Sanjay Prakāśan, 2006.

Bryant, Kenneth E. *Poems to the Child-God: Structures and Strategies in the Poetry of Sūrdās.* Berkeley: University of California Press, 1978.

Busch, Allison. "The Anxiety of Innovation: The Practice of Literary Science in the Hindi/*Riti* Tradition." In Sheldon Pollock, ed., *Forms of Knowledge in Early-Modern South Asia,* 45–59. *Comparative Studies of South Asia, Africa, and the Middle East* 24:2 (2004).

———. "Hidden in Plain View: Brajbhasha Poets at the Mughal Court." *Modern Asian Studies,* forthcoming.

———. "Hindi Literary Beginnings," in Yigal Bronner, Whitney Cox, and Lawrence McCrea, eds., *Language, Culture, and Power: New Directions in South Asian Studies,* forthcoming.

———. "Questioning the Tropes about '*Bhakti*' and '*Riti*' in Hindi Literary Historiography." In Monika Horstmann, ed., *Bhakti in Current Research, 2001–2003,* 33–47. New Delhi: Manohar, 2006.

Case, Margaret H., ed., with photographs by Robyn Beeche. *Govindadeva: A Dialogue in Stone.* Delhi: Indira Gandhi National Centre for the Arts, 1996.

Caturvedī, Sītārām. *Mahākavi Sūrdās aur unkī Pratibhā.* Allahabad: Hindī Sāhitya Sammelan, 1978.

Dave, K. N. *Birds in Sanskrit Literature.* Delhi: Motilal Banarsidass, 1985.

Delvoye, Françoise "Nalini." "Les Chants *dhrupad* en langue braj des poètes-musiciens de l'Inde moghole." In *Littératures médiévales de l'Inde du Nord,* edited by Françoise Mallison, 139–185. Paris: École Française d'Extrême Orient, 1991.

———. "The Thematic Range of Dhrupad Songs Attributed to Tānsen, Foremost Court-Musician of the Mughal Emperor Akbar." In *Studies in South Asian Devotional Literature,* edited by A. W. Entwistle and Françoise Mallison, 406–429. Delhi: Manohar Books; Paris: École Française d'Extrême Orient, 1994.

Deol, Jeevan. "Sūrdās: Poet and Text in the Sikh Tradition," *Bulletin of the School of Oriental and African Studies* 63:2 (2000), 158–186.

Dharwadker, Vinay. *Kabir: The Weaver's Songs.* New Delhi: Penguin Books, 2003.

Dudney, Arthur. "Colonial Knowledge and the Greco-Roman Classics: Resituating the Legacy of Sir William Jones in a Humanist Context." M.A. thesis, Columbia University, 2008.

Edgerton, Franklin, ed. *The Mahābhārata,* vol. 2. Poona: Bhandarkar Oriental Research Institute, 1944.

———. *The Panchatantra Reconstructed.* 2 vols. New Haven: American Oriental Society, 1924.

Entwistle, Alan W. *Braj, Centre of Krishna Pilgrimage.* Groningen: Egbert Forsten, 1987.

Gonda, Jan. *Medieval Religious Literature in Sanskrit.* Wiesbaden: Otto Harrassowitz, 1977.

———. *Viṣṇuism and Śivaism: A Comparison*. London: Athlone Press, University of London, 1970.

Gosvāmī, Rūp. *Bhaktirasāmṛtasindhu*, translated with introduction and notes by David L. Haberman. Delhi: Indira Gandhi National Centre for the Arts and Motilal Banarsidass, 2003.

———. *Ujjvalanīlamaṇi*. Edited by Puridās. Vrindaban: Haridās Śarmā, 1954.

Gupta, Kiśorīlāl. *Sūr aur Sūr Navīn*. Allahabad: Hindustani Academy, 1991.

Hawley, John Stratton. *At Play with Krishna: Pilgrimage Dramas from Brindavan*. Princeton: Princeton University Press, 1981.

———, ed. *The Bhakti Movement—Says Who? International Journal of Hindu Studies* 11:3 (2007), 209–324.

———. *Krishna, the Butter Thief*. Princeton: Princeton University Press, 1983.

———. *Sūr Dās: Poet, Singer, Saint*. Seattle: University of Washington Press; Delhi: Oxford University Press, 1984.

———. *Three Bhakti Voices: Mirabai, Surdas, and Kabir in Their Time and Ours*. Delhi: Oxford University Press, 2005.

Hawley, John Stratton, and Kenneth E. Bryant. *Sūr's Ocean*. 2 vols. New York: Oxford University Press, forthcoming.

Hawley, John Stratton, and Mark Juergensmeyer. *Songs of the Saints of India*, 2nd revised edition. Delhi: Oxford University Press, 2004 [originally 1988].

Hospital, Clifford G. *The Righteous Demon: A Study of Bali*. Vancouver: University of British Columbia Press, 1984.

Hudson, D. Dennis. *The Body of God*. New York: Oxford University Press, 2008.

———. "Vāsudeva Kṛṣṇa in Theology and Architecture: A Background to Śrīvaiṣ-ṇ avism," *Journal of Vaiṣṇava Studies* 2:1 (1993), 139–158.

Inden, Ronald, Jonathan S. Walters, and Daud Ali. *Querying the Medieval: Texts and the History of Practices in South Asia*. New York: Oxford University Press, 2000.

Ingalls, Daniel H. H. "The *Harivaṃśa* as a *Mahākāvya*." In *Mélanges d'indianisme à la mémoire de Louis Renou*, 381–394. Paris: Éditions de Boccard, 1968.

Jhā, Narendra, ed. *Bhaktamāl: Pāṭhānuśīlan evam Vivecan*. Patna: Anupam Prakāśan, 1978.

Jones, Sir William. *The Works of Sir William Jones*, edited by A.M.J. (Anna Maria Jones). 6 vols. London: G. G. and J. Robinson; and R. H. Evans, 1799.

Kale, M. R. *The Hitopadesa of Narayana*. Delhi: Motilal Banarsidass, 1967 [originally 1896].

Kane, P. V. *History of Dharmaśāstra*, vol. 5, part 1. Pune: Bhandarkar Oriental Research Institute, 1974.

Klostermeier, Klaus K. *A Survey of Hinduism*. Albany: State University of New York Press, 1994.

Kumār, Ajit, ed. *Ācārya Śukla Vicār Koś*. Delhi: National Publishing House, 1974.

Kutuban. *Kutuban kṛt Mṛgāvatī (Mūl Pāṭh, Pāṭhāntar, Ṭippaṇī evam Śodh)*. Edited by Parameśvarī Lāl Gupta. Varanasi: Viśvavidyālay Prakāśan, 1967.

Mahābhārata. Critically edited by V. S. Sukthankar et al. 19 vols. Poona: Bhandarkar Oriental Research Institute, 1927–1959.

Maiṭhāṇī, Umā (Kālā). *Sūr-Sāhitya ke Paurāṇik Prasaṅg*. New Delhi: Naman Prakāśan, 1997.

Mann, Gurinder Singh. *The Making of Sikh Scripture*. New York: Oxford University Press, 2001.

McGregor, Ronald Stuart. *Hindi Literature from Its Beginnings to the Nineteenth Century*. Wiesbaden: Otto Harrassowitz, 1984.

———. *Nanddas: The Round Dance of Krishna and Uddhav's Message*. London: Luzac, 1973.

Miller, Barbara Stoler, trans. *The Bhagavad-Gītā: Krishna's Counsel in Time of War*. New York: Bantam Books, 1986.

———. "The Divine Duality of Rādhā and Krishna." In *The Divine Consort: Rādhā and the Goddesses of India*, edited by J. S. Hawley and Donna M. Wulff, 13–26. Boston: Beacon Press, 1985.

Mītal, Prabhudayāl. *Braj kā Sāṃskṛtik Itihās*. Delhi: Rājkamal Prakāśan, 1966.

———. *Braj ke Dharma-Saṃpradāyoṅ kā Itihās*. Delhi: National Printing House, 1968.

———. *Braj kī Kalāoṅ kā Itihās*. Mathura: Sāhitya Saṃsthān, 1975.

Mukherjee, Tarapada, and Irfan Habib. "Akbar and the Temples of Mathura and Its Environs," *Proceedings of the Indian History Congress*, Goa, 1987 [published 1988], 234–250.

Nābhādās. *Śrī Bhaktamāl*, with the *Bhaktirasabodhinī* commentary of Priyādās and the *Bhaktisudhāsvād* commentary of Sītārāmśaraṇ Bhagavānprasād "Rūpkalā." Lucknow: Tejkumār Press, 1961 [originally 1910].

Nandadās. *Nandadās-Granthāvalī*. Edited by Brajratnadās. Varanasi: Nāgarīpracāriṇī Sabhā, 1957 [originally 1949].

Ojhā, Dharmanārāyaṇ. *Sūr-Sāhitya meṅ Puṣṭimārgīya Sevā Bhāvanā*. Allahabad: Śodh Sāhitya Prakāśan, 1973.

Olivelle, Patrick. *The Pañcatantra: The Book of India's Folk Wisdom*. Oxford: Oxford University Press, 1997.

Parīkh, Dvārakādās, ed. *Caurāsī Vaiṣṇavan kī Vārtā*. Mathura: Śrī Bajarang Pustakālay, 1970 [originally 1948].

Parry, Jonathan P. *Death in Banaras*. Cambridge: Cambridge University Press, 1994.

Pauwels, Heidi R. M. *In Praise of Holy Men: Imagining Religious Communities in Medieval India. Hagiographical Poems by and about Harirām Vyās*. Groningen: Egbert Forsten, 2002.

———. *Kṛṣṇa's Round Dance Reconsidered: Harirām Vyās's Hindi Rās-pañcādhyāyī*. Richmond, Surrey: Curzon Press, 1996.

Pollock, Sheldon. *The Language of the Gods in the World of Men*. Berkeley: University of California Press, 2006.

———, ed. *Literary Cultures in History: Reconstructions from South Asia*. Berkeley: University of California Press, 2003.

Richman, Paula. *Extraordinary Child: Poems from a South Indian Devotional Genre*. Honolulu: University of Hawai'i Press, 1997.

Rogers, Alexander, trans. *Tāzuk-i Jahāngīrī or Memoirs of Jahāngir (1605–1624)*. Revised and annotated by Henry Beveridge. New Delhi: Munshiram Manoharlal, 1978.

Ryder, Arthur W. *The Panchatantra*. Chicago: University of Chicago Press, 1964 [originally 1956].

Sanyal, Ritwik, and Richard Widdess. *Dhrupad: Tradition and Performance in Indian Music*. London: Ashgate, 2004.

Schwab, Raymond. *The Oriental Renaissance: Europe's Rediscovery of India and the East, 1680–1880*, translated by Gene Patterson-Black and Victor Reinking. New York: Columbia University Press, 1984 [French original, 1950].

Seṅgar, Śivsiṃh. *Śivsiṃh Saroj*. Edited by Kiśorīlāl Gupta. Allahabad: Hindī Sāhitya Sammelan, 1970.

———. *Śivsiṃh Saroj*. Edited by Trilokīnārāyāṇ Dīkṣit. Lucknow: Tejkumār Book Depot, 1966.

Sharma, Prem Lata. *Sahasarasa: Nāyak Bakhśū ke Drupadoṅ kā Saṅgrah*. New Delhi: Saṅgīt Nāṭak Academy, 1972.

———. "Sahasarasa," *Indian Music Journal* 8–10 (1972–1974), 41–48.

Sheth, Noel, S.J. *The Divinity of Krishna*. Delhi: Munshiram Manoharlal, 1984.

Siddiqi, Iqtidar Husain. "Shaikh Muhammad Kabir and His History of the Afghan Kings (A.D. 1451–1555)," *Indo-Iranica* 19:4 (1966), 57–78.

Smith, Barbara Herrnstein. *Poetic Closure: A Study of How Poems End*. Chicago: University of Chicago Press, 1968.

Snell, Rupert. "Devotion Rewarded: The *Sudāmā-carit* of Narottamdās." In *The Indian Narrative: Perspectives and Patterns*, edited by Christopher Shackle and Rupert Snell, 173–194. Wiesbaden: Otto Harrassowitz, 1992.

———. *The Hindi Classical Tradition: A Braj Bhāṣā Reader*. London: School of Oriental and African Studies, 1991.

———. "Metrical Forms in Braj Bhāṣā Verse: The *Caurāsī Pada* in Performance." In *Bhakti in Current Research, 1979–1983*, edited by Monika Thiel-Horstmann, 353–384. Berlin: Dietrich Reimer, 1983.

Soifer, Deborah A. *The Myths of Narasiṃha and Vāmana*. Albany: State University of New York Press, 1991.

Śukla, Rāmcandra. *Hindī Sāhitya kā Itihās*. Banaras: Kāśī Nāgarīpracāriṇī Sabhā, 1929. 2nd ed. Varanasi, 1940.

———. *Sūrdās*. Edited by Viśvanāthprasād Miśra. Varanasi: n.p., 1948.

Sūrdās. *Pad Sūrdāsjī kā/The Padas of Sūrdās*. Edited by Gopal Narayan Bahura and Kenneth E. Bryant. Jaipur: Maharaja Sawai Man Singh II Museum, 1982 [actually appeared 1984].

———. *Sūrsāgar (Śrīkṛṣṇa Līlātmak* and *Dvādaś Skandhātmak)*. 5 vols. Edited by Kiśorī Lāl Gupta. Allahabad: Lokbhāratī Prakāśan, 2005.

———. *Sūr-Granthāvalī*. 4 vols. Edited by Sītārām Caturvedī. Varanasi: Akhil Bhāratīya Vikram Pariṣad, 1974–1978.

———. *Sūrsāgar*. Edited by Mātāprasād Gupta and prepared for publication by Udayśaṃkar Śāstrī. *Bhāratīya Sāhitya* 15:1–2 (1970), 145–472; 16:1–2 (1971), 149–184; 17:1–2 (1972), 155–196; 17:3–4 (1972), 195–203; 18:1–2 (1973), 145–205; 18:3–4 (1973), 163–210; 19:1–2 (1974), 159–208; 19:3–4 (1974), 173–220.

———. *Sūrsāgar*. Edited by Mātāprasād Gupta and prepared for publication by Udayśaṅkar Śāstrī. Agra: Agra University, 1979.

———. *[Sūrsāgar] Śrīsūrsāgar*. Edited by Rādhākṛṣṇadās. Bombay: Khemrāj Śrīkṛṣṇadās, 1957.

———. *Sūrsāgar*. Edited by Jagannāthdās "Ratnākar," Nandadulāre Vājpeyī, et al. 2 vols. Varanasi: Kāśī Nāgarīpracāriṇī Sabhā, 1972 and 1976 [originally 1948].

———. *Sūr's Ocean*, volume 2. Edited by Kenneth E. Bryant. New York; Oxford University Press, forthcoming.

Ṭaṇḍan, Premnārāyaṇ. *Brajbhāṣā Sūr-Koś*. 2 vols. Lucknow: Lucknow University, 1962.

Tawney, C. H. *The Kathā Sarit Sāgara or Ocean of the Streams of Story*. 2 vols. Delhi: Munshiram Manoharlal, 1968 [originally 1880–1884].

Tulsī Dās. *Rāmcaritmānas*, with a Hindi paraphrase by Hanumānprasād Poddār. Gorakhpur: Gita Press, 1947.

Vālmīki. *Rāmāyaṇa*. Critically edited under the general direction of R. T. Vyas. Baroda: Oriental Institute, 1992 [originally 1960–1975].

———. *Rāmāyaṇa*. Vulgate edition. 7 vols. Bombay: Gujarati Printing Press, 1914–1920.

Vaudeville, Charlotte. *Pastorales par Soûr-Dâs*. Paris: Gallimard, 1971.

———. *A Weaver Named Kabir: Selected Verses with a Detailed Biographical and Historical Introduction*. Delhi: Oxford University Press, 1993.

Wakankar, Milind. "The Moment of Criticism in Indian Nationalist Thought: Ramchandra Shukla and the Poetics of a Hindi Responsibility." In *The South Atlantic Quarterly* 101:4 (2002), 986–1014.

———. "The Prehistory of the Popular: Caste and Canonicity in Indian Modernity." Ph.D. dissertation, Columbia University, 2002.

Zimmer, Heinrich. *Hindu Medicine*. Baltimore: Johns Hopkins University Press, 1948.

List of Poems by English Title

	BRYANT EDITION	NPS EDITION
A bellyful	§384	NPS 52
A boor from Braj	§191	NPS 3797
A cataract of arrows	§325	NPS 4780
A letter has arrived	§248	NPS 4107
A mass of delight	§42	NPS 1245
Aflame at both ends	§206	NPS 4723
All my symptoms	§212	NPS 3880
An offering of lights	§429	NPS 371
At dawn	§20	NPS 821
Autumn alone	§230	NPS 3961
Aviary	§31	NPS 984
Awake!	§19	NPS 820
Back from the woods	§33	NPS 1094
Begging bowl	§201	NPS 3844
Better mothers than Yaśodā	§28	NPS 968
Black braid	§15	NPS 792
Black storm clouds	§65	NPS 1806
Blind to the sun	§428	NPS 368
Body like a flagstaff	§360	Not in NPS
Brindavan's splendor	§172	NPS 3465
Broken horoscope	§413	NPS 298
Butter thief	§22	NPS 901
Celebrating the birth	§3	NPS 642

	BRYANT EDITION	NPS EDITION
Circle dance	§62	NPS 1757
Clad with the sky	§261	NPS 4184
Clogged with my letters	§219	NPS 3918
Confluence	§433	NPS 455
Cooked like an eggplant	§416	NPS 320
Crawling	§8	NPS 720
Daddy, Daddy	§187	NPS 3734
Danced too much	§400	NPS 153
Dancing on the snake	§36	NPS 1193
Dirty trick	§278	NPS 4282
Disastrous leaves	§192	NPS 3807
Dragged him from the blueing vat	§289	NPS 4380
Dvaraka's so close	§337	NPS 4843
Dwarf at the door	§361	NPS 440
Elephant clouds	§220	NPS 3921
Exact whatever punishment	§171	NPS 3441
Feeding his reflection	§17	NPS 796
Filling her pots	§64	Not in NPS
Flutist	§73	NPS 1995
Forest fire	§38	NPS 1233
Ganges	§432	NPS 454
Gopāl has stolen my heart	§102	NPS 2490
Great crowds of clouds	§56	NPS 1487
Hari's chariot	§326	NPS 4782
He conquered Jarāsandh	§336	NPS 4834
He loves butter	§7	NPS 717
Hero of the cow-clan	§55	NPS 1481
His and hers	§105	NPS 2522
His boyhood friend Śrīdāmā	§338	NPS 4846
His fabulous feet	§10	NPS 749
Holi	§173	NPS 3471
Homecoming	§339	NPS 4854
Hunchback	§276	NPS 4256
Ignorant eyes	§90	NPS 2401
In Rādhā's dress	§83	NPS 2298
In the birth canal	§389	NPS 77
Inaccessible in Dvaraka	§347	NPS 4873
Jamunā	§431	NPS 4823

	BRYANT EDITION	NPS EDITION
Jarāsandh bound us	§335	NPS 4831
Kālindī, do what I say	§333	NPS 4821
Kaṃs he killed	§186	NPS 3705
Krishna, the Ganges	§87	NPS 2376
Last rites?	§321	NPS 4735
Lines with her fingernails	§241	NPS 4023
Lord of the Milkmaids	§277	NPS 4265
Lost	§72	NPS 1989
Mādhav, control that cow	§386	NPS 56
Mādhav, in anger	§356	NPS 273
Mathura the bride	§183	NPS 3640
Maybe	§223	NPS 3928
Muralī makes him dance	§46	NPS 1273
Muralī transfixes	§47	NPS 1276
Muralī's kingdom	§45	NPS 1271
Nothing I could do	§1013	NPS 2498
Nothing now remains	§355	NPS 247
No-trait philosophy	§254	Not in NPS
Only this mantra	§165	NPS 3399
Overeager acrobat	§412	NPS 292
Overwrought	§315	NPS 1367
Peddling yoga	§266	NPS 4208
Proper hospitality	§170	NPS 3440
Rādhā disbelieves	§110	NPS 2741
Radiance	§74	NPS 1998
Rāvaṇ roars in battle	§370	NPS 574
Red in the morning	§148	NPS 3299
River of tears	§319	NPS 4730
Scholar at your door	§362	NPS 441
Serpent and vine	§67	NPS 1814
She's going mad	§324	NPS 4764
Similes lost their nerve	§86	NPS 2374
Sing the song of God	§417	NPS 323
Slammed the door	§137	NPS 3150
So many other sinners	§402	NPS 158
Such good advice	§253	NPS 4132
Sūr's twenty-five	§418	NPS 325
Teaching him to walk	§9	NPS 733

	BRYANT EDITION	NPS EDITION
Ten-day trial	§300	NPS 4501
Thank goodness he's come	§316	NPS 4721
The black	§290	NPS 4368
The breaths	§367	NPS 536
The color of dusk	§38	NPS 1234
The dark Jamunā's blackened	§193	NPS 3809
The deer in his face	§93	NPS 2415
The dust of Brindavan	§34	NPS 1107
The elements	§81	NPS 2286
The fever of being apart	§196	NPS 3815
The gaze	§88	NPS 2379
The gift of your devotion	§391	NPS 106
The gopis complain	§23	NPS 909
The lure of Dvaraka	§327	NPS 4783
The master list	§409	NPS 193
The memory of love	§369	NPS 545
The memory of that passion	§197	NPS 3821
The night he was born	§1	NPS 629
The onslaught of love	§60	NPS 1744
The season of rains	§224	NPS 3935
The tyranny of love	§163	NPS 3393
The view from Ayodhya	§374	NPS 611
The wheel in his hand	§357	NPS 279
The worn-out world	§377	NPS App.205
The wrong address	§340	NPS 4855
They say you're so giving	§399	NPS 135
This bee—and that	§288	NPS 4378
This jungle	§366	NPS 507
Those feet, that lake	§420	NPS 337
Thoughts of him stalk me	§214	NPS 3886
Today Rām is raging in battle	§372	NPS 602
Toiling like a dog	§390	NPS 103
Topknot	§16	NPS 793
Toward Badarī	§359	NPS 383
Truth in advertising	§397	NPS 124
Turban of deceit	§287	NPS 4364
Turn away	§419	NPS 332
Ūdho, go	§244	NPS 4045

	BRYANT EDITION	NPS EDITION
Uncanny resemblance	§246	NPS 4077
Utterly soiled	§313	NPS 4690
We marvel at your arms	§58	NPS 1584
Wine in the red of his eyes	§332	NPS 4819
With love	§217	NPS 3908
Working on ourselves	§283	NPS 4340
Yaśodā answers	§24	NPS 913

List of Poems by Brajbhāṣā Title

	Bryant Edition
Antarajāmī ho raghubīra	§377
Ati malīna briṣabhāna kuṅvārī	§313
Apanī bhagati dai bhagavāna	§391
Aba e aiseī dina mere	§192
Aba kachu aurai hai calī	§196
Aba kachu nāhinai rahyau	§355
Aba kai rāṣi lehu gopāla	§37
Aba mo kuṅ jāniye su kījai	§171
Aba rādhe nāhina braja nīti	§163
Aba hauṅ nācyau bahuta gupāla	§400
Aṣiyāṅ ajāna bhaī	§90
Āja ati kope hai rana rāma	§372
Āja braja mahā ghaṭani ghana ghero	§56
Āju avara chabi nanda kisora	§148
Āju saṣī hauṅ prāta samai dadhi mathana uṭhī akulāi	§17
Ihā aura kāsauṅ kahauṅ garuḍagāmī	§335
Upamā dhīraja tajyau niraṣi chabi	§86

	Bryant Edition
Ūdhau tuma jānata gupitahi yārī	§287
Ūdhau vegihī braja jāhu	§244
Kajarī kau paya pīvahu gupāla baini baḍhai	§15
Kamala muṣa sobhita sundara bainu	§73
Kara kapola bhuja dhari jānuni para liṣati hai māi naṣani kī reṣani	§241
Karata kachūvai na banī	§103
Kahā na kījai apanai kājai	§300
Kahi na sakati tuma sauṅ ika bāta	§337
Kahīyata rāma tyāgī dāni	§399
Kānha sauṅ āvata kyauṅ ba risāta	§31
Kālyandrī kari kahyau hamārau	§333
Kālyandrī kesau kī pyārī	§431
Kāhe ko gopīnātha kahāvata	§277
Kite dina hari sumirana binu ṣoe	§384
Kidhau ghana garajata nahi una desani	§223
Kubijā hau yaduvara bhalau kiyau	§276
Kou vaisī hī unahāri	§246
Gagana uṭhī ghaṭā kārī bica baga panti ninyārī	§65
Gupāla dure haiṅ māṣanu ṣāta	§22
Gopāla jū hauṅ na caraṇa taji jaihauṅ	§187
Gopālahi pāuṅ to jāuṅ uhi desa	§201
Cakaī rī cali caraṇa sarovara jahāṅ na pema viyogu	§420
Cahuṅ disi taiṅ ghana ghore	§220
Citai rādhā rati nāgara vora	§88
Chāḍi mana hari bimuṣana kau saṅga	§419
Janama sirānau aṭakai aṭakai	§412
Janu jina kai saṅga ura gāyau	§409
Jaba tai śravana sunyau terau nāma	§165
Jaba lagi satya sarūpa na sūjhata	§428
Jasodā kaba bāḍhaigī coṭī	§16
Jāgau braja rāja kuṅvara kaṅvala kosa phūle	§19

	Bryant Edition
Jītyau jarāsindha bandi chorī	§336
Jai ho jai mādhau bainī	§433
Jaise tuma aura bahuta ṣalu tāre	§402
Joga ṭhagaurī braja na bikaihai	§278
Jau pai rāṣati hau pahicāni	§191
Tumhārai biraha brajanātha nainani nadī baḍhī	§319
Tumhārau bacana meṭyau na jāi	§360
Terau taba tihi dina ko hai hitu hari bina sudhi dhūṅ kari kripana tāhi cita āni	§389
Dina dvārāvati deṣana āvata	§327
Duhu disi kau ati biraha birahinī kaisai kai ba sahai	§206
Dūri hī taiṅ deṣe balabīra	§338
Dena āe ūdhau matu nīkau	§253
Deṣata bana brajanātha āja ati upajata hai anurāga	§173
Deṣata bhūli rahyau dvija dīna	§339
Deṣi rī deṣi ānanda kanda	§42
Deṣi rī hari ke cañcala tāre	§93
Deṣi saṣī bana taiṅ ju banai braja āvata hai nanda nandana	§33
Deṣiyata kālindī ati kārī	§193
Deṣe yaha gati jāta sandesau kāhāṅ hauṅ kahauṅ	§367
Deṣau brindāvana śrī kamala naina	§172
Deṣau rī saṣi āja nayana bhari hari ju ke ratha kī sobhā	§326
Deṣau hari jaisau rāsa racyau	§62
Dvāraiṅ ṭhāḍhe haiṅ dvija bāvana	§361
Nadīyā jamunā kai taṭa	§64
Nahi bisarati vaha rati brajanātha	§197
Nāṅhinai sudhi rahī hiyai	§321
Piya pada kamala kau makaranda	§432
Prāta samai uṭhi sovata suta kau badana nihāryau nanda	§20
Prīti tau marana hī na bicārai	§217
Barajati kāhe tai nahī	§23
Bariṣā ritu āī hari na milai rī māī	§224

	Bryant Edition
Bali bali bali mohana mūrati kī bali kuṇḍala bali naina bisāla	§72
Bātai būjhata yau baurāvati	§324
Bāruṇī bala ghūrama locana biharata bana sacu pāye	§332
Bāla binoda ṣare jiya bhāvata	§8
Bilagu jini mānau ūdhau pyāre	§289
Braja bhayau mahara kai pūta jaba yaha bāta sunī	§3
Bhādoṅ kī raini andhyārī	§1
Bhūlati hau kata mīṭhī bātani	§288
Bhūlyau dvija deṣata apanau gharu	§340
Mathurā aisī āju banī	§183
Mathurā ke logani sacu pāyau	§186
Manā re mādhau sauṅ kari prīti	§418
Mādhau kopi cakra kara līnau	§356
Mādhau jī ke badana kī sobhā	§74
Mādhau naikuṇ haṭako gāi	§386
Mānau megha ghaṭā ati gāḍhī	§325
Muralī ati garva kāhu vadati nāhi āju	§45
Muralī adhara saji balabīra	§47
Muralī tau gupālahi bhāvai	§46
Merau kau tau vinatī kībī	§369
Merau mana matihīna gusāī	§390
Merau manu gopāla haryau rī	§102
Maiṅ jānyo rī āe hai hari jāgi pare tai pachitānī rī	§212
Maiṅ hari sauṅ māna kiyau	§137
Motini kī māla manohara	§87
Rājā ika paṇḍita pauri tumhārī	§362
Rādhā ke basana syāma maṇi cīnhī	§83
Rādhikā hari atithu tumhārai	§170
Rādhe bhūli rahī anurāga	§60
Rādhe milehu pratīti na āvati	§110
Rāvana tau lauṅ hai rana gājata	§370
Rāṣi lehu gokula ke nāyaka	§55
Liṣī brajanātha kī āī chāpa	§248

	Bryant Edition
Vā paṭa pīta kī paharāni	§357
Vai dina visari gaye ihāṅ āye	§416
Vai deṣau raghupati hai āvata	§374
Sandesani madhubana kūpa bhare	§219
Saba ṣoṭe madhubana ke loga	§266
Sabani saneho chāḍi dayau	§413
Sabai braja jamunā kai tīra	§36
Sarada samai hū syāma na āe	§230
Saṣī vai syāma kahā hitu jānahi	§290
Sāṅvare ho tuma jini jāhu kahūṅ	§24
Sāṅvare bali bali gaī [re] bhujani kī	§58
Sāṅvarau manamohana māī	§38
Siṣavati calana jasodā maiyā	§9
Su kahā ju maiṅ na kīyau jo pai soi soi cita dharihau	§397
Sundara syāma piyā kī jorī	§105
Sunata tumhārī bāta udhau cūi cale dou naina	§315
Sunahu anuja nija bana itanainu mili hai jānukī harī	§366
Sobhita kara navanītu liyai	§7
Hama kauṅ supanai hī maiṅ socu	§214
Hama na bhaye bṛndābana kī renu	§34
Hama hū tau ūdhau apanau sau karati kaṭhina mana nisi dinu	§283
Hari aba ihai su kahā	§210
Hari ura mohana beli lasī	§67
Hari ke badana tana dhauṅ cāhi	§28
Hari jū āe su bhalī kīnī	§316
Hari jū kī āratī banī	§429
Hari muṣa niraṣi nimeṣa bisāre	§261
Hari sauṅ hauṅ kahā kahauṅ	§359
Hari hita hita merau mādhaiyā	§10
Hauṅ kaisai kai darasana pāuṅ	§347
Hauṅ sāṅvare kai saṅgi jaihauṅ	§81

Index

Abū'l-Fazl 'Allāmī, 21–22
Advaitan orthodoxy, 206
Afghan rulers, 19
"Aflame at both ends," 116, 230
Afsānah-i-Shāhān "Tale of Kings," 19–20, 23
Agra, 7, 23
Ā'īn-i-Akbarī (Abū'l-Fazl 'Allāmī), 21
Airāvat, 209
akāsa (*ākāśa*, ether), 213
Akbar (emperor), 5–6, 6n4, 21–23, 43
Akrūr, 108, 225–26
"All my symptoms," 117, 230
Amber (Jaipur), 5, 7, 23
amorous love (*madhurati*), 88, 210, 214
amṛt, 204
amulet, 52, 201
anger, 72–73, 82, 98, 208, 218–19
  Bhṛgu's, 90, 215
  "dressed in," 182
  "Mādhav, in anger," 160, 256–57
  pleasure mixed with, 99
  Rādhā's, 103, 222
  Shiva's, 104, 222–23
ankle-bells, 182
antelope skin, 140, 241–42
anurāg (devotional sentiment), 79, 209–10
Arabic, 19
Arjun, 256. *See also Mahābhārata*
arms
  four, 137, 239
  mighty, 77, 108
arrow, 75, 80, 82, 211–12. *See also* bow and arrow
  "straight in the face," 140, 242
Aṣṭachāp ("eight seals"), 12
Āṣāḍh, 201
ascetic, 131, 237
ass, 191
astrologer, 109, 186, 226, 274
astrology, 48
"At dawn," 60
Aurangzeb, 25
authorship, collective, 24–28
"Autumn alone," 124, 233
Avadhī, 4–6, 7, 7n7, 21
Avadh region, 5
avanī (earth), 213
"Aviary," 65
"Awake!," 31, 59, 204
Ayodhya, 172, 264–65

Bābā Rāmdās, 21–23
"Back from the woods," 66
Badarī forest, 163, 258
Badā'ūnī, 'Abd al-Qādir al-, 22–23
Bairām Khān, 22
Balarām, 54, 57, 74, 155, 203, 206, 208, 253–54
  Kālindī and, 151, 249
  plow-bearer, 29, 203
  in wrestling match, 226
Bali, 55, 165, 173, 202–3, 258–60
bali (sacrifice), 83, 212–13
bali jānā (to sacrifice oneself), 84, 212–13

bamboo, 69
banana tree, 104, 222
basant (spring), 104–105, 222–224
basil
leaves, 71, 208
-tree, 206
battle, 147, 246–47. *See also Mahābhārata*
Krishna v. Kaṃs, 107, 225
Rām in, 171, 264
Rāvaṇ in, 170, 263–64
beauty, 104, 222
of Mathura, 107, 225
bee(s), 31, 51, 59, 64, 70, 86, 89, 96–97, 104, 139, 152, 222, 241, 250–51
bhramargīt, 128, 235
militia of, 85, 213
pair of pair of, 91, 216
river eddies and vortices like, 112, 228
"This bee—and that," 137, 239
"bee messenger" poems, 16–17, 127–46
"Begging bowl," 115, 229–30
"Beguiler of the Mind," 70, 108, 165, 207, 225–26
Beguiling One, 165
Behl, Aditya, 5n3, 19n22
"A bellyful," 175, 266
betel leaves, 77, 99, 209, 219
"Better mothers than Yaśodā," 64
"bewildered as a snake," 143, 244
Bhādoṅ, 47, 49, 199, 201
Bhagavad Gītā, 253
Bhāgavata Purāṇa, 15–18, 16n18, 236, 247, 253–54, 256–57
Bhaktamāl "Gardland of Lovers of God" (Nābhādās), 8
Bhaktavijaya (Mahīpati), 12n11
Bhaktavinod (Miyāṅsiṃh), 12n11
bhakti (devotion), 55, 202, 226, 257
bhaṇitā (poet's signature), 23–27, 24n31, 29, 32, 37, 120, 231–32, 256–57
Bhaum (demon), 152, 250–51
bheri drum, 50, 105, 201, 224
Bhikhārīdās, 20–21
Bhīśma, 256–57
bhramargīt (songs of the bee), 128, 235
Bhṛgu's scar, 90, 215
bimba fruit, 70, 207
binoda (games), 53, 201. *See also* game(s)
birth, 47, 48–51, 179
"In the birth canal," 177, 267–68
bitter flavor, 102, 134, 221, 278
bitterness, 103
"The black," 139, 241
"black body," 130
"black bucks," 139, 241
"black Jamuna," 112, 228
"black snake," 57, 203
"Black storm clouds," 82, 211–12
"blanket dyed black," 191
blindness, 12–15, 120, 152, 181, 231–32, 250–51
"Blind to the sun," 193, 277–78
blood, 160, 177, 267
blueing vat, 138, 240
boats, 144, 245
Bodiless One, 80, 100, 211, 220
"Body like a flagstaff," 163, 258
"A boor from Braj," 110, 227
bow and arrow, 104, 222
arrows, 75, 80, 82, 140, 211–12, 242
bow of Kaṃs, 108, 225
Sāraṅg bow, 170, 171
bracelet, 48, 99
Brahmā, 17, 18, 55, 72, 84, 151, 160, 171, 187, 194, 208, 256–57
Brahmin, 156–157, 254
cows given to, 50, 201
"food for a Brahmin feast," 101, 221
Brahmin dwarf, 164–165, 258–59
Brahmin's braid, 131, 237
Brajbhāṣā
Krishna speaking, 6
as literary medium, 7
oaths in, 55, 203
Sanskrit v., xiii, 5
Brajbhāṣā *pads*, 28–29
poem analysis, 31–40
rules governing, 28–30
sample poem: "Awake!," 31
Brajbhāṣā poets, 8, 21
Braj region, 6–7, 30, 48, 56, 62–63, 76, 100, 110, 134
"A boor from Braj," 110, 227
after Krishna's departure, 112, 113, 227–28
Mathura as capital of, 107, 225
people of, 53–54, 69, 105, 203, 208–9, 224
spell cast over, 80, 210
traditions of, 105, 224
breast, 48, 94, 97, 143, 217, 244
"The breaths," 168, 261–62
Brindavan, 67, 206
"Brindavan's splendor," 104, 222–23
"Broken horoscope," 186, 274
Bṛṣabhānu's daughter, 141, 243
Bryant, Kenneth, vii–viii, 26, 34, 38, 40, 42n58, 43
Burhanpur, 24

burning
"brilliant warriors," 171
"burned myself alive," 179
fire-oblation, 101, 221
fire of Holi, 153, 252
"Forest fire," 69
funeral pyre, 170, 178, 188
"lonely woman sets herself on fire," 119, 231
from longing, 112, 117, 124, 141, 227–28, 230, 243
moth to the flame, 119, 188, 230
Busch, Allison, 6–7n5–7, 20n25, 21
butter, 53, 110, 201–2, 227. *See also* ghī
"He loves butter," 52
Krishna's offering to himself of, 58, 203
-thief, 61

caesura (*yati*), 29, 32, 37
Caitanya Sampradāy, 31
cakaī, 112, 228. *See also* sheldrake
cakor bird, 60, 71, 79, 91, 104, 149, 192, 204, 207, 222, 248
"calf" emotion (*vātsalya bhāv*), 34–35, 40, 54, 202
cāmīkara (gold color), 83, 212
campā blossom, 96, 167, 260
camphor, 111, 191
Candāyan (M. Dāūd), 5, 7
Cānur, 108, 226
"captain of the gods," 77, 209
cātak-bird, 71, 139, 207, 241
"A cataract of arrows," 147, 246–47
Caurāsī Vaiavan kī Vārtā "Accounts of Eighty-four Vaishnavas," 12
cavalry, 104, 222
"Celebrating the birth," 48–51
"the chains were loosed," 47, 200
chalk, 49, 200
chāp (poet's seal), 12, 29, 36
chariot, 68, 72, 93, 104, 148, 160, 172, 222, 247–48
churning, 58, 60, 204
"Circle dance," 80, 210
city/woman metaphor, 107, 225
"Clad with the sky," 131, 236–37
"Clogged with my letters," 120, 231–32
clothes, 155, 159, 175, 253. *See also* yellow garments
cloud(s), 48, 70–71, 146, 207, 208–9
archer, 147, 246–47
"Black storm clouds," 82, 211–12
"Elephant clouds," 121, 232
"Great crowds of clouds," 76
storm, 147, 246–47
thickening, 121, 232
club, 90, 216
cobra, 115, 125, 191, 229, 234
crown, 143, 243–44
collyrium, 144
compassion, 39
concentration, forms of, 135, 238–39
conch, 90, 148, 216, 247–48
"Confluence," 197, 280–83
"confluence of child and youth," 99, 219
"connoisseur of love," 158, 255
"Cooked like an eggplant," 187, 274
cow(s), 56, 74–75, 203, 208. *See also* gopī
"calf" emotion, 34–35, 40, 54, 202
given to Brahmins, 50, 201
"Mādhav, control that cow," 176, 266–67
running toward their calves, 59
of the senses, 266–67
wealth, 64, 205
Yaśodā preoccupied with, 110, 227
cow-clan, 74–75, 208–9
cowherds, 49, 63, 74–75, 208
enchanting, 113, 228
crane, 56, 69, 203
"Crawling," 53
cremation rites, 221. *See also* funeral pyre
crocodile, 71, 90
crossdressing, 88, 214
crow, 79, 139, 210, 241
crown, 86, 128
cobra, 143, 243–44
cuckoo, 79, 82, 104, 111, 146, 149, 210, 222,246, 248
"never begging elsewhere," 188
rainy season associated with, 122–123, 233
"shouting love," 119, 230
"sweet pure sound of," 105, 224
curse, singed with, 130
cymbals, 105, 224

"Daddy, Daddy," 109, 226
Dādū, 21
dancing, 68, 80, 194, 206, 210
"Danced too much," 182, 271
"Dancing on the snake," 68, 206
"dancing street performer," 125, 234
ḍaph (frame drum), 105, 224
"The dark Jamuna's blackened," 112, 227–28
Dark Jewel, 88, 214
Dark Lord, 134, 138, 142, 145, 149, 240, 243, 245, 248, 278
Dark One, 68, 77, 96, 102, 115, 124, 206, 229, 233
darśan (seeing), 52, 71, 201, 207

Daśarath, 172
Dāūd, Maulānā, 5, 7
dawn, 58, 99, 114, 229
death, 131, 161, 237, 257
city of, 179
fear of, 175
messengers of, 190
deer, 74, 93, 113, 119, 167, 183, 216, 228, 230
black bucks, 139, 241
"The deer in his face," 93
"enduring the arrow," 187–188, 274
demons, 152, 176, 183, 194, 250–51
Rāvaṇ, 13, 170–171, 263–64
sent by Kaṃs, 77, 209
desire, 98, 179, 219
pulling at mind, 189
"destroyer of the wicked," 66, 205
Devakī
Krishna's revelation to, 200
released by Krishna, 108, 226
wail of, 47, 199
Yaśodā addresses, 110, 227
devanāgarī, xiii
devotion, 179, 181, 268–69
anurāg, 79, 209–10
dewdrops, 64
Dharwadker, Vinay, 26
dhrupad, 41
diamond, 52, 89, 201, 215
"Dirty trick," 134, 278
"Disastrous leaves," 111, 227
discus, 160, 256–57
disk, 90, 216
distress, Devakī's, 47, 200
doe, 69
dog, 178, 186, 191, 268
dohā, 21
dove, 119, 143, 149, 188, 230, 244, 248
"Dragged him from the blueing vat," 138, 239–40
Draupadī, 183, 255–56
dreaming, 118, 230
"dressed like a fine actor," 108, 225–26
drums, 50, 104, 201, 222
battle, 147, 246–47
of Holi, 105, 224
drunkenness, 152, 250–51
dūb grass, 49, 77, 201, 209
Dudney, Arthur, 4n1
Duhśāsan, 159, 255–56
dusk, 70, 87, 207
"The dust of Brindavan," 67, 206
duty, 94
Dvaraka, 6, 148, 248 149
"Dvaraka's so close," 154, 252–53
dwarf, 164, 165
"Dwarf at the door," 258–59

earrings, 48, 71, 86, 89, 215
earth (element), 87, 213
earth (planet), 69, 72
"Island Earth," 194
"shuddered fearfully," 160
"three and a half steps worth of," 164, 165
ego, 188, 190
eight seals, 12
elements
"The elements," 87, 213–14
five, 177
three, 176, 267
elephant, 108, 147, 183, 225, 246–47
"Elephant clouds," 121, 232
elixir, 71. *See also* nectar
embarrassment, 81, 89, 215
emptiness, 115, 229–30
ether (*akāsa*), 87, 213
"Exact whatever punishment," 103, 222
eyebrows, arched, 71, 85, 103, 222
eyes, 92, 93, 111, 216, 227
blindness, 12–15, 120, 152, 181, 231–32, 250–51
cakor-bird, 71
"haṭha-yoga eyes," 131, 237
like pair of bees, 91, 216
like wagtail birds, 65–66, 205
"Wine in the red of his eyes," 150, 248–49

"false poets," 89, 215
fame
mark of, 130, 136, 236, 239
"The worn-out world," 173, 265–66
family
honor, 94
merits, 48
Fatehpur manuscript, 23–24, 23n9, 41
father, 109, 148, 199, 201, 226–27, 248. *See also* Brahmā
fear, 47, 160, 175, 180, 183, 199
"frighten my heart," 124, 233
when "youth and life are spent," 190
"Feeding his reflection," 58, 203
feet, 55, 67, 202, 206, 258–59
"I touch your feet," 103
lotus-, 178
"merciful," 183
"Those feet, that lake," 192, 276–77
touching of, 114, 172, 229
"feud with the moon," 61, 204
"The fever of being apart," 113, 228

fever of longing (*viraha*), 112, 117, 124, 141, 227–28, 230, 243
"Filling her pots," 81, 211
fine magic (*sumāyā*), 80, 210
fingernails, 125, 234
fire-oblation, 101, 221. *See also* burning
fish
  eyebrows like, 86
  without water, 127, 128, 188
flags, 136, 171
flagstaff, 163, 258
flavors (*ras, ṣaḍras*), 63, 102, 134, 205, 221, 238
flowers, 73, 96, 104–105, 111, 145, 167, 222, 224, 245, 260. *See also* lotus
  garland, 50, 70
flute, 66, 72. *See also* Muralī
"Flutist," 85, 213
foam, 67
food, 110, 176, 187, 227
  "diet of foam," 112, 228
  "Feeding his reflection," 58, 203
  "for a Brahmin feast," 101, 221
  "gorge yourself," 104
  "rare flavor," 102, 221
forehead mark, 48, 70, 144, 175
forest, 66, 104, 162–163, 222, 257–58
  "Forest fire," 69, 206
four ages, 195
four goals, life's, 181
fourteen worlds, 176, 266
"frighten my heart," 124, 233
frog, 146, 246
frost, 141, 243
funeral pyre, 170, 178, 188, 221

gagarī (waterpots), 80, 211
game(s), 53, 114, 201, 229
  of dice, 189
  "game that's played at Phālgun time," 105, 224
Gang, 20-21
Ganges river, 55, 202, 215–216
  "Ganges," 196, 279–80
  "Krishna, the Ganges," 90
Ganges water, 191
"Garg's words," 109, 226–27
garland, 50, 70
Garuḍ, 152, 250
Gautam, 183
"The gaze," 91
geese, 104, 148–149, 222, 247–48
Ghaus, Sheikh Muhammad, 23
ghī, 49, 63, 102, 200, 221. *See also* butter
"The gift of your devotion," 179, 268–69
Gītagovinda (Jayadeva), 230
"girl's plea," 104, 222–23
"glistening new boats," 144, 245
god(s), 72, 213, 256–57
  "all the host of," 194
  ashamed, 179
  born as, 67, 206
  Brahmā, 17, 18, 55, 72, 84, 151, 160, 171, 187, 194, 208, 256–57
  "captain of," 77, 209
  devanāgarī, xiii
  household, 54
  Indra, 1, 13, 75, 77, 121–122, 170–171, 208–9, 232–33
  Kāma, 80, 82, 85, 88, 100, 104–105, 210–12, 214, 223–224
  "River-of-the-Gods," 196
  Shiva, 104, 115, 151, 157, 171, 194, 196, 211, 222–23, 229
  Vishnu, 9, 17, 18, 72, 90, 143, 165, 202, 208, 215, 243–44, 259–60
God of Love, 82, 102, 142, 211–12, 221, 243. *See also* Kāma
Gokul, 30, 48, 144, 200, 206
Gokulnāth, 12
gold color
  cāmīkara, 83, 212
  kañcana, 80, 211
  vine of, 96
Gopāl, 56, 61, 69, 73, 84, 109, 161, 213, 226, 257
  "Gopāl has stolen my heart," 94, 217
gopī (cowherdess), 16–17, 35, 44, 112, 115, 120, 132, 204, 228–229, 237–38
  "The gopīs complain," 62
  letters from, 120, 231–32
  memories of Krishna, 114, 229
  in rainy season, 121, 231–32
Gorakhnāth, 115, 229
Goswami, Shrivatsa, 38
Govardhan, 76, 109, 183, 208–9, 232–33
Govind, 98, 159, 255–56
grass
  dūb grass, 49, 77, 201, 209
  hair like, 112, 228
  kāṃs grass, 124, 233
  kuśa grass, 49
"Great crowds of clouds," 76
great flood, 76, 209
greed, 185, 188
Greek classics, 3–4, 4n1
"Growing too slow," 56
gudara (tribute), 104, 223

Gujarat, 30
guñjā berries, 49
Gurū Granth, 26
Gwalior, 6–7

hair
  Brahmin's braid, 131, 237
  braided hair like snake, 57, 203
  in braids, 48, 56, 167, 203
  breeze-blown curls, 85, 213
  disheveled, 112, 228
  like grasses and reeds, 112, 228
  śrīvats, 90, 215
  tangled, 86
  thick locks, 71
  "Topknot," 57, 203
  in unkempt mound, 115, 229
hand(s)
  with bracelets, 48
  flower-petal, 73
  gesture of, 104, 223
  left-hand side, 88, 214
  lotus-like, 33–34, 59, 77, 204, 209
Hanumān, 168–169
happiness, 159, 255–56
  giver of all, 54, 202
  Krishna's touch bringing, 75, 209
"happy knot," 96, 217
Hari ("remover of distress/sin"), 13, 55, 58, 64, 80, 83, 87–89, 92–93, 95, 97, 131, 200, 237
  "Hari has come," 143, 243–44
  "Hari's chariot," 148, 247–48
  "ignoring," 189–90, 266
  playful acts of, 9, 14, 18, 108, 192, 225
Haridās, 22
Harirāmvyās, 18, 23
Harirāy, 12
Harivaṃśa, 236, 247
Harnahadgalli, Karnataka, 201
"haṭha-yoga eyes," 131, 237
headman (of Gokul), 48, 200
heart, 94, 137, 163, 239, 258
  dyed with color of love, 188
  frightened, 124, 234
  Hari in charge of every, 178
  -lotuses, 111, 228
  lotus home of, 95, 217
  made whole, 172
  thievery, 91, 216
"heavenly mansions," 147, 246–47
hell, 179
heron, 122, 233
heron woman, 75, 183, 209
"Hero of the cow-clan," 75, 208–9
Himalayas, 90
Hindavī, 19–20
Hindi, Modern Standard, xiii–xiv, 4, 8
"His and hers," 96, 218
"His boyhood friend Śrīdāmā," 155, 253–54
History of Hindi Literature (Śukla), 8
Hit Harivaṃś, 25
Holi
  crackling fire of, 153, 252
  "Holi," 105, 224
"Homecoming," 156, 254
honey, 83, 85, 97, 213. *See also* bee(s); nectar
hopelessness, 124
horoscope, 186, 274
hunchback woman, 129, 136, 235
hunter/huntsman, 65, 187
husband, 47, 68, 82, 107, 144, 200, 206, 221–22, 225, 244–45
  gone, 185, 274
  Sītā's, 168

"Ignorant eyes," 92
"Inaccessible in Dvaraka," 158, 255
Indra, 1, 13, 75, 77, 170–171, 208–9
  Lord of Airāvat, 121, 232
  rain associated with, 122, 232–33
"In Rādhā's dress," 88, 214
intellect, 94, 97. *See also* mind
"In the birth canal," 177, 267–68
Islām Shāh, 19, 23
Istanbul, 20

Jahāngīr, 19, 33
Jaipur, 5, 7, 23
Jai Singh II, 25
Jamunā river, 5, 47, 50, 68, 81, 101, 124, 138, 140, 158, 200, 233, 240–42, 255
  blackened, 112, 227–28
  "Jamuna," 195, 278–79
  as Kālindī, 151, 249
  "standing still," 72, 74
Jānakī, 167, 260
Jarāsandh, 147, 246–47
  "He conquered Jarāsandh," 153, 251–52
  "Jarāsandh bound us," 152, 250–51
javelin, 147, 246–47
Jayadeva, 230
Jāyasī, Malik Muhammad, 6, 21
jewel(s), 66, 68, 96, 130, 156

Krishna like, 62, 88, 138, 204, 214, 240
"of a friend," 177
śikhar jewel, 89, 215
sweat/blood as pearls/rubies, 160
Jones, William, 3
joy, 172
of bees, 188
"capturing every," 87, 213–14
inner, 196
of Nanda, 54, 66, 202, 205
ocean of, 192
"of singing your praise," 183

Kāma, 104, 222
Kabīr, 8, 21, 26
Kabul, 7
Kachvāhā, Mānsingh, 5
Kachvāhā rulers, 5–7, 23, 25
Kadamb tree, 79
Kailāś, 157, 254
Kaiṭab, 152, 251
Kālindī, 151, 249
"Kālindī, do what I say," 151, 249
Kāliya, 68, 206
Kāma (god of passion/lust), 80, 82, 85, 100, 210–12
basant as chief courtier of, 105, 224
cowering/imploring, 104, 223
Radha/Krishna and, 88, 214
Kamalā, 155, 253–54
Kaṃs, 47, 56, 77, 107, 152, 199, 209, 251
"Kaṃs he killed," 108, 225–26
kāṃs grass, 124, 233
kaṃval, 33
kañcana (golden) pitchers, 81, 211
Kānh, 54, 65, 70, 76, 81–82, 100, 125, 202
Kanhāvat (Jāyasī), 6
kaṇṭulā (infant's necklace), 52, 201
karma vipāk, 162, 257–58
karmic past, 177, 267–68
Kaurav army, 256
Kavīśvar, Pundit, 43
Kavitāvalī (Tulsīdās), 21
kavitt, 21
Kāvyanirṇaya (Verdict on Literature), 20
Keśavdās, 20–21
Keśī, 56, 152, 203, 250–51
killing, 108, 225–26
king, 39, 123, 158, 163, 183, 220, 233
Bali, 55, 165, 173, 202–3, 258–60
Kaṃs, 47, 56, 77, 107, 108, 152, 199, 209, 225, 251
Krishna exhorted to become, 107, 225
"minions mimic kings," 100, 220
Rām, 5–6, 9, 13, 171, 181, 215, 264
royal delights, 110, 227
"Tale of Kings," 19–20, 23
Yādav, 123, 233
"kingdom of Krishna," 72, 105, 224
koel (bird), 111, 139, 145, 167, 241, 245, 260
Krishna, 6, 89, 114, 215, 229. *See also* Hari; *specific metaphors*
to battle Kaṃs, 107, 225
butter-ball lifting icon of, 52, 201
"dancing street performer," 125, 234
"dark as raincloud," 121, 232
daybreak poem to, 30–31, 30n2
"dressed like a fine actor," 108, 225–26
"headman's son," 48, 200
"His and hers," 96, 218
"his lovely image," 98, 218–19
Kaṃs killed by, 108, 225–26
kingdom of, 72, 105, 224
līlā of, 9, 14, 18, 108, 192, 225
Lord of Love, 221
"Lord of the Milkmaids," 133, 238
"The night he was born," 47, 199–200
outwitting Bali, 55, 202–3
poetry about, 7, 9, 13–15
poetry by, 25
potentially present, 44
Rādhā as mantra for, 101, 220–21
Rādhā's offerings to, 102, 221
"sea of compassion," 159, 173, 256
Sūrdās observing Rādhā and, 11*f*
Sūrdās singing for, 9–10, 10*f*
"Teaching him to walk," 54
temples, 5, 7, 9–10, 10*f*
virtues of, 125, 234
"wish-fulfilling jewel," 62, 204
"Krishna, the Ganges," 90
kūṭ (riddle poem), 29
Kūbjā (the hunchback), 129, 235
kumkum (vermillion powder), 48, 66, 113, 182, 200, 228
kumudini, 33
kuśa grass, 49

ladybugs, 122, 233
Lahore, 7
"language of animals," 165, 259–60
"Last rites," 145, 245. *See also* funeral pyre
Latin, 3–4, 4n1
laughing, 71, 118, 230
left-hand side, 88, 214
"left him at a loss," 156, 254
"A letter has arrived," 129, 235–36
letter-writing, 120, 231–32
liaison, 136, 239
libation, 101, 221

lightning, 71, 89
"like a great yogi," 101, 220–21
līlā (play), 9, 14, 18, 108, 192, 225
"Lines with her fingernails," 125, 234
lions, 146, 246, 257
lips, 70, 98–99, 148, 207, 247–48.
See also mouth
of nectar, 103, 222
"little bites," 102, 221
"lonely woman sets herself on fire," 119, 231
longing, 112, 117, 124, 141, 227–28, 230, 243
Lord of Airāvat, 121, 232
Lord of Braj, 144, 244–45
"Lord of the Milkmaids," 133, 238
"Lost," 84, 212–13
lotus, 61, 89–90, 137, 208, 239
Braj women like, 48
feet, 178
garland, 50, 70
hand(s), 33–34, 38, 59, 77, 204, 209
heart, 95, 111, 217, 228
Krishna like, 31–34, 36–39, 59, 64, 93, 104, 204, 216, 222
mouth, 72
primeval, 38–39, 160, 257
love, 52, 80, 100, 110, 119, 227, 230.
See also gopī; Kāma
amorous (*madhurati*), 88, 210, 214
associated with spring, 104, 222
connoisseur of, 158, 255
costliness of, 119, 230–31
as "essence of every other essence," 189
first stage of, 221
God of Love, 82, 102, 142, 211–12, 221, 243
memory's connection to, 44, 114, 169, 228–29, 262–63
onslaught of, 79, 209–10
romantic associations, 111, 227
"The tyranny of love," 100
Lucknow, 41n55
"lunar steeds," 93, 216
"The lure of Dvaraka," 149, 248

Mādhav, 55, 86, 103, 188, 202, 222, 274–76
"Mādhav, control that cow," 176, 266–67
"Mādhav, in anger," 160, 256–57
Rādha's identification with, 116, 130
Madhu, 152, 251
Madhumālatī (Mañjhan), 5
madhurati (amorous love), 88, 210, 214
Mahābhārata, 6, 152, 250–51, 255–256
Mahīpati, 12n11
male offspring, 201
Mandākīnī, 169
Maṇikhambh genre, 58, 203
Mañjhan, 5, 23
mansion, 157, 255
mantra, 101, 220–21
"mark of hardship," 129, 235
marriage vow, 212
mascara, 48, 99
"A mass of delight," 71, 207
"The master list," 184, 273
maternal role, 34–35, 202
Mathura, 5, 24, 199
Krishna's escape from, 200
"Mathura the bride," 107, 225
māyā (divine magic), 200. *See also sumāyā*
"noose of illusion," 185
"Maybe," 122, 232–33
meditation, 74, 101, 135, 238–39
memory, 155, 177, 253–54
love's connection to, 44, 114, 169, 228–29, 262–63
"The memory of love," 169, 262–63
"The memory of that passion," 114, 228–29
mercy, 58, 179, 190
Merciful One, 67, 184
"meshed windows," 145, 245
metaphor, 89, 96, 107, 225
milk, 49, 57, 63
"Lord of the Milkmaids," 133, 238
ocean of, 58, 60, 204
mind, 58, 95, 176
cakor-bird, 71
desire pulling at, 189
"a drum pasted with the dough of confusion," 182
Ganges' effect upon, 196
intellect, 94, 97
Mind-Beguiler, 70, 108, 165, 207, 225–26
"Turn away," 191, 276
"minions mimic kings," 100, 220
Mirabai, 115, 229
mistreatment, 109, 116
Modern Standard Hindi, xiii–xiv, 4
Mohan, 84, 85, 213
monkey, 168–169, 172–173, 191
monsoon season, 47, 121–122, 146, 199, 207, 232–33, 246. *See also* rainy season
moon, 59, 71, 89, 111, 196, 216
"feud with the moon," 61, 204
full, 79, 83, 212
Krishna's face like, 60, 113, 204, 228
-light, 71

"lunar steeds," 93, 216
peacock feather's, 70
Rādhā's face like, 88, 214
moonbeam pollen, 60, 124, 233
mother, 34–35, 109, 148, 202, 226–27, 248. *See also* Devakī; Yaśodā
Ganges as, 195
womb, 177, 189
moth to the flame, 119, 188, 230
mountain-lifter, 73, 84, 208
Mount Govardhan, 76, 109, 183, 208–9, 232–33
mouth, 72, 85, 213. *See also* lips
mṛdaṅg drum, 50, 68, 201, 206
Mughal Empire, 4–5
Muhammad Kabīr, 19–20, 23
muṇī bird, 48, 200
Mur (demon), 152, 251
Muralī, 11, 11*f*, 70–71, 73, 84–85, 93, 137, 208, 239
like buzz of bees, 86
"Muralīs kingdom," 72
"Muralī transfixes," 74
musicians, 68
musk, 111
Muṣṭik, 108, 183, 226
mynah bird, 149, 248

Nābhādās, 8–9, 18, 23, 26
Nāgarīpracāriṇī Sabhā, 8, 11, 28n40, 36, 39–40, 43
Nal Daman, 41n55
Nānak, 26
Nanda, 49–50, 53, 60, 66, 69–70, 73, 75, 96, 99, 201, 205
"Daddy, Daddy," 109, 226–27
darling girl of, 141, 243
delight of, 108, 225–26
feet of, 67, 206
joy of, 54, 66, 202, 205
Krishna's safety with, 48, 200
Nandadās, 16n18, 22, 128, 235
Nandalāl, 182
nandīmukh rite, 49, 201
Nārad, 149, 176, 248, 267
Naraharidās, 23–24
Nāth Yogi, 115, 229
necklace, 48, 99
infant's, 52, 201
"of passions," 182
string of beads, 101
nectar, 71, 85, 98, 103, 137, 188, 204, 222, 239
"nectar of life," 88, 214
neti neti (not that, not this), 66, 86, 205–6, 213
night, 114, 148, 229
"The night he was born," 47, 199–200
nirguṇ school, 206
nisān drum, 50, 201
"Nothing I could do," 95
"Nothing now remains," 159, 255–56

oath, 55, 87, 203, 213. *See also* vow
false, 136, 239
ocean of joy, 192
ocean of longing, 124
ocean of milk, 58, 60, 204
offering, 55, 95, 202–3, 217
fire-oblation, 101, 221
"food for a Brahmin feast," 101, 221
Krishna's offering to himself, 58, 203
"An offering of lights," 194, 278
Rādhā's, to Krishna, 102, 221
sacrificial, 165, 259–60
six flavors (*ṣaḍras*), 102, 221
"unexcelled," 194
Yaśodā offering six tastes, 63, 205
offering plate, 77, 209
"Only this mantra," 101, 220–21
"The onslaught of love," 79, 209–10
Oudh, 5
"Overeager acrobat," 185, 273–74
"Overwrought," 142, 243

pad (lyrics), 28–29, 28n40, 31–32. *See also* Brajbhāṣā *pads*
palās plant, 105, 224
"parading it around," 129, 235–36
Paramānanddās, 18, 22, 25
parasol, 72
parents, released, 108, 226
parrot, 69, 70–71, 149, 248
"parting that cuts two ways," 116, 230
paṭah drum, 50, 201
peacock, 69, 82, 104–105, 111, 149, 201, 222, 224, 248
feather moons, 70
rainy season associated with, 122–123, 233
pearls, 65, 134, 160, 205, 278
of freedom, 192
"Peddling yoga," 132, 237–38
performance, 37, 37n8, 44
range of, 38–40
Persian language, 4, 5, 19, 19n22
or Urdu, 104, 223

Phālgun time, 105, 224
pigs, 69
pinnacle-gems, 89, 215
plague, 100
planets, 48
playful acts (*līlā*), 9, 14, 18, 192. 108, 225
"pleasurable mixture," 99, 219
"pleasures of mating," 132, 237–38
poet's seal (*chāp*), 12, 29, 36
poet's signature (*bhaṇitā*), 23–27, 24n31, 29, 32, 37, 120, 231–32, 256–57
pomegranate, 83, 167, 212
 śikhar jewel resembling, 89, 215
pots
 filling of, 80, 211
 golden, 83, 212
Prahlād, 13, 181
Prajāpati, 194
pride, 82, 177, 188
"Proper hospitality," 21, 102
prostitute, 183
pungent flavor, 102, 221
punishment, 103, 222
Purāṇa, 176, 190, 206
"Purifier of the Fallen," 180
pūrvarāg (first stage of love), 221
Pūtanā, 75, 209

Qutban, 21

Rādhā, 11*f*, 91, 100, 145, 212, 217–218, 245
 anger of, 103, 222
 anurāg exemplified by, 79, 210
 "His and hers," 96, 218
 "In Rādhā's dress," 88, 214
 in Krishna's absence, 116, 230
 Krishna's offerings to, 101, 221
 "Only this mantra," 101, 220–21
 "Rādhā disbelieves," 97, 218
 Sūrdās observing, 11*f*

Rādhā/Krishna, 11*f*, 88, 116, 214, 230
"Radiance," 86, 213
Radiant One, 88, 214
rāg (raga), 24, 28
 malhār, 233
 of war, 108, 225–26
rain, 76, 89, 122, 208–9, 232–33. *See also* cloud(s); monsoon season
 like tears, 121, 232
rainbow, 82, 123, 233
rainy season, 50, 70, 121, 201, 207, 232. *See also* monsoon season
 birds associated with, 122–123, 233
 "The season of rains," 123, 233

Rajasthan, 5, 24
Rajput rulers, 5
Rām, 5–6, 9, 13, 181, 215. *See also Rāmāyaṇa*
 "Today Rām is raging in battle," 171, 264
Ramāpati, 143, 244
Rāmāyaṇa, 5, 21
 "Rāvaṇ roars in battle, 170, 263–64
 "The breaths," 168, 261–62
 "The memory of love," 169, 262–63
 "This jungle," 167, 260–61
 "Today Rām is raging in battle," 171, 264
 "The view from Ayodhya," 172, 264–65
 "The worn-out world," 173, 265–66
 Rāmdās, Baba, 21–23
Rasārṇava-sudhākara (Siṅgabhūpāl), 210
rās dance, 80, 210
Rāvaṇ, 13, 171, 181
 "Rāvaṇ," 170, 263–64
 "Rāvaṇ roars in battle," 170, 263–64
"Red in the morning," 99, 219
"red *muṇī* birds," 48, 200
remembering, 155, 177, 253–54
rescue, 69, 206
respect, 172
rhyme, 38–40
rhythms, 182
rice, 77, 155, 209, 253
rites, 49, 145, 201, 221, 245
river. *See also* Ganges river; Jamuna river
 blackened, 112, 227–28
 poems to rivers, 195–97, 278–83
 "River of tears," 144, 244–45
 "River-of-the-Gods," 196
robbery, 61, 91–92, 100, 188, 204–205, 216, 220
 "Gopāl has stolen my heart," 94, 217
roosters, 59
rubies, 160
Rukmiṇī, 155, 253–54
Rūp Gosvāmī, 18, 210, 255

ṣaḍras (six flavors), 63, 102, 205, 221
saffron, 111
sage, 72
saguṇ school, 206
salty flavor, 102, 221
salvation, 75, 209
Samson, 203
Sanak, 149, 176, 192, 194, 248
Sanātan Gosvāmī, 18
sandal, 111
"sandal-paste designs," 90, 215
sandalwood, 145
 mark, 66, 90, 215

powder, 113, 228
Saṅkarṣaṅ, 68, 206
Sanskrit, 3–4, 21
Brajbhāṣā v., xiii, 5
city/woman metaphor in, 107, 225
devanāgarī, xiii
as language of gods, 17–18
memory and love connection in, 44
Sanskrit verse (*śloka*), 18
sārang, 88, 214
sapphire, 66, 88, 96, 214
sari, 48, 95, 217
kohl-black, 112, 228
"Scholar at your door," 165, 259–60
scribe, 120, 231–32
seal, poet's (*chāp*), 12, 29, 36
"sea of compassion," 159, 173, 256
"The season of rains," 123, 233
secret liaison, 136, 239
"Serpent and vine," 83, 212
Śeṣ, 125, 194, 203, 234
"set foot inside your home," 156, 254
"set off with the sun," 253
Shaikh Muhammad Ghaus, 23
sheldrake, 112, 118, 228, 230
"She's going mad," 146, 246
Shiva, 115, 151, 157, 171, 196, 211, 229
anger toward Kāma, 104, 222–23
dancing, 194
shivering, 142, 243
signature, poet's (*bhaṇitā*), 23–27, 24n31, 29, 32, 37, 120, 231–32, 256–57
śikhar gem, 89, 215
Sikh guru-poets, 26
silk, 208. *See also* sari; yellow garments
similes, 89, 215
"Similes lost their nerve," 89, 215
Siṅgabhūpāl, 210
singing, 48, 105, 183, 224
Sūrdās, for Krishna, 9–10, 10*f*
Śivsiṃh Saroj, 22
Sītā, 9, 168, 169, 171–172
six tastes, 63, 176, 204–5, 266
"Slammed the door," 98, 218–19
sleep/sleeplessness, 118, 175, 230
śloka (Sanskrit verse), 17–18
smara, 44
smiles, 99. *See also* lips
Smith, Barbara Hernstein, 34
Smṛtis, 190
snake, 68, 83, 142, 206, 209, 212, 243
"bewildered as a snake," 143, 244
braided hair like, 57, 203
"Dancing on the snake," 68, 206
"Serpent and vine," 83, 212
Śeṣ, 125, 194, 203, 234
Ūdho like, 130
Snell, Rupert, 38
sobriety, 94
"So many other sinners," 183, 271–73
"sophisticated act," 108, 225
soul, 95
sour flavor, 102, 221
spices, 102, 221
spring season (*basant*), 104–105, 222–224
Śrī, 72, 208
Śrīdāmā, 155, 253–54. *See also* Sudāmā
śrīvats, 90, 215
śruti chandana, 66, 206
stars, 48, 194
storm, 147, 246–47
strength, 150, 248–49
"stretto" technique, 37
"Such good advice," 130, 236–37
Sudāmā, 13, 154–57,181
sudarśan, 256–57
Sufi writers, 6, 19, 21, 23
Sugrīv, 172
Śukla, Rāmcandra, 8, 8n9
sumāyā (fine magic), 80, 210. *See also māyā*
sun, 8, 165, 170, 189, 193–194, 253
"Blind to the sun," 193, 277–78
sunbeams, 86
Sūrdās
blindness of, 12–15, 120, 181, 231–32
courtly frames for, 19–23
divine lineage for, 17–18
more than one, 22, 24–28, 27n9
observing Rādhā and Krishna, 11*f*
signatures of, 23–24, 24n31, 25–27, 37
singing for Krishna, 9–10, 10*f*
"sun" of Brajbhāṣā poets, 8
"translator" of *Bhāgavata Purāṇa*, 15–18, 16n18
Sūrsāgar, 13, 24. *See also* Fatehpur manuscript
as anthology, 17–18
"bee messenger" section of, 16–17
Bryant edition of, 40–41
collective authorship of, 24–28, 27n9
Krishnaite portions of, 10–11, 11*f*, 14, 24
relationship to *Bhāgavata Purāṇa*, 15–18, 16n18
"Sūr's twenty-five," 188, 274–76
swan, 167
sweat, 48, 103, 112, 141–142, 222, 228, 243
rivulets of, 112, 228

sweet flavor, 102, 221
Śyām, 88, 120, 145–146, 154, 245

tactics, 132, 237–38
Tānsen, 21–22
Tāntarang Khān, 22
"Teaching him to walk," 54
tears, rain-like, 121, 232
teeth
  angry, 103, 222
  diamond-like, 89, 215
  lightning-like, 86
  like pomegranate seeds, 167
ṭek (title line), 34, 37n8, 42
"Ten-day trial," 140, 241–42
ten directions, 97, 218
"Thank goodness he's come," 143, 243–44
"They say you're so giving," 181, 269–70
thief, 61, 91–92, 100, 188, 204–205, 216, 220
  "Gopāl has stolen my heart," 94, 217
"This bee- and that," 137, 239
"This jungle," 167, 260–61
"Those feet, that lake," 192, 276–77
"Thoughts of him stalk me," 118, 230
"three worlds," 57, 196
thunder, 122–123, 232–33
tihāī (thirds), 37, 37n8
tilak, 70. *See also* forehead mark
  -mark tree, 144
"timid captain of the gods," 77, 209
title line (*ṭek*), 34, 37n8, 42
"Today Rām is raging in battle," 171, 264
toenails, 192
"Toiling like a dog," 178, 268
"Topknot," 57, 203
"Toward Badarī," 162, 257–58
translation, 15–18, 32, 40
traveling, 122, 158, 233, 255
Treasure of Grace, 172
tree, 69, 79, 104, 111, 144, 206, 222
  Veda-, 176
  wishing-, 157, 173, 255
tribhaṅg pose, 73, 208
trivacan (threeutterances), 37
Trivikram, 197, 282–83 "Truth in advertising," 180, 269
Tulsīdās, 5, 20–21, 22
"tulsī leaf in exchange," 154, 252–53
turmeric, 49, 200
turban, 84
  "Turban of deceit," 136, 239
"Turn away," 191, 276
turtle dove, 119, 143, 149, 188, 230, 244, 248

"The tyranny of love," 100

Ūdho, 112, 130, 162, 257–58
  black flag of, 136
  as Krishna's messenger, 127, 128, 134–43, 227–28, 234–46
  "Ūdho, go," 127, 234–35
Ugrasen, 108, 225–26
umbilical stem, 160, 257
"Uncanny resemblance," 128, 235
universe, 53, 57, 203, 267
"unknowable, untellable, unmeasurable," 129, 235
"Utterly soiled," 141, 243

Vaishnavas, 220
Vallabhācārya, 12, 15
Vallabhite worship, 12, 16n18, 25, 200
Vallabh Sampradāy, 12, 14–15, 31
Vaiṣṭha, 172
Vasudev, 147, 199–200, 246
  released by Krishna, 108, 226
vātsalya bhāv ("calf" emotion), 34–35, 54, 202
Veda (wisdom), 66, 86, 160, 190, 200, 206
  brushing aside, 161
  "fragrance of," 192
  "-tree," 176
  "tripping off his tongue," 165
vermilion, 113, 228
  "of greed," 182
  saindur, 48, 66, 200
Vibhīṣaṇ, 13, 172–173, 181
Vidyāpati, 230
"The view from Ayodhya," 172, 264–65
Vinayapatrikā (Tulsīdās), 21
vine, 31, 82, 83, 104, 212, 222
  golden, 96
viraha (longing in separation), 112, 117, 124, 141, 227–28, 230, 243
virahiṇī (lonely woman), 115, 124, 229, 233
  sets herself on fire, 119, 231
virāma (mark for break between verses), 1
virtues, 125, 180, 234
Vishnu, 9, 17–18, 38–39, 72, 165, 202, 208, 215, 259–60. *See also* dwarf, Krishna, Rām, Trivikram
  Ramāpati, 143, 243–44
  "sandal-paste designs" adorning, 90, 215
VishnuPurāṇa, 236
vizier, 100
vow, 161, 179, 183, 257. *See also* oath
  marriage, 212
  ritual, 102, 221–22

of silence, 82, 212
yogic, 136
Vṛṣṇis, 247

wagtail (bird), 65–66, 89, 122, 149, 205, 215, 233, 248
waist-bells, 80–81, 211
water
great flood, 76, 209
waterfalls, 104–105, 222, 224
"water of good deeds," 192
whirlpool, 147, 151, 246–47, 249
waterpots (*gagarī*), 80, 211
wayfarer, 112, 227–28
"We marvel at your arms," 77
wheel, 160, 256
"The wheel in his hand," 161, 257
wife (wives), 110, 221–22, 227
Kāliya's, 68, 206
Mathura as Krishna's, 107, 225
wildflowers, 145, 245
wind, 121
window, 145, 245
"Wine in the red of his eyes," 150, 248–49
"wish-fulfilling jewel," 62, 204
wishing tree, 157, 173, 255
"With love," 119, 230
woman/city metaphor, 107, 225
womb, 177, 189
women of Braj, 35, 48, 59, 77, 93, 144, 244–45. *See also gopī*
Holi celebrated by, 105, 224
virahiṇī, 115, 229
"Working on ourselves," 135, 238–39
world(s)
fourteen, 176, 266
"three worlds," 57, 196
"The worn-out world," 173, 265–66
"The wrong address," 157, 254–55

Yādav king, 123, 233
Yaśodā, 34–36, 49, 54–57, 64, 77, 109, 200, 202, 226
Devakī addressed by, 110, 227
offering "six tastes," 63, 205
"Yaśodā answers," 63
yati (caesura), 28n40, 29, 32, 37
yellow garments, 136, 239
Krishna's, 80, 84, 99, 108, 161, 211, 219, 225
of Ūdho, 128
yoga, discipline of, 129, 134, 148, 278
fifth stage of, 140, 242
"haṭha-yoga eyes," 131, 237
"Peddling yoga," 132, 237–38
yogi, 74, 101, 115, 131, 220–21, 229, 237
yogurt, 200